Still West of Nowhere

More Tales from The Cimarron:
The Continuing Saga of the
Quinn Family's Montana Homestead

NANCY QUINN

HELLGATE PRESS  ASHLAND, OREGON

STILL WEST OF NOWHERE

Published by Hellgate Press
(An imprint of L&R Publishing, LLC)

Hellgate Press
PO Box 3531
Ashland, OR 97520
email: sales@hellgatepress.com

Cover and Interior Design: L. Redding
Cover Photo: Nancy Quinn

ISBN: 978-1-55571-992-0

Printed and bound in the United States of America
First edition 10 9 8 7 6 5 4 3 2 1

Lovingly Dedicated to:

My family,

And all my kindred spirits, including those who walk on two legs, or four, or soar into the skies with beating wings.

A Personal Note to You, the Reader

I'M GLAD YOU ARE holding this book in your hands, for I consider it a privilege to tell you stories about our unique way of life, and I trust that you will enjoy spending some time with me and my family.

People often ask me why we choose to live on a rural mountainside with all its inherent difficulties. There is no single simple answer, and so it is through these continuing stories that I hope to further illustrate my sincerest thoughts and feelings about our somewhat offbeat lifestyle. As an artist I am more used to painting a story with a brush, but here I must paint my ideas with words. In so doing I hope you will feel as though you are sharing our experiences along with us. If these stories uplift you, arouse your pioneering spirit, or inspire you to pursue your dreams, then I have achieved my primary goals.

I have heard it said that authors and artists are dreamers. Whether it's a painting or a story, in my work I like to weave reality and creative thought together. The written word is a powerful influence, therefore I believe I have a responsibility to my readers, as does any author, to write about what I truly understand from personal experience. For this reason hope and faith are two recurring themes throughout my books, along with perseverance and the need to cultivate a humorous perspective on life. I once read that the highest mountains are not formed without earthquakes. On both a physical and emotional level I have found this to be true. Perhaps one day in the distant future, long after I am gone, someone will find a dusty copy of my book sitting on a shelf, and my family's experiences will be brought to life once more to ignite the pioneer spirit in another generation of adventurers.

Lastly, my favorite aspect of being an author is building a connection with my readers. I'm truly grateful for those of you who have taken this journey with us through my books, art, radio programs, and videos. I hope to meet you someday, perhaps at a book signing or other future event. In the meantime, if you have a question, comment, or just want to introduce yourself, feel free to contact me through my website. I would be delighted to hear from you and include you in our expanding circle of friends.

Much obliged,

—Nancy Quinn (*www.quinnwildlifeart.com)*

Contents

"What lies behind you and what lies in front of you, pales in comparison to what lies inside of you."

—Ralph Waldo Emerson

Prologue

LIVING ON A MOUNTAIN in Montana is not for the faint of heart. We have resided here for well over a decade, and I still believe this statement rings true. Montana is a place of incredible beauty. Being surrounded by the raw, unapologetic ways of the natural world, one begins to have a better understanding of the circle of life. It is simultaneously stunningly resplendent, serene, harsh, and unforgiving.

Even though the years have turned us into more seasoned and prepared modern day pioneers, there remain numerous challenges we face daily. I continue to look at our experiences with a hefty dose of humor. We expect the unexpected, and there is rarely a dull moment on our high mountain homestead. I continue my expostulation of blending my urban perspectives and social norms into our daily life in this remote area. Although it's not easy, I have adapted to most circumstances without changing the core of who I am. It does demand the price of a certain amount of isolation, but there is a rewarding feeling of contentment as well, being "far from the madding crowd".

This is the third book in my *Go West, Young Woman*! series. It continues the timeline from the second book, *Stay West, Young Woman!* My goal of blending our city deportment with a wilderness lifestyle remains an unending work in progress. I'm pleased to share our ever-growing collection of true stories about our frontier living, using a touch of style, more wild animal encounters, extreme weather, our "growing" and changing family, animal rescue work, mistakes, triumphs, cultural differences, and just the business of living. This is my invitation to all of you to share our life in the modern and still very Wild West.

1

Home Is Where Our Story Begins

I FIND BEING IN my kitchen extremely comforting. I enjoy the moments of thoughtful meditation while stirring batter, the fragrance of butter when it sizzles in the pan, and the sound of utensils clinking as I search each drawer for just the right implement. Over the years I have had the opportunity to bake, broil, barbecue, and burn meals in many states across this continent. But having settled into a Montana lifestyle for thirteen years, at least I can enjoy the oasis of serene predictability that my kitchen offers me. This day was no exception; my mind was at ease. I was not worrying about my family's future, any health issues, or if we might have to relocate someplace else. I suspected Mother Nature and Old Man Winter were conspiring and would soon come knocking, but the pantry was well stocked for the frigid days ahead, and this added to my sense of security.

Sonja, my youngest daughter, was helping me in the kitchen. Sandy, her older sister, was upstairs deeply engrossed in writing a college theme paper. Nothing would deter her focus save for the scent of vanilla drifting in the air. I waited expectantly for it to waft up the stairs and seep into her room.

Despite now being a young teenager, Sonja happily sang and hummed like a child as she stirred the cookie batter. I listened quietly to the intermittent sound of her soft rendition of Silver Bells. It was Christmas time, not just in the city, but on our mountain as well.

"The dough's thick enough," I said. "Now roll them into balls and put them on the sheet."

"Mom, I'm not a kid anymore; I know how to do this," she snapped back.

"Sonja, just because you're now taller than me doesn't mean you have the right to be disrespectful."

Sonja's face sank and her voice softened. "I'm sorry, Mom. I just thought you didn't trust me."

"Of course I trust you; that's why you're making the cookies. I'm only trying to help. My Gram taught me how to make them when I was smaller than you, and I want the tradition to be passed to your children someday."

"I'm not going to have any kids. I may not even get married."

"Now you're starting to sound like Sandy."

"Hey, I enjoy making cookies; Sandy just enjoys eating them."

"True enough, but practice makes perfect. That's why you have to combine the right quantities of Amish butter, flour, ground pecans, and vanilla."

"I know, and then we bake them for a few minutes and roll them in powdered sugar while they're still warm so they'll look like little snowballs."

"That's right, Honey Girl, and we would never think of wasting them by throwing them at each other!" The moment of tension had passed and Sonja was again relaxed and laughing. Her features may have been maturing, but her emotions remained a mix of childhood and budding young womanhood. Two teenagers in the family at the same time – would I survive the drama?

The hours passed quickly, and it was late afternoon when I heard the doorbell. I wasn't surprised because we often had packages delivered to our door by UPS, particularly at this time of year. Additionally, being a rural route, we didn't have any mail delivered to our home, but were required to retrieve it from the tiny Mullan Post Office.

Sonja stopped humming and asked, "Do you want me to get the door?"

"No, keep stirring; I'll get it. I don't want you seeing any Christmas surprises."

I hurried down the hall while wiping away the dough from my fingers with a holiday cloth. As a precaution I peered through the large oval glass of our front door. The textured beveling made it impossible to discern who was there, but I could tell it was not the outline of our usual deliveryman, Jim. It was somebody much larger, whose features were so distorted that I could not fathom who it might be. I cracked the door just an inch and peered through the opening. There stood our white gelding, Wilson. Puzzled, I immediately scanned the vicinity, but saw no one else. I opened the door further and looked down the road where our other horse, Whiskey, was slowly walking toward us. His dark reddish color stood out against the brilliant white of the snow, but all around him was stillness.

Curious, Sonja came up beside me and peeked outside. "Who is it? Oh, hi Wilson. Where's Jim?"

"It's not Jim, just Wilson," I replied, rather puzzled.

"No packages?"

"Not unless Mr. Wilson brought them." He perked up his ears at the mention of his name, clearly pleased by our company, and took a step closer to the door where he began to nibble at the green wreath we'd hung next to it. As he nipped away I saw his lips brush against our doorbell, a green cast iron frog that was a memento from our first home in Florida.

Sonja laughed in disbelief, "Wilson likes to ring doorbells?"

"Maybe he heard about the cookies."

"Or just smelled them cooking. Did you do that on purpose, Mr. Wilson?" she teased.

The look on his face as he lifted his head and snorted, confirmed our suspicions. *Well, yes, I knew you were baking, and our afternoon meal is late, so I came to the door to wait for you. Whiskey said we could. Just ask him when he gets here. He walks a little slower than I do as you can plainly see.*

By the way, this wreath isn't as good as last years. I do wish you would taste them first and choose the best one before you bring them home. Last year's had more flavor; this one is not as sweet.

I mused at the thought of this information exchange between us. Did Wilson have a penchant for tasting all of our previous Christmas wreaths? Personally, I loved the fragrance of our locally grown evergreens, but I'd never bothered to taste one. No doubt the explanation was much simpler than this. Normally the horses stayed in the front meadow, but sometimes hunger or the need for company drove them to our front door, or to my art studio where they would stare at me through the picture window as I worked. More than once I had spied Wilson tasting the bird feeder from the dining room window, or been startled by his presence while I was concentrating on some painting at my drafting table. He would patiently stand a silent vigil until I took notice of him, then snort with pleasure when I acknowledged his presence and asked him what he wanted. Food, naturally, was the most common reply.

"I guess that mystery is solved," I said as I peered down the road, "but perhaps Jim is still on his way."

"I hope so; Christmas in nearly here."

"It's about more than gifts, you know," I gently reminded her.

"Oh, I know what it's really about, but I'm still excited to see your face when you open my gift."

Looking at her maturing face, I found it hard to believe that a scant few years ago I was holding her in my arms at Bethesda Naval Hospital. I cherished every moment with my girls. How many more years would we spend together baking and preparing our favorite holiday dishes? The only constant in our lives was change, and the pace of it was increasing. I intended to enjoy every minute I could with them.

I snapped out of my melancholic daze and said, "Sonja, why don't you feed the boys. I'll keep an eye on the oven until you get back. We still have a couple of sheets of cookies to make."

"Will do!" She turned and darted out the door, never one to saunter.

"Wear a coat and hat," I called after her, but it was too late. She was already halfway down the hill. I watched her trot toward the barn, the boys quickly falling in line after her. They knew her presence meant good feed and sweet treats. The horses kicked up clouds of snow around their feet as they hurried along against the faint pink sky of the setting sun. It was a comforting sight, this picture perfect moment. How many more would I enjoy before the girls were young women seeking their own paths in life, perhaps far from our sanctuary? Sandy would soon finish college and Sonja was learning how to drive. I sighed; *am I getting old?*

I was beginning to feel the cold air seep into my bones. I debated whether to go back inside, when the high pitched beeping of the oven timer decided matters for me. I reluctantly returned to the kitchen and removed the freshly baked cookies with my oven mitts. As I lifted the baking sheet out of the oven, I accidentally brushed my arm against a hot oven coil. I let loose a cry and had to consciously force myself not to drop the cookie sheet. I quickly set it on a trivet before glancing at my arm. A streak of skin had turned fire-engine red and was about to bubble. I dashed to the sink and pushed the tap to the cold setting as I placed my elbow and forearm under the faucet. The cool water soon ran ice cold, and with it came a modicum of relief.

Bill had heard my agony and came down to investigate. "What did you do to yourself this time, Quinn?" I briefly lifted my arm, and his expression became more serious. "That looks really bad; do you want some aloe or egg white?"

"Egg white, please. Will you whip one up for me? And hurry!"

Bill quickly located the hand mixer and fumbled under the counter for a bowl. I watched in pain as he separated an egg white in it and began whipping it into a lather. I listened to the whirring sound and focused on the egg white as it transformed into an opaque fluffy mass.

"How does this look?"

"Fine, let me dry my arm." I gently pressed the area with a paper towel and spooned the mixture onto my arm, leaving it to do its magic. I winced as I spoke. "This always worked before…I hope it does now."

"Is this the trick you learned from your grandmother years ago?"

"Yes…it really helps me not to blister and scar…I still don't know how it works…maybe the protein in the egg?"

"How are you feeling? Is it having any effect?"

"I think so…the pain is easing off." It still hurt and felt like someone was holding a match to my delicate skin, but it wasn't getting any worse. I continued leaning over the sink, supporting my left arm with my right hand.

"Are you feeling sick?"

I looked up at Bill and frowned. "No, it's just a burn; I'll be okay now."

I barely heard the front door open and close, and took little notice of it until Sonja entered the kitchen.

"Oh, no, what happened?"

"Your Mom burned herself."

"Again?"

"Yep."

"Hey, what do you mean 'again'? It's been years since this last happened."

Sonja and Bill exchanged knowing glances. I looked at them both and rolled my eyes at their sense of humor. "I'll be fine; it's no big deal, but I'd appreciate it if you would bake the rest of the cookies, Sonja. Your dad can help."

Bill managed a pathetic smile. "Whatever you say, Dear."

As the cookies baked, I kept basting my arm with more egg white, replacing the batter every twenty minutes, while checking the progress of my healing. I was rewarded for my persistence, and within two hours most of the redness had disappeared, and no blisters formed. The skin was still delicate and sore, but it could have been much worse. You have to give credit to some of the old wives' tales; there are times when such remedies work.

By now I had stopped using the egg white, and was applying both Aloe Vera cream and ice to my injury. Sonja watched me intently for a while before cautiously saying, "Mom, you know I want to be a nurse."

"That's a very noble choice," I replied without any conviction.

"No, really. I've already begun studying first aid, but I didn't know anything about using an egg on a burn. Do you think home remedies are better than modern medicine?"

This time I looked at my daughter instead of my wound. "I'm sorry, Honey, I didn't mean to sound dismissive. I'm still in a bit of pain. I think nursing is a good idea, but it takes a lot of dedication and hard work."

"But what about home remedies?"

"Huh?"

Sonja appeared exasperated. "Home remedies, are they better than modern medicine?"

"Well…I have to say yes and no."

"That's not much of an answer."

"They each have their place. I would say I want most of what today's medicine has to offer, but sometimes the medications can cause more harm than good. You've seen some of the reactions I've experienced. On the other hand, you know I've spent a fair amount of time in hospitals, and the doctors have helped me a lot. Sometimes I react better to natural remedies, but even herbs can have side effects, so I'm careful what I choose, and I do a lot of research before I decide to try anything. At least nowadays we have a better idea of what works and what doesn't. Did you know that a long time ago the early pioneers would rub cow manure into a burn or place butter on it?"

"Oh, butter please," Sonja quickly injected.

"Do you know how they cured a cold? They ate an onion sandwich and washed their hair. Sometimes they carried an onion in their pocket to ward off small pox. They also caught leaves in their hands, and they treated the chills by running a broom down the patient's back in the sign of the cross."

Sonja just snorted, "No one believes that now, Mom."

"But they believed it back then. They also believed you should put a spider web on a cut to stop it from bleeding. I'm sure when people far in the future look back on us, they will think we had some pretty silly treatments as well. So I like to blend the old and new – whatever works best and is handy."

"How's your arm?"

"Take a look."

"Wow, it really worked."

"Yes. I don't know exactly why. I'm sure if some scientist researched it, he'd find the answer. Just the same, sometimes the old remedies are still good choices. Either way, I'm glad your Dad isn't a rancher."

"Why's that, Mom?"

"Because he might have run into the field to get me a fresh cow pie."

2

Classic Christmas

THIS WAS THE YEAR. The girls were old enough for me to finally unpack two of my most beloved Christmas ornaments without fear that they might be accidently broken or damaged by little helping hands. Each one was an old-fashioned tabletop ceramic Christmas tree containing a small lightbulb in its base. When turned on, a smattering of soft colored glows emitted through each of the tiny plastic "bulbs" or "birds" that adorned them, simulating Christmas tree lights. They were very popular at one time, but now are considered vintage décor. I made the first one myself the year Bill and I were married. I cast it from a mold and painstakingly painted it several shades of green before firing it in a ceramic oven. The second tree was inherited from my paternal grandparents after they died. It was of similar size and shape as the first, but was glazed in a frosted white finish. I never knew my paternal grandparents very well because we moved away from Michigan a few years after my father's untimely death. We maintained a sparse relationship over the intervening decades, but were never very close. I acquired their ceramic ornament so my children would have some connection to them, no matter how tenuous. My plan had always been to give each of my daughters one of the trees in order to maintain that thread to the past every holiday season. Today they would see each tree for the first time.

Now I was unconsciously holding my breath as Bill cautiously descended the steep loft staircase with the first large box containing one of these precious ornaments. He could not see over or around the box and had to feel his way down each step. Once he reached the floor, my apprehension was replaced by a surge of excitement, and I began to breathe again. We carefully unpacked the box and I caught a glimpse of an opaque pearlescent white spire I had not seen in a decade. They had been packed away by the moving company we hired when we left Washington, D.C., and had remained untouched all these years.

The tree shimmered as Bill lifted it out of the box, its tiny blue, yellow, green, and red plastic birds with outstretched wings perched on the edges of the branches.

"I can't wait to get them set up," I said as I peered into the large box looking for the tree base and cord.

"You can start on this one while I get the other box open, then you can put them together," Bill replied. He soon returned with the second box and placed it gently on the floor. As he opened the top I heard a light tinkling sound. We both froze and looked at each other.

"That doesn't sound good," I cautioned.

Bill opened the box and looked inside. "Nancy, I don't see any packing material in here." He leaned closer to the box and began to rummage. I could hear more tinkling and I cringed at the thought of what this meant. "Damn!" He lifted out a large chunk of green ceramic, followed by another and another. "There isn't any packing material in here, none at all. This tree is in pieces; I can see shards at the bottom of the box." He moved a few of them around, and I heard them scuff and clank as his hands touched what was left of my poor beautiful tree.

I looked into the box and I saw all my hard work and memories shattered at the bottom. "I can't believe this! Not even a scrap of paper to wrap this in? They just threw it into the box? They knew it would never arrive intact; they just didn't care! We paid for this?" I was angry and on the verge of tears.

"Maybe I can fix it," Bill replied as he began fitting the large pieces together.

"I doubt it. Just look at this mess! How are you going to fit these small pieces together?" I picked one up in my hand and turned it over thoughtfully.

"I'll see what I can do; I know how much it means to you." He stared into my eyes and gave me a sympathetic smile. Bill picked up the box, and I mentally cringed when I heard the ceramic pieces clink against each other. "I'll take it to my shop and see if I can glue it back together."

The next two days we all kept busy cleaning, decorating, wrapping gifts, and cooking. Despite the rush, pesky hands still managed to find time to raid the cookie jar, and I soon found myself having to bake more confections. Otherwise, our supply would be depleted before Christmas Day. This time I decided to make a different kind of Christmas treat, my painted cookies, which I made by combining extra vanilla with a basic sugar cookie recipe. My daughters would use an assortment of cookie cutters to form the dough into stars, wreaths, bells, and horses which we then painted with my artist brushes and a food coloring mixture. When they came out of the oven the results were always (well, usually) soft cream-colored cookies with glossy hard icing. They looked like small works of art which I considered too pretty to eat. My family harbored no such inclination, and it wasn't long before I found myself hoarding some for our ranching neighbor, Chase.

Each Christmas we would prepare a basket of assorted goods and small gifts for him to show our appreciation for all the help he freely gave us during the year, not the least of which would be pulling Bill's tractor out of a snow drift at least once during the winter. Chase enjoyed chocolate cake, so this season I decided it would be the centerpiece of his basket. I would surround the cake with my snowballs and painted cookies. To this we added a utility knife and a camouflaged watch cap with built-in LED lights so he could calve during the bitter cold winter nights with both hands free.

In past years I had made the cakes for his entire family, but he once sheepishly admitted to me that the cakes rarely got to their house in one piece, if at all. I laughed when I thought about this, until I remembered how close his mother Gail and I used to be. I treasured our friendship during those early years on the mountain, but this had abruptly ended several years ago for reasons I never understood. She simply stopped returning my phone calls or dropping by to chat. It had been and remained a painful experience, and I truly missed our camaraderie. Now I was suddenly feeling melancholy. I guess this happens to everyone at some point in the holiday season. Be it Thanksgiving, Christmas, or New Year's Eve, we can't help but remember absent friends and family. I still had my family, but the girls were becoming more independent. Before long Sandy would leave, then in a few more years it would be Sonja. "Stop it Quinn," I mumbled to myself. "You're making yourself miserable over nothing."

I heard the back door open and felt a sudden blast of cold air. Bill came in carrying a large cardboard box. He stomped the snow from his muck boots and set the box on the dinner table. "Merry Christmas, Nancy," he beamed. Then his countenance grew more serious once he saw my face. "What's the matter, Honey? What did Sandy do this time?"

"Nothing. She did nothing wrong. Everything's fine; everyone's fine. It's just me—as usual."

"What's that supposed to mean?"

"Oh, nothing. I'm just feeling sorry for myself over nothing. Here I have everything to be thankful for and I'm upset over nothing."

"Well it must be something. Do you want to talk about it?" He came closer and held my arms, staring intently into my face.

"No, you'll think it's silly." He gave me one of those "looks", the raised eyebrow, coupled with a scolding frown. He knew I could never resist that expression. It was his silent way of telling me that anything I said would be taken seriously and not dismissed or ridiculed. "I was just thinking about Gail."

"Ah, I see." He gave me a big hug and continued. "Well, I can't do anything about that, but I do have something here that might make you feel better." He guided me to the table and told me to close my eyes. I could hear the rustling of paper and the sound of something like a dinner plate being placed on the table. "You can open your eyes now."

There sat my green ceramic Christmas tree, all in one piece again. Suddenly I was ecstatic. "You fixed it! That's amazing!" I smiled and grabbed him around the waist and squeezed as hard my little frame could.

"Well, it's not exactly fixed, but I did manage to get about 95% of it back together. The rest I puttied in. You'll still have to paint it to hide the seams, but I think it'll be alright after that."

I studied the cracks which appeared as fault lines spreading over several major surfaces. They were white from the glue that had seeped into the small caverns formed when putting the pieces together. It reminded me somewhat of a stained glass window or a jigsaw puzzle, and I marveled at how he was able to find the smaller pieces and reassemble them into their original three-dimensional shape. I knew I wouldn't be able to paint and re-fire the tree, and the paints I used for canvas were unsuitable to this task. I pondered how I could hide the cracks without making the repair obvious. Then it came to me. "Nail polish," I said firmly. "Green glitter is in style now. I'm sure I can find some in the stores. I'll paint over the cracks and the glue. I know it'll stick. It's glossy when it dries, and I won't have to re-fire it. It's the perfect solution!"

"See, I knew you'd think of something creative, Quinn. I'll put sparkly green nail polish on the shopping list. Who would have thought? Just one thing though," he added as he wrote it down.

"What's that?"

"Well, you'd better come with me when I get it. You have a better eye for color than I do." Then he added in a fake Arnold Schwarzenegger accent, "And I don't want anyone at Walmart thinking I'm a girly-man."

Within a few days I was sitting at the round table in our loft and "polishing" my labor of love. The green ceramic tree began to look more like my original creation with every stroke of glittery green lacquer. Personally, it was not the right choice for my fingernails, but it was the perfect choice for bringing our little Christmas tree back to its former glory. Carefully, I dabbed and ran the brush along each crevice, filling in the white areas, which then seemed to magically disappear. It was working, and even if upon close inspection you might see a minuscule seam, that only added to the history of the piece. After all these years, my tabletop Christmas tree was adding another chapter to its story…and ours.

3

The V-8 Debate

I STOOD ON THE front porch inhaling as much cold fresh air as I could hold. It rejuvenated me even as its dry crispness stung my lungs and made me wince. It was a ritual I practiced every season, and I remember how Bill laughed at me whenever I did it. I tried to explain to him that each season has a scent of its own. The smell this time had a note of sweetness, a sure sign of harsh winter.

Bill popped his head out the door and inquired, "Are you done sniffing the air? Penny must have picked up that trait from you." Penny wagged her tail in agreement and peeked outside, her nose twitching as she scanned the immediate area.

"Yes, it smells like winter is here."

"I've got news for you; it arrived yesterday." Technically he was correct, but I paid him no heed, for it was only two days until Christmas, so I had more important matters to attend to. Chase's Christmas cake was ready for pickup and we expected him at any moment. Our gift exchanging schedule varied from year to year. Sometimes Chase would spend Christmas Eve with us, but when his family was having a gathering, we'd see him a day or two earlier.

Penny's ears perked up as she alerted to something. I glanced in the direction she was looking. "I think Miss Wiggles hears something. Could it be Chase's truck?" I could neither hear nor see anything. The snow dampened most sounds and partially obscured the view. The fact that his truck was white would only make it that much more difficult to spot.

"Here he comes," announced Bill.

"I can't see anything."

"That's because you're too short, Quinn. Give it a minute."

I waited a few seconds before I detected movement in the snow. The GMC pickup rounded the corner and drove up the embankment before stopping a dozen yards in front of the house. Chase always parked further back than necessary, as though fearful he might hit the front porch if he came any closer. When he opened the door, I saw him emerge with two large, brightly wrapped boxes stacked one on top of the other. He approached the house warily, weaving slightly like a drunken sailor. It was then I realized he could not see where he was going. "Chase, is that you? I recognize your boots."

He chuckled, "I'm here; it's me."

"Let me help you," I responded as he reached the door. "Watch out for Penny; she's trying to sniff you. Bill, please take Penny inside." I lifted the top box and carried it to the kitchen counter. I was pleased to see it was wrapped with his traditional silver duct tape. If Chase ever wraps his presents with invisible tape, Christmas won't be the same. Chase placed the second box on the countertop next to the gift I had prepared for him, an extra chocolate German chocolate cake. He plopped onto the bar chair and eyed the plastic carry container that held his gift.

"I'm glad you let me know ahead of time you were coming. I have your 'surprise' cake ready."

"So I see, the best gift ever." He removed the lid and continued. "Chocolate and coconut frosting, my favorite. You know it'll be gone by tomorrow and I won't be sharing it with my family." He carefully returned the lid without smudging the side of the cake. "These gifts can wait, but here's something you can eat now." He produced a gallon sized Ziploc bag of his homemade deer and elk jerky from a pocket in his coat and placed it on the counter top.

"Thanks, Chase."

I unsealed it and the aroma of smoked meat gently swirled into my nostrils. "Chase, do you know where the name 'jerky' comes from?"

"No, but I bet you do."

"Funny. Do I bore you too much with my facts?"

"No, I always learn something. Where does the name come from?"

"Well, the origin is actually from the ancient Incas of Peru. The word was 'charqui', which meant dried meat. Over time it got shortened or corrupted, depending on how you look at it, to jerky."

"Huh, I've been making it for years, but never thought about the name."

"So tell me, what are your plans for Christmas?"

"Mom is celebrating tomorrow night, so I thought I'd come over now."

I understood, but tried to hide my disappointment. We had no family or other friends close by to celebrate with, so we welcomed his company all the more. In the past, Gail would come bearing gifts for all, and I would respond in kind. When that ended, she never received her last Christmas gift from me, a singing cow, which now sat quietly on the counter of my studio kitchenette. Even friends from Florida, who used to visit when the girls were younger, had not been seen for years. Understandably, not many people want to travel to Montana in the winter, and they have their own commitments elsewhere. But I was missing those happy times and saddened by the realization they might never come again.

"Anything wrong, Nancy?" I snapped back to reality when Chase spoke. "You had a faraway look in your eyes."

"No, I was just wondering if you are looking forward to tomorrow night. I hope the weather holds and your sister can make it from Billings."

"It'll be great to see her, but I'm not sure Mom will let me in the door."

"Why?"

"Well, it'll be a big shindig this year. Mom told me to bring a vegetable tray. I was so busy yesterday that I only just managed to get to the store as they were closing the doors. I begged the guy to let me in and I told him I only needed one thing. I ran down one of the aisles and came to a dead stop. I suddenly couldn't remember what I needed to buy. They were already sweeping the floors and some of the lights were shutting off, and I stood there desperately trying to remember the one thing I needed to buy. My mind was completely blank."

Bill had gone into the back to retrieve some ginger ale. As he returned and handed one to Chase he asked, "What did you do?"

"I saw a can of V-8 and grabbed it, and ran to the checkout."

"That's…sort of…vegetable-ish," I offered hopefully.

"Mom will kill me. She's expecting a lot of people this year. Why did I buy that? I don't even like to drink it, and I grabbed the biggest bottle I saw!"

I could detect the desperation and frustration in his voice, yet at the same moment I saw the humor in it and tried not to smile. "She'll forgive you; perhaps she'll be filled with the holiday spirit. Maybe you can all have a glass of V-8 for a Christmas toast—you know, a new tradition," I gently teased. "She can't get too upset; they are vegetables, just in liquid form. You almost got it right."

Chase moaned, shook his head, and placed one hand on his forehead. "Nope, she's gonna kill me."

Trying to think of a way to console him, I encouraged him to taste his soda. "Here, try this new ginger ale from Australia. It's my favorite."

"I'm sure it'll be fine; I'm not really worried," he sighed before tasting his drink. "Say, this is really good."

"It contains real cane sugar. You can taste the difference."

"But the real question is," Bill added, "will your family notice the difference when you serve them V-8?"

Chase shook his head again. "Mom's gonna kill me for sure."

Penny is ready for Santa.

🐎 🐎 🐎

Somehow Chase survived Christmas; at least there was no obituary notice. I continued with my post-Christmas routine. Time to take down the tree and put away the ornaments. It always bothered Bill. His family never took down the tree until New Year's Day. I prefer a decluttered home, so the 26th is always cleaning day. But this year I relented. Bill wanted to take advantage of the post-Christmas sales. "It's the best time to buy tree lights and decorations. They're practically giving them away."

I dreaded the thought of rushing from store to store. I don't like crowds, so I try to visit businesses during their off-hours when I can have a little peace and quiet. Even though my fears soon proved warranted, it was fortuitous that we ventured into that cold day. At the seasonal section of one local grocery store Sonja and I wandered the aisles, admiring all the treats and festive decorations still remaining, mostly brightly colored stocking stuffers and candies in decorative boxes. As I gazed at a shelf near the bottom of the display, a small gold-domed object caught my eye. I picked it up and looked it over. It somehow seemed familiar to me, but I couldn't think of a reason why.

Sonja approached and saw me engrossed in my thoughts. "What do you have there?"

"A chocolate covered cherry."

"Mom, you act like you've never seen one before; they're really good with that white cream inside."

"No, it's not the white cream."

"What are you talking about?"

"It's clear red juice inside." Then I remembered. A thoughtful, melancholic smile spread across my face. "Honey Girl, these particular Cella's brand of cherries have a special meaning to me. I remember when I was about five years old or so, my Dad used to bring them home in his pockets just for me. He died only a year later." I continued to stare at the shiny foil as images flashed before me, taking me to places I had left long ago. "They were always the same kind, in this gold wrapper. Sometimes he would leave them for me on the kitchen counter as a surprise, or he would reach into his pocket and take one out to place in my hand for no reason really. It wasn't my birthday; it was just because...he loved me."

"Mom, what a wonderful story. Is that why you do things like that for me and Sandy?"

"I'm sure it is." I was reluctant to put that piece of chocolate back on the shelf. I even contemplated buying it for myself. Somehow, it would not have been the same, and I feared it would lose some of its meaning, so I gently placed it back in the box with the others and held the memory close to my heart. "Let's go find your Dad and Sandy; they must be wandering about somewhere." As we turned to walk away, I looked back over my shoulder for one moment. I wondered if that chocolate would find its way to some other little girl who would remember it fondly many years later. Christmas was over, but I still had received a cherished gift, a pleasant memory from my past. Thanks, Dad.

4

Thirty Below and Nowhere to Go

WINTER RAGED WITH A vengeance. We were experiencing both record cold temperatures and snowfall. I was right; Old Man Winter and Mother Nature had produced the worst weather ever. National news, local radio, and even social media were all focused on the snowstorms that came in waves. There was no rest from the pummeling Montana and other northwestern states were experiencing. Bill was having a difficult time clearing the snow from our mile of mountain road. He was regularly plowing in treacherous conditions up to five times a day, and I was concerned for his safety. I pleaded with him to reconsider and not plow so often.

"Nancy, if I don't keep plowing, the drifts will build up to the point I can't move them, much less find the road. The snow's nearly stopped now, so I'm going to take advantage of it. I'll be back in a couple of hours."

"Just be careful; it's so slick out there with the ice and snow accumulation." I checked my watch, a safety measure I had been practicing for years. I needed to keep tabs on how long Bill was away from home.

"Are you going to listen to your CDs?"

"Not this time, I need to stay focused on finding the center of the road. Keep the fireplace going; the temperatures are going to drop even more once evening starts setting in."

"Try to get home before dark. I know the cell service is hit and miss, but take your phone anyway in case you need me."

"I will, but there isn't anything you can do if I get stuck."

"At least I'll know what's happening and where you are if there's a problem."

Bill finished bundling up in his parka, watch cap, scarf, snow boots, and gloves. As he opened the door I glanced at the thick dark clouds hovering low over the landscape, ready to unleash another flurry of snow. A cold blast of subzero air stung my face and sent a tingling chill throughout my body. I instinctively wrapped my arms around myself and shivered.

"Stay warm, Nancy." Bill's voice was cheerful. "I'll be back soon; love you."

"Love you; be careful. I'll get supper started; you'll need something warm when you get home."

Within minutes I heard the low rumble of the diesel engine and the shrill warning beeper as the tractor backed out of the garage. Bill spent precious minutes pushing snow from the parking area before turning onto the road. I stood by the loft window and watched the lights disappear as he crawled down the mountain. Once out of sight I went downstairs and placed another log in the fireplace. The firebox had a built-in fan that activated automatically and filled the room with warm dry air. I wanted to sit by the fire and enjoy the flicker of its yellow and orange flames, but I had laundry waiting in the dryer and another load of clothes sitting in the hamper. The endless cycle of cleaning and cooking could not wait for long. But the sound of the burning, cracking, popping, and sizzling had a mesmerizing effect on me. I decided to rest a few more minutes before returning to my mundane chores. *Better get on your feet, Nancy; there's much to be done.* I was sharply awakened by the phone ringing. Where was it? How much time had passed? I didn't bother looking at the clock; I just lifted myself out of the cozy chair and fumbled for the phone. I immediately recognized Bill's voice.

"Nancy, the tractor slid off the road and I'm stuck at the bottom near the highway. I plowed a wide enough path for you to drive the truck down and pull me out. The tires are already chained up and the tow cables are in the bed. Stay in four-wheel-drive and be sure to keep a bit to the right so you don't slide off the hill. A little bit of snow will give you some traction. But don't go too far over or you'll get stuck in the drainage ditch."

I was trying to assess everything he said while I called to Sonja on the intercom. She was excited by the prospect of a rescue mission. My first instinct was to decline her offer of assistance, but Sandy was away visiting friends and Sonja was older now, and I could use the extra pair of eyes and hands. We bundled up and headed for the truck bay. I rarely drove the truck in the summertime and never in the winter. It was so wide I could lay across the front seat and still have room to stretch. But its height was my biggest challenge. I could barely reach the pedals even with the seat pulled all the way forward, and I could only see over the hood by sitting on a pillow. Sonja offered to drive.

"I'm bigger than you now, Mom. I can handle it."

"I appreciate the offer, Dear, but I'll manage. Just get me a pillow."

After we backed the truck out of the garage, the snow began to fall heavily and the wind picked up considerably. I could feel it slamming the left side of the truck. *Oh well, at least it will push me in the ditch instead of down the cliff side.* I silently said a prayer as we slowly began to crawl down the icy hill. I could hear the crunch of the chains biting through the snow and into the ice. This was a good sign; it meant I was gripping something. I kept the left side tires in the plowed path and the right side tires along the edge of the snow. *Don't go in the ditch, Nancy; don't go in the ditch. Where is the ditch?*

"Sonja, you need to watch the edge on your side; I can't see that well from the driver's side. If my wheel gets too close to the ditch, tell me. It's there somewhere under the snow. I want the tires to barely be in the snow. If we get stuck, we can't help Dad. I'm in low gear and four-wheel-drive, so we should be fine."

Sonja wanted to roll down her window, but it was much too cold and I feared the defroster would not keep up. Even with the windows closed it was just managing to provide me with enough visibility to see the road. We both remained quiet while I concentrated on my driving. We continued to crawl down the mountain. The wind did not abate; it struck us like pounding waves, blowing snow over us and temporarily blinding my view. I would stop each time and wait for it to subside. The heater was running full blast, but it was still cold in the truck. I began to shiver and I was worried about Bill because the temperature continued to drop.

"I'm freezing, Honey Bear. How are you doing?"

Sonja did not reply. She was having just as much trouble seeing the road as I was. We were almost in whiteout conditions when we reached the first cattle guard at the entrance to our property. I paused the truck. It taxed my nerves not being able to see clearly in front or to the sides. If I misjudged the centerline of the crossing by ten inches either way, we risked falling into the culvert. I lined up as best I could and started to cross slowly.

"Mom, go to the left; you're too close to the edge!"

"Thanks…this mile of road feels like ten miles today."

We made it safely across and continued our trek down the mountain. I felt my spirits lift as the snow and wind began to ebb. It was a relief; the six-foot wide path of plowed snow became visible again and I could see much better. Despite the chains, I still found myself slipping from time to time in the pockets of drifts the wind had created. I tried navigating around the worst ones, but some were unavoidable. We were over halfway down now and approaching the second cattle guard when I felt the truck suddenly stop.

"Sonja, am I off the edge?"

"No, Mom."

"Why are we stuck?"

She opened her door and looked back. "It's the rear tire, Mom. It's buried."

"We can get out." I sounded more confident than I was. I put the truck in reverse and it barely moved. A wave of anxiety passed through me. I looked down at the four-wheel-drive indicator. I had not engaged it after all. My heart sank. I flipped the switch on and heard a distinctive clunk as it locked all four wheels. I eased down on the gas pedal. The truck moved rearward only an inch before the tires began to spin. I raised my foot.

"I'll have to rock us back and forth, so we don't dig in deeper. We can do this." I tried moving forward, but the spinning continued. *You can do this; you're smarter than snow. C'mon Nancy, just a little more gas; Bill is waiting. I hope his heater is working. Stay focused; Bill is a soldier; he knows what to do. Now back up a little more. Now forward again. Keep rocking; build up momentum. Why aren't the chains gripping this ice? I'm in a snow drift; it's like powder. Try once more; this time it'll work. Come on, do it…do it!* On the last forward thrust the tire lurched free of its imprisonment and we continued moving forward.

"You did it Mom!"

"Well, aren't we the mountain rescue women! Keep watching the road for me."

We crossed the second cattle guard without incident and were again on our way. After a few cautious directions from Sonja we rounded the corner and could see the tractor two hundred yards ahead. "Thank goodness he's on flat level ground."

We crossed the final cattle guard and drove to where the tractor sat idle near the highway. I stopped five yards in front of it. I was wrong about the ground being level. The tractor was actually canted slightly to one side, resting on a shallow berm beside the road, partially buried in a large drift.

Bill jumped out and approached the truck. I rolled down my window so I could hear his yelling over the now steady wind. "It took you awhile; I was getting worried."

"We had a rough time. Are you okay?"

"Yes, let's get going." Bill guided us closer to the tractor, making certain we remained in the center of the road. He connected the tow cable to his front bucket and the tow hooks under the truck, then came up to the window again.

"Nancy, keep the truck in low gear. When I waive my arm, give it some gas and start backing up. There's not a lot of slack in the cable, so expect some resistance almost immediately. Just keep applying gas. If you start to spin, you can stop and honk at me." He returned to the tractor.

I looked at Sonja and said, "That doesn't make sense. I can't be in low gear. I have to be in reverse."

Sonja shrugged, "Do what Dad says."

"If I do that, I'll run right into him."

"You want me to go ask him?"

"No, I'll figure it out."

I put the truck in reverse and waited for his signal. I could see the exhaust bellowing from the tractor, so I knew he'd started the engine. Then it began to roar and I saw him wave his arm in the air. I accelerated, steadily pushing on the gas pedal.

"He's moving!" Sonja called out.

The chains tightened and the tractor popped right out of the drift. As soon as it was safely level in the middle of the road I hit the break and stopped.

"Good work!" Bill called as he walked up to the truck.

"I'm glad. I was a bit worried when you told me to put the truck in low gear and back up. I couldn't do both."

"Huh? No, Honey, I meant you should put the truck in low four-wheel-drive, not low gear. You've got a high and low setting for it."

"Now I'm confused. Well, it doesn't matter; we got you out."

"Yes…well if I wasn't freezing my tuchus off I'd explain it to you, but right now I need you to back up to the intersection <u>after</u> I take the tow cable off. I'll pass you and plow you a wider path on the way up. Stay about hundred yards behind me. I'll have to make a series of passes to clear these drifts and open up the road, so I'll be going back and forth. I want to get this done by dark. Better to have you nearby in case I run into trouble again."

There was no time for any further discussion; we were losing daylight and the temperature was still falling. The snow had begun again and we experienced another brief whiteout along the way up, but at least we were parked when it hit. We waited and watched as Bill widened the path. It was a very slow trudge home that took over ninety minutes of stopping and starting. We watched him methodically clear a 100 yards of road at a time in a series of passes. I kept back and only moved forward after he started each new section. This was the first time I'd ever actually seen how he plowed the road beyond the house. As darkness settled in, I had to judge our separation mostly by following the glow of his rear lights. By now I estimated the temperature was a good twenty degrees below zero.

"Are you warm enough, Sonja?"

"Oh, fine, but I'm young and strong. You must be cold though."

"Because I'm old and frail?"

"Stop it, Mom. I just know you get cold a lot."

We were managing the deep freeze, but despite the inside cabin temperature and the defroster spewing full blast, the wiper blades kept freezing to the windshield. Each time this happened, Sonja would reach out and free them. Ice began forming on the windshield and side windows. I could only see out of the two small holes the defroster created for me. Snow was now blowing hard again and caking on the windows as well. The vicious wind never ceased, the darkness grew, and I prayed for our safe return. The thought of sitting by the fireplace with a pot of steaming hot tea, lots and lots of hot tea, sustained me. Sonja dreamed of hot cocoa. We both envisioned chocolate sweets to go with our drinks. It was better than thinking about our cold feet, cold hands, and cold noses. Then I saw the lights from home ahead. Only 150 yards to go. We made it. By the time we'd put the truck away and gone inside, I had developed a mild headache. There was no warm supper like I had promised, but I was satisfied that we were all home safe and sound once more.

"Sonja, you were wonderful today. I think we need superhero names and capes! You can be Super Girl."

"Thanks, Mom, but I would rather be a pirate."

"Okay, Captain Jacqueline Sparrow. Let's get dinner ready; we're all hungry."

It wasn't our worst day on the mountain, and it wouldn't be the only challenge this winter. It was more like the opening salvo of things to come, events that would test our resolve as the winter progressed.

Once more unto the breach!

5

Wildlife Rodeo

IT'S HARD TO EXERCISE during the winter months, so my more exotic hobbies like knife throwing and archery have to be curtailed. I don't go hiking since snowshoeing holds no allure for me. Even working with the horses is out, so I have to find other ways to avoid a sedentary state. I've tried Tai chi, yoga, and stationary bicycling, which all work, but aren't particularly fun. Bill fenced in college, and suggested I try it. I acquired a proper foil and a video, but without a partner, the appeal was limited. I asked Bill to participate, but he no longer fenced due to a shoulder injury he sustained years ago while downhill skiing. When I pitched the idea to Sonja, she shook her head vigorously and proclaimed, "You'll put out an eye out with that thing." There is no excitement associated with shadow fencing, so I guess I was foiled. I finally settled on something completely different—ribbon dancing. It is impossible to be gloomy when long, multicolored, silk streamers are gracefully flying through the air overhead. I put on suitable music, grasp a ribbon stick in each hand, and just have fun. It is quite the cardio workout, and after a half hour I am breathless. When I'm through having fun with flags (as Bill puts it) I sit down by the front windows and rest for a spell

On this day, after finishing my workout, I was watching the wind blow snow across the gently rising front meadow. Intermittently, they formed small drifts which took on the appearance of waves upon a white lake. Each time a strong gust blew through, billowy waves of white powder would rise into the air and resettle on the roadbed. If it continued much longer, Bill would have to plow through the barriers with the tractor.

Down by the corrals the drifts were already several feet high. They reminded me of the walls we used to make for our snow forts when I was a child in Michigan. We built similar walls to serve as a boundary for our backyard skating rink every winter. My brother and his friends would line the rink with plastic before filling the pool with water from our garden hose. One year it was too cold to remain outside while the rink was filling, so he connected a sprinkler to oscillate during the night, thinking it would fill the rink, and we would all be skating by morning. He didn't realize that overnight it got so cold that the water froze in the air. In the morning we awakened to the sight of a frozen water arch that passed through the middle of the overhead power lines and down into our small skating rink. My mother had to call the electric company to come remove the ice. Even though I was about seven years old, I still remembered it fondly.

As I continued to gaze at the drifts I caught a glimpse of Wilson off to the left, raising his head sharply, transfixed by something I could not see, but he could sense. I scanned the field ahead of his gaze as Whiskey, now alerted, spun on the ice and began running in the opposite direction. Wilson quickly followed him, and both horses stumbled in the drifts and on the slick ice underneath. Only Wilson fell, smacking his hip, but he quickly recovered and stood up to face the unknown threat. He didn't appear to be injured, but my big fellow, who wasn't afraid of anything and who took life in stride, was now quite nervous. Both geldings returned to the perceived safety of the corral, but continued to run in small circles inside the paddock. They tossed their heads back dramatically and whinnied loudly.

I sent Bill down to investigate. Sonja insisted on going along, so I asked Bill to take a rifle in case there was a dangerous animal about. I watched from the window for several minutes as they searched the area. Satisfied the danger had passed, they took to feeding the horses. The drama over, I went to my desk to write. I had emails to answer and became engrossed in them to the point that I was unaware a half hour had passed before Bill and Sonja came through the front door. Bill called up to me, "Nancy, did you see them?"

"Who?"

"Oh, no, you missed it," Sonja added.

"Missed what?" I said as I clambered down the stairs, still sore from my workout.

"We didn't see anything at the barn and there were no unusual tracks in the snow, but the horses were still bothered by something. I assumed it was some unfamiliar scent that alerted them, but suddenly Wilson's ears shot up, so I followed his stare and saw something rising over a snowbank like a periscope."

"What was it?"

"I couldn't tell. It was fifty yards away and blended too much with the trees behind it. It sank back down, and then another periscope slowly rose up next to it. Whatever it was, there were two of them. Then the other periscope slowly raised up again and went back down. Finally both of them raised together. It was a pair of heads that looked like a couple of camels at first, but we don't normally get those around here." Sonja rolled her eyes as her Dad continued. "It was the funniest thing, a couple of young moose—or is it mooses?"

"Why didn't you call me? I'm so sorry I missed it."

"We thought you were still watching."

"I would love to have gotten that on video. It must have been Lady Moose's twins. You can't mistake a moose face."

"Yeah, they were pretty young, so I suspect Mama Moose was nearby. I think they were as scared of the horses as the horses were of them, but they were curious just the same. They kept bobbing up and down and hiding from us—we had to laugh."

"It sounds like something you'd see in a cartoon. I wish I could have seen them; they must be darling, such a curious couple. I'm relieved to know that they're safe. I often wonder how well the little ones do in such brutal weather."

"They were sure talking things over between themselves," Sonja chimed in. "They acted kind of goofy, Mom."

"I can just imagine…'You look at them.' 'No, you look at them.' 'Okay, we'll both look at them…one… two…three—up!' I just wish I had seen it." It was such a rare treat, and I always enjoyed studying the behavior of our native visitors. Each one has its own personality, and seeing them in their natural surroundings brings out those traits. Be they predators or prey, all the different species have unique behavior patterns of their own. In this regard they are not unlike humans.

With the excitement now passed, I went into the kitchen to prepare lunch. As I inspected my cupboard in search of inspiration for a meal, I wondered if our hay stores were what really attracted the moose calves. Perhaps they too were formulating dinner plans.

Uninspired by the assortment of canned and boxed food in the pantry, I now stared blankly into the refrigerator, hoping an idea would pop out at any moment. Each thought I had was stymied by the fact I was always short one or two ingredients. I closed the door and sighed. We were growing short of food stocks, so I would have to be creative. The driving conditions had been so poor that we were making fewer trips to town. Fearing Bill would suggest an ice cream supper, I settled on making potluck soup. It went over fairly well, that is they ate it.

As we dined, Sonja informed me that she thought the hay stores looked a bit low, and that she believed some bales were missing. It was a mystery. Regardless of the cause, we were running dangerously low on hay and now needed to ration it. I told her to supplement their feed with concentrates until we could figure out a solution. This cold winter was proving to be very expensive. Although we kept our spirits up, we were paying a price for it in more than one way.

6

Cold Case

WINTER CONTINUED ITS ASSAULT. It seemed to last forever. We played our board games, baked, and had our usual pizza and movie nights, but we were still all in need of some cheering up. I decided a colorful table setting might change the mood, so I got out a set of green, hand-blown, textured glass plates. To me they evoked a feeling of springtime. Perhaps if I made it look like spring inside, spring would arrive outside. It was wishful thinking, but I was also working on the theory that food tasted better on pretty plates and a beautiful table cloth.

I glanced out the dining room window to see if perchance my plan had worked. All I saw was snow and the occasional chipmunk popping his head out of one of their many hidden tunnel entrances. It was a comical sight; he would appear from nowhere, then disappear, only to reappear moments later several yards away. Life was a game to him in any kind of weather.

The front door squeaked as it opened, telling me Bill was home from plowing. When I saw the look on his face I knew it wasn't good news.

"Nancy, I'm stuck again."

"Oh no, that's the third time this week. How far did you have to walk?"

"From the end of the road. The truck is all ready to go. I'll drive you down and you can pull me out."

I nodded, folded the last cloth napkin, and placed it on the table. Even this was becoming a predictable, if somewhat tedious, routine.

Early the next morning Sonja and I went to the barn to feed the boys. Wilson was his usual plump and easygoing self, bobbing his head in a friendly greeting. I was concerned about Whiskey though; he was eating, but I felt the unusually long winter was taking a toll on his 31 year old body. I encouraged him and rubbed his back, reminding him how important he was to the family. In truth I thought all the wildlife were suffering this year. The deer were so hungry they were digging up my iris rhizomes in the garden and eating them. They had nibbled all the lower tree branches and eaten my shrubbery to the ground. I couldn't complain about it; I could see how difficult it was to find food when the terrain was in such a barren state.

As we were leaving the corral, we noticed the horses alert and trot to the far end of the paddock. Just then a large elk effortlessly jumped over the fence, strode into the hay storage area, and began munching. She pulled at the bales and quickly consumed one mouthful after another.

"Look at that!" Sonja exclaimed.

"I see her; there's our hay thief. She certainly is brazen." As we started toward the stable, the elk saw us. At that moment I wondered if I was making a mistake. Elk can be dangerous if they feel threatened, and this one was clearly hungry. The horses decided not to tangle with her, and I had nothing more than my hickory walking staff. My concerns quickly abated, for as soon as we began our approach, she turned, jumped over the gate, and fled into the forest.

"Mom, she's so hungry."

"I know; I feel bad for her, but she looks well fed. We'll have to talk to Dad about hanging another set of gates above these to keep her out. She'll have to find her food elsewhere. I'm sorry, but we simply can't afford to feed her. Clever gal though, I'll give her an 'A' for initiative."

Return of the hay thief.

The elk tried several times that day to finish her breakfast. Each time we were able to frighten her away. We had to wait for a break in the weather before we could go to town and purchase two extra gates to fasten above the existing ones so we could fully enclose the hay. I hoped it would be soon because we couldn't watch the stable twenty-four hours a day.

Four days later our opportunity arrived and we made the much needed trip to Helena. Near the state capitol we saw a curious sight that further emphasized how rough the winter was on the wildlife. Deer were everywhere to be seen in search of food. This was a year-round phenomenon, but the count was higher than normal. As we waited at a stoplight, I watched three deer standing at the curbside, judging traffic.

The first doe stepped onto the street and looked in both directions. Satisfied there were no approaching cars, she confidently walked across. The next doe followed suite, and the third deer did the same. I was amazed that all three of them had learned to watch for traffic so they could avoid being hit by a moving vehicle. It left quite an impression on me, and on the drive back home we debated whether or not the deer had learned how to read traffic signals.

As we topped the Continental Divide, the snow blew across the road in a ghostly mist. Surrounded by ice coated trees, the atmosphere they created had a surreal quality to it. No matter how often we made the trip, and no matter the season, the view from here made me feel as though I was on top of the world.

We arrived at Cimarron without incident and erected the gates to secure the hay. Despite Sonja and me helping Bill, the task proved frustrating enough for him to invoke a bit of color into his dialogue, but we did eventually finish the job. I yearned for spring, but it would be a long wait. It had no intention of arriving on time, though it did take devilish delight in teasing us.

7

The Mild, Wild West?

"I'M SO TIRED OF college; it will never end." I listened to Sandy bemoan her long hours of study. She rested her head in her hands at the dining room table and looked rather glum.

"It will be over faster than you think. You'll be graduating with honors the first week in July."

"How do you know I'll keep my honors' status? I still have one semester to go."

"I know you; even if you're weary you won't let your grades slide."

"Working part time at the Stratford Café is more fun than college. Maybe after graduation I can work there fulltime while looking for a job. But that doesn't help me get through the next few months."

"Enjoy the false spring we've been having the last two weeks. It's glorious. We don't usually have mild weather this time of year. Maybe winter's really over."

She looked at me with a blank expression. We both knew it wasn't true; it was just another trick by Old Man Winter to get us to lower our guard. Winter was far from over, but I was trying to find something to brighten Sandy's outlook. I decided to take a different direction. "Be proud of yourself; you'll be the first student in the University of Montana system to have an AA degree at eighteen years old. It's amazing."

Sandy just rolled her eyes at me. All she could think about was freedom from tests, due dates, and term papers. I understood. "I know what will cheer you up. Let's read the Police Blotter. Perhaps something in it will make you smile. If that fails, I'll break out the chocolate. Let me see…" I picked up the county newspaper from the table and rustled through it, searching for the Blotter, then quickly scanned it for something humorous. "Oh, listen to this. 'A woman called and reported her husband is not letting her out of the garage.'"

Sandy did not respond; she just gazed ahead, completely disinterested. I continued scanning silently until I found another possible candidate. "How about this one? 'A woman at a gas station requested to speak with an officer regarding the theft of a case of pop from the store. She said she had a video of the incident. An officer advised it was the Pepsi delivery driver picking up overstock.'"

Sandy remained mute, so I searched some more. "Here's one. 'A caller advised they had been trying to trap a feral cat and instead they caught a skunk.'"

Sandy cracked a smile and asked, "Is there another one?"

"Perhaps, let me see…'A caller stated a kid got his arm stuck in a cup holder at the theatre. The person called back and stated they were able to get the kid's arm out.' 'A caller requested to speak with an officer regarding a subject that was metal detecting on school district grounds and had dug several holes.' But wait, there's more. 'A man requested an officer check on a female that is in the front yard of her residence, standing in one place, and swaying back and forth. A responding officer advised the woman was trying to get a Wi-Fi signal and everything was okay.'"

Sandy snorted, "I could dance all over the meadow and not get a signal in our front yard."

The conversation was not going the way I had hoped. I was nearly finished reading when more entries caught my eye. "Here we go. 'A caller reported a man walking on the highway who was wearing a baseball hat and did not appear to be a hazard.' Hang on, Sandy, this is the best one yet. 'A child called 911 stating he wanted to turn in a little girl for pinching him. He would not give his name.'"

I heard a small giggle and knew Sandy was feeling a little better. "I see one last entry. 'A caller reported a man jogging, and the caller said he would follow the individual until an officer got there.'"

This time Sandy burst out laughing. My goal achieved, I started to fold the paper, when suddenly the sun disappeared and the dining room went surprisingly dark. "I don't like the looks of this." I turned to Sandy and added, "Have you checked the weather lately?"

"No, not today."

"I wonder if a snow storm's moving in."

Within minutes the wind picked up. It ranged between a whistle and a howl. We placed draft blockers by each door plate to keep out the dreaded cold. News reports indicated an Arctic front was moving in from Canada and blizzard conditions were expected, with temperatures plunging to between -35 to -54 degrees. We were now practiced hands at dealing with foul weather, so I knew we could comfortably ride out the coming storm, but I was concerned for our two horses, Wilson and Whiskey.

"They'll be okay," Sonja reassured me. "They've got thick winter coats and the stable to shield them from the wind."

"If they'll stay in it. Most of the time they just stand in the corral and let the snow fall on them."

"If it's bad enough, they'll go inside."

"Sonja, do they have any hay?"

"Yep, I filled the feeder and checked the waterer for ice. I also gave them a bit of sweet feed to keep them warm."

"How about filling the bird feeder." It wasn't much, but I hoped my feathered friends would continue to get some sustenance in the wicked storm. The dreaded white parachutes began to fall and once again I felt like I was living in a snow globe. I watched through the picture window as Sonja refilled the hanging feeder in the high wind. Ice quickly built up on the windowsill and tiny frost patterns, resembling lace, were etching themselves onto the glass.

My daughter rushed back in and threw off her coat. "Yikes, that was fun." She edged over to the fireplace and warmed her hands."

"You should have brought the feeder inside to refill it."

Sonja shrugged, "My way was faster, but that wind! It must be gusting over forty."

The tempest was pushing the powdery snow horizontally. It was as beautiful as it was deadly. When snow falls vertically, it coats the land evenly. But wind like this will create heavy drifts wherever it encounters a sudden rise in terrain. I knew the result would be heavy snow drifts on parts of our road. Even with this knowledge I was fascinated by the air that had come alive, and I watched the flakes swirl and dance in the icy gale. Then came a flash of feathered movement as a Downey Woodpecker landed on the birdfeeder. Clinging desperately and pecking the seeds, she found a morsel or two before flying back to the shelter of a large evergreen tree near the house. She repeated this mission several times, and I had to marvel at how she was able to maintain her grasp when the feeder was blowing almost sideways. It twisted precariously on its shepherd's hook, which itself was frozen into the ground.

All I could do was watch the poor gal grab a seed and continue her quest as the wind whipped at her feathers. I often felt sad for the wildlife that endured such hardships, and found myself watching for signs that indicated my little neighbors were well and safe. Each morning I would look for tracks in the snow and nibbled tree branches. Finding such signs eased my mind and reassured me that nature would endure with or without my help. All I could do now was wait for tomorrow and the passing of the storm.

The morning was bright, clear, and sunny. Bill had gotten up early to clear the parking pad and plow a path for us down the mountain. Fearing a little cabin fever might set in, I decided to brave the cold. I stepped onto the front patio and surveyed the heavy blanket of snow. It measured nearly a foot deep, but would settle some now that the sun was out. A long continuous mound of dirt, gravel, and snow snaked its way down one side of the roadway. It was always a challenge to keep the road open, and I constantly feared the bank would get too large, leaving no place to put the new powder. Even now parts of this wall were almost seven feet high. As I walked across the fresh plowing I could feel older compacted snow and ice crunch beneath my feet. It was somehow satisfying to me as I listened to the steady rhythm of the sound. It was almost musical. Wilson and Whiskey heard me and began to call. They wanted their breakfast. The snow was stacked so high I couldn't see them, nor could I climb over the debris field between me and my horses. My only option was to return to the house and use the pasture Bill had not plowed. This meant stomping through ten inches or more of fresh powder, but there would be no tall mounds or ice to deal with, and it was all downhill. Experience had taught me to leave a large wake in the snow so I'd have an easier time coming back up. This meant going back inside to don more wintry attire.

When I again emerged, it was from the back of the house, wearing my parka, snow pants, and tall muck boots. Despite looking like Nanook Nancy of the North, my horses must have recognized me because they started to whinny again in loud shrieks. I plodded down the hill much to their delight. Their heads now hung over the corral panels and they followed my every movement. As I approached closer I heard much snorting and similar reminders that clearly indicated I wasn't spending enough time with them. I often told them that we humans were not bred for such cold, and it really limited our time at the barn. Other than a quick inspection and feeding, we couldn't spend much time socializing with our boys during the winter. But my pleas fell on deaf ears. Food and companionship were the order of the day. No excuses!

Twice a day, regardless of the biting temperatures, the horses had to be fed and checked for signs of discomfort. In subzero weather like this they were given a special feed mix that we had concocted. It contained vitamin supplements, minerals, and sugars, the latter of which provided them much needed extra calories to burn so they could stay warm without losing weight. They also enjoyed it immensely.

We did not blanket our horses, relying instead on their natural ability to grow heavy winter coats with which to regulate their body temperatures. A blanket would impair this normal bodily process. However, if I saw signs they were struggling, or if they looked sickly, I had a horse blanket on hand to warm them. The inevitable effect of placing this blanket on one horse was that the other was always taken aback. *Who are you? What did you do with my friend? Are you an alien?*

I called to my companions, "Settle down, boys. I'm here to feed you. My, you two put on quite a spectacle. You'd think you hadn't eaten in ages." I received reassuring nods and snorts as they followed me gleefully to the tack room. Soon all would be well again.

After placating them, I began the long trudge back up the hill. I had placed a muffler over my nose to keep out the searing cold air, but it was now coated in ice formed from my breath. I paused partway up the hill to rest. I turned to admire the sparking, snow-laden trees and noticed something small flutter on the branch of one of them. I thought it must be my woodpecker, so I took a few steps closer to the tree and stood gazing up its massive trunk. All was now still and silent. I searched the branches for the familiar dark silhouette of a woodpecker, but saw nothing. I kept focusing on the branches, inspecting each one in minute detail. Nothing. I quietly moved closer and surveyed the brown and white branches again. As I peered up the tree trunk, my efforts were rewarded. I spied a Pygmy Owl. He was about the size of my fist and was as still as a statue, completely camouflaged against the bark of the tree. He reminded me of a painting of a pair of screech owls I had created years ago. It always amazed me how well they could blend into their surroundings. What a treat it was to see this fellow alive and well!

I watched him for a full minute, before the stinging in my gloves reminded me the cold was creeping through my clothing. If I didn't want frostbite I needed to get back inside at once. Reluctantly, I said goodbye to my new little friend and continued up to the house. As I entered the warmth of my chalet, I glanced at the clock on the wall. Now it was time to feed the two-legged animals. It was a very comforting thought to know that, despite our daily routines, something wonderful and unique was always possible, even likely, on our mountain.

He's a real hoot.

8

Wheeler of Fortune!

ALFRED WHEELER, OUR RESIDENT Professor of Animal Psychology and noted swine connoisseur, sat at our dining room table suspiciously eyeing my apricot oatmeal bars. I knew he wanted to try one, but even after I offered him a tender sweet cookie, he declined. After several minutes of watching Bill and the girls enjoying the treats, he finally reached out to the plate. "Well, I suppose I should see how these taste. You have been practicing with your recipes, right, Nancy?"

"Oh, yes, I hope you like them, Alfred."

He bit into one of the bars and tried to hide his delight. "This is better, not the way I would have prepared it, but you're improving."

"I'm glad you approve."

"Perhaps 'approve' isn't quite the word I would use, but it's an honest effort." He put two more cookies on his plate and quickly changed the subject. "I see Sonja and Sandy are still enjoying their horses. But what about you, Nancy? Did you ever decide on one for yourself?

"No, I've had to give up riding, Alfred. It's too hard on my back."

He replied as he munched, "That's a pity. If you ever do decide to get another one, I promise to stay away for a while so he doesn't attach himself to me and rebuff all of you. That could happen you know."

"I didn't know you had a way with horses, Alfred. I thought your specialty was pigs."

"Well, I don't work with horses, but all animals immediately like me. There's just something about me that creates that instant bond."

"Maybe it's your scent," Bill added.

"Yes, it could be. They seem to pine when I'm not around. They refuse to connect with anyone else and simply become despondent without my company. It's a shame really, a blessing and a curse."

The conversation lagged for an uncomfortable moment as I recalled the less than warm reception Alfred had received in the past from some of our animals. I decided not to refute his premise and offered no comment. Bill, on the other hand, had that amused look of a cat that was just about to pounce on a canary. I had a hunch as to what he was thinking, but I quickly gave him "the look" and he relaxed. Alfred did not appear to notice our reactions and continued chatting nonchalantly. "I'm glad we're nearing the end of winter; it really got my pigs quite upset. You know, the ex-wife never did like the cold or pigs. That's one of the reasons I moved here, so I could experiment with my swine in peace. Of course, they are the most intelligent creatures -"

I had to break in; I had heard this lecture too many times. "Alfred, may I refill your tea?"

"No, no," he muttered. "I have plenty. I prefer Earl Grey anyway. However, I did want to share my good fortune with all of you."

"What's that?" I asked.

"The local university has requested me to give a series of lectures for their spring semester on raising champion pigs."

Bill pounced. "Well congratulations, you must be in hog heaven!"

Alfred did not join in the laughter. He gave us a practiced smile that suggested he was tolerating our humor. "It's for their agricultural department and they are expecting a large turnout. I proposed they book an auditorium to accommodate the crowd. I plan to bring my best trained pigs to demonstrate their many abilities."

"What would those be?" I automatically asked before instantly regretting my question.

"Well, they make excellent pets and they are easier than dogs to train as sentries, drug sniffers, bomb sniffers, and the like." Alfred looked down at Penny and continued. "What's more, unlike dogs, they can be trained to relieve themselves in a litter box like a cat. They are quite remarkable you know. Why the average pig -"

"Sorry to interrupt, Alfred," Bill responded. "When do your lectures begin?"

"Next month. They wanted enough time to get the program set up. Everyone is looking forward to it. I expect it will be the most popular event on the college calendar this year."

"Who's catering it?" I inquired.

Alfred appeared slightly irritated. "No one. We won't be having food or drink. This is to be an academic endeavor, not a social gathering. Of course, not all the ladies may see it that way." Alfred allowed himself a sly smile. "They do seem to compete over me. Why only yesterday after our faculty meeting I found a phone number in the pocket of my overcoat."

"Placed there by a secret female admirer?" I quizzed.

Bill couldn't resist the opportunity. "What makes you think it was a female?"

"What's that supposed to mean?" Now Alfred was offended.

Bill felt compelled to clarify his remark. "I mean it could have been anyone who's interested in swineology."

I squinted seriously at him. "Bill, is that a real word?"

"I don't know, Honey, but I've heard it used before."

Alfred sniffed, "It's not a term professionals would use."

"Maybe I should have said Oinkophile."

"Very clever. Hmm, now that I think of it, maybe I should come up with a term for a swine aficionado. Thanks, Bill, I have to give this some thought. It would look good on the lecture posters—Alfred Wheeler, Swineologist."

Bill was a bit baffled, but replied demurely, "You're welcome, Alfred."

After Alfred departed, I chastised Bill for his remarks. He defended himself by claiming, "I only said what you were thinking."

"That's beside the point."

"Ah-hah! Then you were thinking it."

"Not exactly. At any rate you should be more respectful of our guest."

"And he should be more respectful of us. I see how he talks down to you, and I don't appreciate it."

"Now don't go claiming you were protecting my honor. You just love taking jabs at Alfred. Did it ever occur to you that he's a lonely man in need of friendship?"

"I thought that's what his pigs were for."

"There you go again."

"Sorry, Honey. I'll try to be nicer next time."

"If there is a next time."

"Of course they'll be a next time. Alfred needs an audience, and we're it."

"Really, why do you think he picked us?"

"He probably likes your cookies."

I just shook my head and tried not to laugh. It would only encourage Bill.

9

The Chimney Sweep

ALMOST IMPERCEPTIBLY, WINTER SLOWLY faded into spring and brought with it the need to clean and reorganize our home. The first weeks of the thaw required us to focus our attentions on the horses. Once the snow melts, the ground turns into a thick pasty black goo. The horses become ankle deep in an unhealthy mix of mud and six months' worth of manure, the latter now softened and aromatic from the warmer temperatures. Their feet and lower legs become covered with it, and if left unattended, health issues will quickly arise. The best way to deal with the muck is to remove it with the front end loader of a tractor.

I watched from the comfort of the house as Bill methodically drove through the corral, scooping up a half-ton of potential fertilizer at a time. Several panels had been removed from the far side of the corral so he could easily exit and deposit it thirty yards away on our ever growing dung mound. The tractor struggled in the black treacle and belched smoke as the engine strained like some ancient dinosaur trying to free itself from a tar pit. At times I feared it might sink into the abyss, not to be seen again for a million years when some future archeologist would dig it up and marvel at how well it had been preserved by a cocoon of nitrogen rich fecal material. I just hoped my husband wouldn't be in it.

The corral cleaning took up the better part of a day, and once completed, it required another hour to hose down the tractor with a pressure washer. A simple water hose lacked the necessary force to remove the muck. The following days would be consumed with road and fence repairs, tack room cleanup, setting out patio furniture, weeding, grass sowing, and a dozen other exterior tasks. Only after all the saddles, bridles, and tools had been cleaned and taken back down to the stable could I focus on traditional spring cleaning. It is time consuming, but worth the effort. When the sun comes out and dries the corrals, my nose rejoices at the loss of all odiferous traces of the previous months. The warmth then brings out the sweetness of honeysuckle mixed with evergreen. All other odors dissipate until they are but faint memories.

It was finally time to tackle the house. Winter coats were placed in armoires and closets. Mittens, gloves, scarves, hats, and snow boots were stored under the staircase or in the upper loft, making room for lighter garments and footwear. Anything no longer needed, yet still serviceable, was placed in a large donation pile for Goodwill. If it was too worn to donate, it was taken to the dump.

The girls had swept the fireplace clean that morning, and placed potted plants around the now unused hearth. My task was to remove the dust from the family room tables, bookshelves, and lampshades, each of which had collected a fine soot from the fireplace over the winter. My efforts seemed futile, for no sooner did I remove the particles than the survivors settled back down to rest in the same spot.

Penny watched me from her bed by the living room sofa, neither bored nor curious. The only time she became ruffled was when I offered to wash her pillow. This she found unsettling, and she would protest by going completely flaccid in it. Her big brown eyes would plead with me not to disrupt her splendor. If that failed, she would bury her face in the bed and pretend to ignore me.

I finished dusting and picked up a broom. As I swept closer to Miss

Wiggles, her eyes never left me, though they retained that indifferent look. "Do you want me to clean your bed, Penny?"

Here came the begging, right on cue.

"No – no, Honey, I have to do it. Your bed smells like corn chips."

Oh-oh, there went the face into hiding.

"Now, Miss Penny! Scoot your buns." With these words she knew her cause was lost, and up she jumped, good-naturedly, wagging her tail fiercely. It continued to spin more than normal and her eyes grew wider.

"What is it girl?"

A faint sound reached my ears. Was it a chirp or a squeak? Penny must have heard it too. She instantly bounded across the floor and onto the fireplace hearth. A wave of dread rolled over me. *It must be a rodent.*

I cupped my ears and stood still. I could barely make out a chirp. I leaned over to watch Penny, who was engrossed in sniffing every potted plant around the fireplace and corner wall. I just knew at any moment a skinny hairless tail would come slithering around the ivy, then a grey furry mass would appear and pounce onto my foot. What if it jumped into my hair? I started to rise, but then a movement caught the corner of my eye. Penny went into a low crouch and cautiously inched forward. Her whole body quivered with the excitement of the hunt. I tightened my grip on the broom and crept forward behind her, still stooped over. I peered over the top of the potted plants which now decorated the fireplace hearth. *What is it?*

A small, frightened, female bluebird blinked her eyes at me from behind the glass door. She was crouched in the corner of the firebox and completely terrified. *Oh, dear girl, how did you get in there?* "We must help her, Penny. She may be injured." Penny's tail wagged in eagerness. She had found the source of the sound, but I knew this delicate bird would be in mortal danger if Penny's hunting instinct kicked in. Right now she was simply curious. I held Penny's collar with one hand and placed the broom down. I realized I could not retrieve the bird with only one free hand, but neither could I let go of the wiggle worm. I scooped up my fearless huntress and carried her, squirming and complaining, upstairs to our master bedroom, where I shut her in. There was much wailing and scratching at the door, but I had no time to deal with her tantrum right now. "Stop it, Penny," I scolded, "you'll scratch the door." I heard a sneeze and the jingle of dog tags as she trotted angrily to her bed and plopped down with a disapproving grunt. Before returning to my frightened friend downstairs, I enlisted the aid of Bill and Sonja.

"I'm going to open the fireplace door and see what condition she's in. I'm hoping she can still fly."

Sonja was looking over my shoulder. "How did she get in there, Mom?"

"She may have been looking for a place to build a nest. Perhaps she fell down the chimney flue. She's not as fat as Santa, and she could have easily taken a tumble."

My humor was lost on Sonja. Her eyes remained fixed on the bird, which was the object of her complete focus. I opened the door slowly, but before I could get it fully extended, the bird shot past my shoulder in a blur and began a jittery panicked flight around the room. She climbed to the vaulted ceiling, then dove down to the loft where she clung to a handrail and chirped. Speaking in a soothing tone, I started to approach the delicate figure. Once more she dashed past me, but flew straight into the window, stunning herself. With a loud thud she bounced back, folded her wings, and dropped to the couch. We ran to her. Bill reached out and gently picked her up. Her little chest was heaving rapidly, so we knew she was still alive. "Do you think she will live?"

I could see Bill's concern, so I tried to offer some reassurance. "I think she's going into shock. I don't think her wings are broken; she can fold them in. Look." Her eyes were blinking, so she was awake. "That's a good sign."

Bill gently cupped her between his hands. "She's trying to get free."

"Don't hold her too close or too tight. Let's get her onto the patio. She may calm down in a more familiar environment."

We all filed out the back door and Bill gently laid her on the concrete.

The Bluebird of Happenstance

The delicate girl rested on her side for a moment and then popped to her feet, slumping slightly forward.

"Sonja, please get some dry meal worms out of the garage. I'm going to stay with our new friend until she's ready to fly again."

"Sure thing, Mom, I'll be right back." Sonja scampered off, and I sat quietly, a few feet from our guest so I wouldn't upset her any further.

I looked at Bill. "I really think she'll be okay, I'm going to sit here with her. I don't want anything to prey upon her in her weakened state."

Sonja returned and dropped a handful of dried worms into my hand. I gently placed a few of them near the little bird and backed up a few feet. I remained quiet and watched her breathing. Slowly her breath began to return to normal, and she was soon able to stand upright on her feet.

"You look better already," I softly remarked.

She cocked her head at me and continued to look me over.

"Just rest and catch your breathe. You are safe now."

It was a beautiful evening. The sun was beginning to set and was casting long shadows from the tree branches across the patio. I watched the natural beauty unfold for about a half an hour while the bluebird and I rested and chatted. Without warning she unexpectedly grabbed a dry worm, and with a flutter of blue feathers, launched herself skyward. She perched on a nearby tree limb, safe from intruders. Watching her there among the leaves, I felt a genuine satisfaction. I supposed she wasn't the first bird who had enjoyed a carry-out supper while dining al fresco. Bill came out to check on me and asked, "What's the prognosis?"

"She's made a full recovery."

"How do you know?"

"Because she just 'flue' away."

10

The Moose Is Loose

I WAS FILLING A plastic bucket with cleaning supplies from the laundry room pantry as my daughters looked on in horror. "Your Uncle Max will be here tomorrow, so we have to freshen up the guest area today." I didn't bother turning to see their expressions. "Yes, I know we just finished spring cleaning, but we didn't dust or change the linen in the spare bedroom, and your father has been using the downstairs bath, so you know what that means. I'll start cleaning it and you girls can begin dusting and vacuuming the bedroom." I heard two groans behind me as I continued filling my bucket with rubber gloves, spray bleach, and grout brushes. Without glancing back I lifted up a toilet brush and added, "Would you prefer my job?" The moaning stopped. I reached into the cabinet and retrieved two clean dust cloths and furniture polish which I handed over my shoulder. "After you finish dusting, clean the windows, the sills, and vacuum the carpets." The groaning resumed. "Would you prefer toilet brushes?" The noise ceased and two pairs of feet shuffled from the room.

I stepped into our moose themed guest bathroom and surveyed the scene. *This shouldn't take too long.* I began by collecting the towels from their racks for laundering. *No telling how many hands have used these for drying.* I added them to my growing stack of laundry awaiting its turn in the washing machine. I then noticed a lone washcloth draped over the face of our moose toilet paper holder. "Sandy," I whispered, exasperated. She considered the foot tall resin sculpture to be creepy and complained that its eyes stared at her when she used the guest bath. Anytime she came in here she would cover his eyes with the closest available hand towel or washcloth. I thought the moose caricature was darling, with its front hooves extended like hands to hold the toilet paper roller; and he had the sweetest expression on his face. It had been a Christmas gift from Chase several years prior, and it fitted the motif of the bathroom perfectly

Now began the hard work. I started by scrubbing the mineral stains from the sink until it was bright and sparkling again. I next moved to the grout between the floor tiles. It was dark and dirty and required vigorous cleaning with a narrow brush. *What made me think this would go quickly?* I certainly hoped Bill's brother Max, also known as "The Moose," would appreciate the effort I was putting into the bathroom he assumed had been named in his honor. Max had gained the moniker from his mother when he was baby. She made up songs to sing her children to sleep when they were young. His song went something like this. *Maxy Moose, the glossy moose, you're my favorite moosey moose.* As he grew, the name Moose seemed to fit him well. Even as a child he was notable for his size and girth. I always considered him more of a bull in a china shop, but I suspect he would not have appreciated being called Bull.

I continued cleaning the bathroom and was working on the commode when Bill walked in. "You must really enjoy your work."

"Why do you say that?"

"You were humming Mom's old baby song."

"Really?" I blushed with slight embarrassment.

Uncle Max and spring were arriving at almost the same time. The crocus flowers had popped out of the ground, but the winds still held us in their frigid grasp. Max had inquired about the weather and assured

me he would be packing his long underwear. He was used to warmer weather. As a pilot for a large commercial airline company, he often flew to Aruba and other tropical climates. Although no one visited us in the dead of winter, Max was the first person to come to Cimarron in early spring.

He arrived late in the evening, tired and weary from a long day of traveling. "We don't have any regular western routes, so I agreed to substitute for a colleague on his normal D.C. run. From there I jump-seated on Delta to Denver, Salt Lake City, and finally here. Not counting work, I've been flying or waiting in terminals for twelve hours."

"You must be exhausted, Max. Your room is prepared in case you'd like to go straight to bed."

He shrugged as he took a huge bite into the sandwich I'd made for him. "I'm used to it. After I finish this snack, I'll probably take a shower and relax for a bit." He looked around and added, "You got any cookies?"

We chatted late into the night about family, flying, and politics. I finally had to make my apologies and go to bed. Bill and Max continued their dialogue unperturbed. I awoke later than usual the following morning to the aroma of bacon frying. By the time I dressed and got downstairs, everyone was sitting around the dinner table listening to Max's tales. "Oh my, everyone's eaten already?"

Bill responded, "We just finished. I didn't want to wake you. I thought you needed the rest. What would you like for breakfast, Honey?"

"What are you having?"

Max was finishing the last few scraps of food on his plate, but still managed to speak through his full mouth. "We had pancakes, bacon, sausage, and hash browns. I told everyone to take what they wanted and I'd eat the rest."

I laughed at his joke, remembering the first time I ever invited him to supper. It was shortly after Bill and I got married. I thought he was teasing back then. He was not. He consumed our entire spaghetti dinner and a loaf of fresh baked bread. Bill had warned me in advance, so at least we each got a plateful of spaghetti and a slice of bread before The Moose devoured the rest. With that memory in mind, I replied, "Pancakes sound a bit heavy for me. I think I'll just have my oatmeal and dried cherries."

Max stopped chewing and thought about it for a moment. He shook his head and finished his last swallow, washing it down with a huge gulp of orange juice. "Ah, that hit the spot." He emitted a mild hiccup and stretched his arms. When he leaned back, his belly bumped the table askew several inches. He was his usual jovial self, and began to entertain us all with the stories of his travels and his various mishaps.

"You know I started out flying small regional turboprops. They were cramped little things." His voice boomed even though we were all together at the table. "I'll tell you how confining they were. I had just finished a couple of quarter pound burgers and a milkshake when I realized I was about to be late for my next flight. The copilot was already doing the preflight checklist when I reached the cockpit. The door was pretty tight, so I had to turn sideways and squeeeeeze myself in." He looked down and patted his stomach the way one greets a favorite pet. "I tried to take a step, but I got wedged in the hatchway. I was stuck."

"Stuck!" The girls responded in unison.

"Yes, it was a bit embarrassing, and my copilot didn't help. He got on the intercom and announced to the passengers 'Ladies and gentlemen, there will be a momentary delay in departure while we free the captain from the cockpit door. He appears to be wedged in it.' Well that caused a roar of laughter in the cabin."

"Is that really true?" Sandy quizzed.

"I'm afraid so," he sighed. "I went on a diet shortly after that."

"Did it work?" asked Bill.

"No, so I switched to flying larger planes. Problem solved."

As the girls were mulling over the story, Bill picked up the local newspaper and asked Max about his old motorcycle. "Do you still have it?"

"No, I sold it and the jeep about the same time. There wasn't room for them and two cars in our garage after I got married."

"It was a Harley, wasn't it?

"Naturally."

"I know you had a few scrapes with it."

"Yeah, one night some clown pulled out of a parking lot without looking and I slammed into him. The bike stopped but I didn't. I ended up bouncing over his trunk, roof, and hood."

"Were you hurt, Uncle Max?" asked Sonja.

"I jammed my thumb and wrecked my bike. The ass—I mean driver, took off."

"Really?" I added indignantly. "Was he ever caught?"

Max shook his head. "Didn't have to catch him. When he got home and his father took one look at the dents I'd left in his car, he made him confess and turn himself in."

"Don't mess with The Moose," Bill added.

"Dam—danged right."

Bill smiled, "I remember that incident, but I bet you never hit a bear."

"Nooo, never did that—what are you talking about?"

"I was reading in the history section of our local paper that just before World War II, two soldiers were driving a motorcycle on a rural highway near Mullan when they collided with a bear. No one was seriously injured, but they were all knocked unconscious, even the bear!"

I teased Max. "That's rather unusual. Most of the animals hit around here are deer and elk, rarely a bear. Just to be safe, don't go walking along the highway here. We wouldn't want anyone to hit our Moose."

The conversation continued to ramble and touch on many subjects. It was, essentially, a continuation of the previous evening's chat. Whenever Bill and Max got together, the oxygen level in the room dropped precipitously. Maybe that's why I felt so tired after finishing my oatmeal. I excused myself from the clamor and returned to the bedroom. I sat by the back window to view the scenery and relax. I pondered how much the fir trees had grown over the decade since we had arrived. One of the trees near the house had fallen in a heavy wind two years earlier and its trunk was nearly broken in half. It would have hit the ground if not for another tree that caught it. Somehow the leaning tree had managed to survive, and it now resembled a primitive bridge pointing skyward. Many times I have imagined myself walking up its trunk to the very tip of the last branch before extending my arm to touch the clouds. Then I would peer beneath me to watch the creek water as it splashed over thousands of rocks and hundreds of broken limbs to join the river a mile below us. The spring melt caused an annual turbulent surge that I enjoyed immensely. The sound was reminiscent of a waterfall, but one that was muted just enough to create a pleasant white noise that blocked out the vulgar cry of cars and trucks on the highway.

I followed the tree line as it stretched for miles up and over one mountain after another until the image blurred into a single green mass. I mentally retraced my steps back until I could once again distinguish individual trees. I imagined myself painting these trees, one by one, until they formed a complete mountain. I examined every feature of this rocky slope, and stopped near the summit to peer at a barren patch among this evergreen horizon. It wasn't a complete void; a lone pine stood in the middle of the small field, stripped bare of all branches but two. *What is killing it? Why is this patch of ground nearly devoid of life when all about it remains lush?* But it was the shape of the tree that really intrigued me. With its two bare limbs extending in opposite directions it reminded me of a towering cross. *Why does such a feature exist in death amid a forest of life?*

I stopped my mental landscape painting and focused on that tree. I felt an immediate connection with it. It was unlike anything around it for miles. It stood upright, holding its own in its singularly unique way, despite its frail appearance among all the other timber. *Why am I always seeing myself in these trees?* I felt like I understood its struggle, and at the same time, it offered me some comfort.

The laughter drifting up the stairs disrupted my musings. I decided to return to the family room and join the fun. When I arrived, the conversation had shifted to the original *Star Trek* television series. I knew this could go on for hours, but for once I had something to contribute. "Max, have you ever heard of the actor Harry Landers?"

He pondered the question for a moment, but I could see he was stumped. "No," he replied, "I don't think so."

"He was in a *Star Trek* episode, and also played on the old medical drama, *Ben Casey*. I was reading some interesting facts about Montana and I came across his name."

"Was he from Montana?"

"No, he was born in New York, but I was hoping you knew something about him. They may be two completely different people, but I read about a Harry Landers who lived on Hwy 59, and topped a mile of his fence posts with over 300 boots."

"What on earth for?"

"There are a few reasons; some ranchers placed them on fence posts to prevent rain rot. Of course, this was long before pressure treated wood was available. Some cowboys used them as a tribute if they lost a valued friend or a favorite horse. Before they had telephones or electricity, they put a boot on the fence post to let visitors know they were finished working for the day and were at home."

Max was amused. "I don't know if it was the same guy, but you know how eccentric those actors can be. I met a lot of them when I was acting." Before Max became an airline pilot, he'd attempted other professions, including the Army, police work, acting, and standup comedy. He even had an agent who helped him find a few small parts in movies.

"Well, it was a long shot, but I thought maybe you had heard of him, with your acting background and knowledge of all things *Star Trek*."

"Well, there's a big universe of actors out there. I did meet Tom Hanks on one movie set."

"What did you say to him?"

"Can I freshen your coffee, sir?"

We all burst out laughing and continued talking until lunch. The sun had come out and it was a cool, clear afternoon. It proved irresistible, and after lunch the family went outside to play with Max's new aerial drone. With it he could take video of our property from the air. Before joining them, I thought it best to stay on top of the laundry, so I entered the guest bathroom to replace the towels. I was surprised to see my moose paper holder once again draped in a brown washcloth. I thought it unusual for Sandy to use the guest bath when we had company, so I quickly scooped up the towel. As I stood up, Max rounded the corner and announced, "I forgot the battery charger…oh, sorry about the washcloth; I just can't stand that moose looking at me!"

"Do you want me to put it back or remove the holder?"

Max thought about it for a moment. "No, it's okay."

"I'll leave an extra washcloth for you; I don't want you to be intimidated by the moose. Or you could just pull the bathroom paper over his head."

Max grunted and moved on. I completed my tasks and returned to clearing away the dining room table. I was removing the last of the dishes when I heard a familiar chirp. I glanced out the window and saw the Downey Woodpecker again, the same one who had clung to the feeder in the vicious wind during the winter. She was happily at the bird feeder sifting through the seeds. Nearly everyone she dropped was quickly picked up by a Mountain Chickadee. An entire family of them was on the ground waiting for the next seed to fall. Here was another sure sign that spring had arrived and life was again renewed. The laughter from outside only confirmed it.

The visit went by quickly and was marred only by one incident. Max was using his drone to record video of our land from the air. This resulted in some dramatic views of the surrounding countryside that we could not duplicate unless standing on the highest ridge above our home. He even managed to capture our horses running across an open field as the drone swooped down over them. He intended to produce more video, but on his last flight of the last day of his vacation, the drone developed a mind of its own and flew off into the wilderness.

Computer coordinates of its last known flightpath placed it somewhere amid a rocky escarpment behind Bill's shop. The two of them set off to find it.

It began simply enough. Max would search the lower terrain amid the pines and Bill would climb up the escarpment to see if the drone had landed on its plateau. Neither of them was suitably attired for the job, and soon Max became entangled in the brush while Bill found himself clinging to a scrawny root as the loose granite gave way beneath his desperate attempts to find sure footing.

"Max! Can you give me a hand?"

"Where are you?"

"Up here!"

"Where is 'here'?"

At that moment the root Bill was clinging to made the decision to depart the soil. "Never mind," he called as he slid down the steep incline. Good fortune followed him, for Max rounded the corner at the base of the hill just in time to arrange an unplanned collision. Both brothers tumbled over and came to a halt.

"Oh, there you are," Max calmly stated.

"Funny running into you," Bill added.

They returned to the house, sans the drone, none the worse for wear, save for their clothes, which were filthy and torn. Bill promised The Moose he would continue to search for the missing drone. Max shrugged it off and instead of lamenting his loss, said, "At least I didn't bring my expensive one."

He left the following day, catching a series of roundabout hops that would eventually land him safely home back in Florida. As for us, we're still looking for that drone.

11

The Great Sniffing Expedition

PENNY HAD CREATED A very particular routine. When she jumped and placed her front feet on the chair, the door, or even our legs, we knew what would follow next. She would begin to spin in a circle and make a series of vocalizations that sounded incredibly like the words "I want."

With her eyes bright and purposeful she would look imploringly into her chosen family member and begin the whole show again until we relented and escorted her outside. Bill shook his head and moaned to me instead of Penny. "Why does she do this every time we sit down together?"

"When was the last time she went outside?"

"A couple of hours ago."

"It's better than her usual time of five minutes," I teased. I was only half joking. Penny had developed another habit. A few minutes after coming inside and devouring her little treat for a job well done, she would again begin her spinning and growling. She logically reasoned that if she split her needs into two trips, she would get two treats. Bill tried, to no avail, to break her of this habit by offering two treats if she did a number one and a number two during the same outing. Penny appreciated the extra reward she received on the rare occasion when she performed both tasks simultaneously, but she still preferred her approach of separate engagements. It meant getting to go outside for longer periods if she milked it just right.

This time was no different and it irritated Bill to no end. "I just took you out two hours ago," he stated flatly, but Penny was undaunted. Her face said it all. *But Father, you must take me out again; you simply must; I have to "go" again. I can't hold it another minute…I want …*

"You just want another treat." Bill looked sternly into her face. Penny's brown eyes became huge as she widened them even more and seemed to answer him. *And this is a problem? I'm holding up my end of the bargain.*

Bill gave up his protesting and once again went to the front door for Penny's leash. He had to protect our precious pup from the local predators. Penny didn't seem to mind being restrained; she just wanted to be outdoors. Within a few minutes Bill and Penny returned inside and she made a beeline down the hall and past the grandfather clock. Despite her diminutive size, every single time she trotted past it, the clock chimed like a drunken Big Ben. She scampered around the corner and into the laundry room where she awaited her biscuit or meat treat reward.

I laughed, "By the looks of it, she went."

"Yes," Bill replied, "but I wish she would do everything all at once."

"And miss out on two consecutive treats? She's an intelligent girl and she's figured out how to game the system."

As soon as she finished eating, Penny returned to the family room and settled down in her bed. All was quiet for several minutes. Bill and I resumed our conversation again, discussing the recent news events. Penny's eyes opened and she stepped out of her bed. "Oh, no." Bill's voice was ripe with irritation. It was the "Penny Stretch."

There was no argument from me. I watched Penny push her body back and raise her spine and tail up. Her forelegs stretched low to the carpet and she formed a furry banana shape. Then she pushed her chest forward and lifted her head up into the air. Her hind legs stretched backward with the toes inverted. The banana had reversed direction. Her stretching now complete, she assumed a normal standing position and looked up to Bill. Her eyes grew larger as she approached him, then leaping up on her hind legs, she grasped his trousers with her front feet. She opened her mouth and began to speak. *Oh, Father…I need to go out again.*

"Not again," Bill snapped. It was a futile gesture. Penny would not be ignored. Bill was helpless to her wiles and had to give into her cute factor.

I placed my hand on Bill's arm. "It looks like you have fallen under the 'cute-a-tonic' spell; she's got you now." Penny agreed and began spinning.

"This is the last time!" Bill muttered as he rose from the comfort of the reclining loveseat. "I long for the days when it's cold and Penny takes one look outside and runs back to her bed." Having won her way, Penny began to prance and sneeze. I don't know quite what that signifies, but she always does it whenever she is triumphant.

From my side of the couch I watched through the window as they stepped into the front garden. Penny ran in circles with her nose to the ground, sniffing everything. Bill quickly tired of being dragged around the boulders and flowers, so he disconnected her leash and let her have a little freedom. I watched in amusement and tried to imagine things from Penny's perspective. She was so serious and intent on reading the signs. It was her daily gazette. What was she learning as she raced from each rock and evergreen shrub? I could only imagine the thoughts that crossed her mind. *Wow, I didn't know the chipmunks were here today. Wait! Is that a new one? Never smelled him before.*

I watched Penny's nose twitch as she inhaled and analyzed each scent. She gave the boulder a quick tiny lick and raced off to inspect a clump of flowers. Another news flash. *So you think I didn't know you were here, Mr. Fox? I know all about your goings and comings and—wait! Squirrel alert!* Penny's head suddenly jerked sideways. *Nope, false alarm. Back to the matter at hand. This requires further investigation. I think Mr. Fox has a lady friend…or is it a mouse? No, definitely a lady fox…wait a minute, do I smell a horse? Wait! Squirrel! Darn, wrong again. I thought for sure I saw one out of the corner of my eye. This is so exciting.*

Bill continued to follow close by as Penny hurried around the garden. He kept scanning the sky for any eagle that might think Penny was the perfect meal. It was nearly twenty minutes before they came back inside. Penny raced by me and headed down the hallway. Big Ben chimed madly. I heard Bill's voice call to her, "No, Penny, you don't get a treat for sniffing."

Penny returned to the family room where Bill had flopped onto the sofa and was now enjoying a cold soda. She was crushed. All that great sniffing surely deserved a reward. Dad got one.

"How about a different kind of reward," I said, knowing exactly her thoughts. "It isn't TV time yet, but let's get you settled between us on your Penny blanket." Penny didn't need additional encouragement, and she waited impatiently while I spread the blanket on the couch between Bill and me. I signaled her and she sprang onto the couch, made a half turn, and plopped down between us. I wrapped the blanket around her and she rested her head on my lap. "How's my little burrito?" She let out a big snort and closed her eyes. An hour later she opened them again as Bill snoozed next to her. She reached out with her front paws and stepped on his chest, startling him awake. Before he could speak, she gave him that look which clearly said, *Oh, Father, I have to go outside.*

12

The Face in the Mirror

IT WAS ONE OF those days where I felt out of sorts. I set aside the book I was reading and willed myself to rise from my chair to water the plants. This experience was becoming more commonplace with each passing year, as was the struggle between mind and body. I had promised myself long ago never to submit to time and aging. Besides, I told myself, it's good therapy to wander the house with a watering can in hand—as long as you don't forget the reason why. *My plants need the water; I need the exercise; and my brain needs to ponder life's problems, both great and small. Now focus—don't splash the leaves; the water will simply fall to the floor and compound the workload.*

Pouring the life giving fluid into a pot of African violets, I smiled when I saw a framed photo of my dad as a young man, standing on a large boulder by the shores of Lake Michigan. Written on the rock with bold blue spray paint was the name "Bill". The photo was beginning to fade, but it was my treasure. Was it mere coincidence or a premonition that drove him to select this particular stone? I would never know and neither would he. I lost him by the time I was six. A defective guard rail cost him his life, but the state of Michigan had saved fifty cents in construction costs.

You think too much. I heard this my entire life from my mother, my brother, my friends, even my husband, Bill. *You think too much.* It is true, my introspective nature rarely allows me time to rest or enjoy the moment. Was I a product of my environment or was it an inherited trait? Am I too sensitive? Is this not the bane of all artistic types? *You're thinking too much – and you're spilling water on the floor!*

After cleaning up my mess and finishing the ritual watering, I removed dead foliage from the house plants, then stopped in the bathroom to wash my hands. The reflection of a flicker of light in the mirror caught my eye. The light shone through a break between the two sheer curtains behind me, with their printed pattern of golden brown tree branches and leaves. They masked the spa tub from view when it was not in use, and diffused the light from the picture window behind it. The spa was more than a mere luxury; I used it for therapeutic massage when ibuprofen was not enough to deal with the pain of tense sore muscles. My spa was my oasis and momentary sanctuary from the realities of life.

The flecks of gold glitter contained in the drapes now sparkled in the mirror. It was one of my small daily joys, spending a minute or two admiring the colored lights and shadows instead of staring at my own reflection. My disparate thoughts became entwined like a tangled ball of yarn as I gazed blankly at my face. Unconsciously I looked into my own hazel-green eyes and pondered the same question I'd asked myself since childhood. *Who am I?* I know I'm not my brother or my mother. I'm not any of my grandparents either. My personality is different from all of theirs. *Who am I?* I am my father's daughter; I must be. Everyone says it is so. We shared the same tastes, the same artistic abilities, the same mannerisms, the same face, the same eyes—those eyes, yes—those eyes. They are my father's eyes. *What's bothering me? What's wrong? Wait – what day is this?* I remember now; it's my father's birthday. He would have been eighty-five years old today. His eyes stare back at me through my eyes. Now I see; now I understand, and now I smile. There is an emotional connection between us, even after half a century. Although I barely remember him, he is always with me, for he is more a part of me than anyone else. With every stroke of a paintbrush, with every instrument I play, with every decision I make or action I take, I know I am acting on my heritage. Most days this would be a great comfort to me, but not today. Today it only adds to my sense of isolation. What if he had lived? How would my life have turned out? I wanted to share all my happiness with him, celebrate the holidays, birthdays, and just sit and talk. How I have yearned for his confidence, advice, and approval. How I have ached to hear his voice and his laugh. How I have longed for him to put his arms around me and tell me, "Everything will work out."

It wasn't meant to be. I had to go it alone through those formative, vulnerable years and for much of my adulthood, until Bill came along. And what about Bill? Would I have been a different person if Dad were alive? Would I have made other life choices? Would I have had children? Would they have been different from Sandy and Sonja? Would the name written on that boulder be prophesy, coincidence, or simply passed off as graffiti?

And what about his life? He had dreams for himself and his family. At one point he had studied to be a concert pianist, but after meeting my mother, he decided not to pursue that path. He wanted to marry and have a family, and he believed a career in art would provide more stability, and not involve as much travel and time away from home. He became a talented, well respected, and successful artist. He was a charitable man who gave much of himself to philanthropic work such as children's charities. I knew he suffered his own private disappointments and heartaches. Watching his infant twin sons die only days apart must have left a scar in his heart. Dad had always wanted to live in Florida. At the time of his death they were planning on relocating there. I often wondered if that was the reason my mother later moved us there after remarrying a far lesser man.

You can't go home again or turn back time. There are no retakes in life, only endless second chances. I scolded myself for my trip down memory lane and the inevitable "What if" questions. I don't like to look back, so I rarely do because it's always the same replay. I don't live there anymore. The past is prologue. Remember the good times and learn from the bad times. *Avanti*! *Avanti*! Always forward. Gain knowledge from those experiences, plan your future, and continue pressing on to bigger and brighter things. Never give up; never give up; never give up. I try, always I try, but the most painful lesson I could not escape was the fact that my life had a gap in it that only my Dad could fill. There are no substitutes for a good father.

13

The Bear Necessities

"ARE YOU AWAKE?" I heard Bill's voice as he entered the bedroom.

"Yes, I'm in the closet folding clothes."

"Come and see this rainbow. You don't want to miss this one."

Bill's assumption was correct; it was a lovely rainbow. The bands of color were thick and bright and shimmered strongly in the sunlight.

"It's a good omen," Bill added.

"It's a great way to start the day. It's worth enduring all the rain if we get a rainbow like this one."

One of the joys of mountain life is to experience what nature has to offer. My work is often interrupted by the sights outside. It might be a wild animal or the shadows of clouds racing each other across the meadows. I often wonder how I ever manage to accomplish any work with the constant interruptions, but then again, it is those interruptions which make my work worthwhile.

As much as I enjoy these interludes, there is always a whisper of caution. Wind means a coming change in the weather. Harmless animals mean the likelihood of predators nearby. I have even read that Montana has been rated number one of all the fifty states in the category of "likely to be killed by a wild animal". Since we have bears, moose, cougars, and wolves living nearly at our doorstep, I understand why Montana has achieved such a status. The odds are still in our favor, but we've always been cautious, particularly when the children were young.

Of all the animals around us, the ones that have most concerned me are the bears, both the Grizzly and the Black Bear. I know of hunters who have been maimed or killed by them, usually while they were walking through deep brush or field dressing their game. Bill doesn't hunt much, so I was always more concerned about a bear coming into our pastures or up to the barn or house. A startled bear is a surprisingly fast animal. They have been clocked at burst speeds of up to thirty-five miles per hour. In a field a person has little chance of escaping them. Climbing a tree will not stop a determined bear. They are better climbers than humans. Early on I made a point of reading as much as I could on the subject, and I tried to separate fact from fiction. In the end I concluded your chances of being attacked or surviving an attack really depended on the personality of the bear. If it was a sow who believed she was protecting her cubs, your chances of attack were high. Startled bears also were more likely to attack if you were very close to them. Fifty to one hundred yards is considered a bear's personal space, assuming you can see one at that distance. Therefore, the farther away they are, the less threat they will perceive you to be. Making noise can alert a bear to your presence in time for him to run away if that's what he decides to do. Yelling and screaming at a bear might save you from an attack or it might provoke the bear to come for you at full speed. If one does attack and you can't escape, know that they don't just bite; they claw, rip, shake, and twist their prey. Their primary target is the head, so if one grabs you, your best bet is to curl into a ball, protect your head, and play dead.

Traveling in large groups is a great way to avoid an attack, but not always practical. To my knowledge there are no documented bear attacks on humans who stayed close together in groups of three or more, but I have never been interested in verifying this information. Just as climbing a tree is no guarantee of safety, neither is being in a car or a home. Bears have been known to pop the windshields out of trucks and cars so they can crawl in to look for food. During this foraging they can completely destroy and partially eat the interior of the vehicle. They have broken in doors and raided kitchen pantries; they have taken off the roofs of houses, stripped off the wood siding of domiciles, and dug up power lines (I'm not sure how well that last one worked for them). There is no way of knowing what incentive might cause such behavior other than possibly prior human contact via trash cans and garbage dumps (a favorite bear hangout). This is why you should always heed signs that say "DON'T FEED THE BEARS." The bear may not attack you, but he may later attack somebody else because of what he learned from you.

The good news is most bears avoid humans whenever they can. Even those that stand their ground will most likely only huff and puff and make false charges. One report I read claimed that 90% of the charges are false charges. Of course, you have no way of knowing if you are in the unlucky 10% that are real charges. This is the kind of situation where Wile E. Coyote opens his ACME umbrella and mutters, "Mother."

To minimize the probability of any encounters near our place, we keep our homestead really buttoned up. We never leave any doors open. All vehicles are stored inside garage bays. Aside from a birdfeeder (unfortunately bears do like seed), we never store or toss any food or garbage outside, including old grease. When we barbecue we do it next to the house by a door and keep a watchful eye out for any uninvited dinner guests. We keep bear spray on the girl's walking sticks, and we go armed if traversing anywhere beyond the front of our buildings. Even though we take precautions, the wildlife on our mountain continually refuse to conform to convention.

It was a pleasant morning with high clouds resembling fog that covered the mountains to the west. We were nearing the end of the school year and all Sonja had left to do was finish reading a book about the life of Daniel Boone. I found pioneer stories about settling the frontier fascinating. It was amazing to me how people could uproot their lives and build new ones in completely uncharted and unfriendly territory. There is nothing today in America that can compare with it. I often wondered how they faced medical emergencies, forged relationships with new cultures, dealt with severe weather, and found their way across the land without any maps or roads to guide them. The rivers were their lifeline, but they don't always run the direction one wishes to travel. Progress was painfully slow.

As we listened to Sonja read aloud, Bill and I sat quietly, each engrossed in our own thoughts. Sonja took one of her frequent breaks from reading and went to the loft windows to check on her horses. She stiffened at the sight and exclaimed, "I see a bear!"

Bill replied, "It's probably a cow."

"No, Dad, it's a bear!"

We ran to the window to see for ourselves. Indeed, there was a large grizzly bear digging in a dirt mound less than twenty-five yards behind the stable and barely one hundred yards from the house. The hump on his back was quite distinctive. Bill grabbed a set of binoculars we kept by the window and peered at him; Sonja ran to get the camera and started taking pictures of him; I ran into the bedroom for a rifle. All I could think about was my horses' safety. They were in the corral, blissfully unaware of the present danger. As long as the bruin remained focused on his digging, they were safe. If he caught wind of them, I did not know what would happen next.

Bill and Sonja came into the bedroom with the still camera and the video camera. "I want to get some video and a clearer picture of him from the deck." He looked at the rifle in my hand and added, "I don't think that will be necessary, but just in case, keep it handy."

Bill opened the door slowly, trying to avoid making any noise. The door frame insulation prevented this, so he was forced to pull on it. The resulting sound alerted the bear, who raised his head and then made a dash for the tree line. For such a large cumbersome-looking fellow, he was fast, and within a few bounding steps he was out of our sight.

"Wow, did you see that?" Sonja exclaimed.

"I didn't get a chance to shoot my video," Bill moaned.

"Thank goodness my horses are safe," I rejoiced.

The horses missed the entire fracas. We wanted to find out what the bear had been doing. Bill brought a rifle on the remote chance he might return. Sonja and I brought along bear spray. We walked to the spot where the bear had been digging and discovered a large ant hill. I had read that ants were a source of protein for bears. Given the time of year, it made sense that a bruin would seek out any source of protein available to him. This left me wondering if he had been here before. We had seen some signs in the past, log stumps overturned and rubbings on tree trunks, but this was one of our very few confirmed sightings. I doubted he had gotten his fill. Hundreds of angry ants were scattered across the grass and desperately trying to rebuild their devastated home. If we had not interpreted his breakfast he would no doubt have consumed most of the colony. I was thankful now that the two apple trees I had naively planted five years earlier in the back yard had died. One of our neighbors had a much less desirable crab apple tree, but the tart fruit turned out to be a favorite of a black bear sow and her cubs. She visited them every spring. I had to consider the possibility our bruin would come back later to finish his meal.

The horses remained calm the entire time, so we returned home and settled back down to finishing our school day. Sonja picked up her book and resumed reading. I watched her as she periodically glanced out the front windows that overlooked the stables. She was nearly finished when she yelled, "I think he's back!"

We all rushed to the window and surveyed the front yard and meadow. I cried out, "I see it!"

Bill replied dryly, "It's a cow. I better call Chase."

I agreed. I didn't want cows in my yard. They ate too much grass and left their calling cards everywhere, but it was still preferable to a grizzly bear.

"Do you think Chase will come out right away?"

Bill winked and said, "He will when I mention the grizz."

I recited my oft used phrase, "This wasn't in the brochure when we bought this land."

"Be glad for that; they might have charged us more."

Nancy Quinn's "Silvertip."

14

What the Hail Is This?

IT WAS ANOTHER GORGEOUS summer day in Montana, the kind of morning that made all the cold, blustery winters worth enduring. I thought of it as my reward for trying to stay cheerful in below zero temperatures that hung on, uninvited, for days on end.

The breeze was warm and my Irises were beginning to bloom. It was the only flower I could easily grow on the mountain. They thrived against all odds and withstood temperatures in the long winters that less hardy flowers could not tolerate. I had planted dozens that numbered now in the hundreds, and were about to be augmented with four new colors, orange-amber, pink mixed with purple, dark magenta, and white with purple stripes.

"Isn't it wonderful, Precious Petunia?" I said as I glanced at the view out our loft windows from the comfort of my glider. Penny sat beside me in her daybed, and I gently stroked her soft ears. She returned my enthusiasm with a loud thumping of her tail. Our beagle/dachshund/Jack Russell mix had acquired many nicknames over the last few years: Penny Pup, Miss Wiggles, Spazz, Spazzine, Puppin, Precious Pup, Panini Penny, Panini Bread, and Penny Person, to name but a few. She responded immediately to any of them. She has been a constant joy for me and my family with her ladylike behavior and endearing loving demeanor. When her "Penny blanket" is placed on the couch, she obediently awaits an invitation before hopping up and joining us. If the television is turned on, or anytime the words "TV time" are echoed, she appears from whatever crevice she has been napping in and scurries around the corner or down the stairs to join us. She rarely watches the program, preferring to be wrapped like a burrito in her blanket, sandwiched between Bill and me. This act is not without its rituals which must be observed. Before she can become comfortable on the couch, she will perform the Penny stretch. This is her signal that she must go outside and relieve herself or, failing that, at least enjoy her morning, afternoon, or evening gazette by cautiously twitching her nose as she sniffs and analyzes the surrounding air.

No matter where I am, Penny is my constant shadow and companion. I arose and moved to the edge of the large picture windows for a better view below. Penny dutifully followed and propped her front paws on the lowest sill, her ever spinning tail barely missing the carpet. The sun was behind the house, so it did not interfere with the view. I began a slow pan from east to west. In front was blue sky, a good sign. But as my gaze moved left toward the west I saw the ominous approach of dark clouds. "So much for our beautiful weather, girl." I glanced down at Penny as though expecting a reply. She looked up and yawned. The house shuddered slightly. "The wind is picking up. That means a change in weather."

It didn't take long. Within ten minutes rain was pelting the glass. I wasn't truly disappointed. The rain would water my garden and save me from performing the task myself. I watched the water droplets stick to the plate glass windows and slowly run down, blurring my view of the pasture and corral. The horses were calmly grazing as they enjoyed the gentle rain shower. It was a peaceful scene, and I decided to share the experience. The gentle tapping was musical, and I was mesmerized by the repetitive sound. Penny wagged her tail with appreciation.

The soothing patter on the metal roof abruptly gave way to a loud crashing of ball bearings. The violence of it startled me. Huge chunks of hail smashed incessantly against our roof, creating a deafening roar.

The rain gutters filled with ice pellets and piled them up like marbles at the base of the drain spouts. In the meadow the horses were now in turmoil, and they dashed wildly about in circles. It must have been painful having stinging chunks of ice, some as large as golf balls, assaulting their bodies.

I ran to the balcony off our bedroom and called to them, gesticulating with my arms. "Go to the stable!" I wasn't sure they could hear me over the tumult. How could they hear me when I couldn't hear my own voice? The noise was now deafening. I shrank back to the safety of the doorway while the wind pelted my face with ice. I retreated back inside and nearly tripped over Penny, who was close at my heels. I closed the glass door and wiped the moisture from my stinging cheeks.

Wilson and Whiskey were in full panic and repeatedly spinning around. Wilson broke and ran to the closest tree line. Whiskey soon followed. Among the dense firs they found sanctuary and relief. I lost sight of them, but assumed they would be alright. Mother Nature was releasing her full fury upon us. All we could do was wait and watch the ice piles grow. The meadows turned completely white. *How long can this go on?* After an eternity of a half hour the din began to wane, the rhythm slowed, and at last a patch of blue emerged. The hail returned to the delightful pitter-patter of rain. The horses refused to leave the safety of the trees. I surveyed the massive snow cone that now coated my yard and front patio. All I could think of was the shaved iced treat I used to look forward to as a child. The only thing missing was cherry syrup, lots and lots of cherry syrup. The sun emerged and the clouds dissipated. Wilson and Whiskey peeked cautiously from the evergreens and slowly emerged back into the sunshine. Their backs were covered with ice, and they looked as if they were wearing white blankets.

"I think all is well again, Penny." I reached down and stroked her head. "The storm is over." A sunbeam pierced the room, and Penny raced to embrace it. Within minutes she was fast asleep amidst the yellow rays. It was just another summer morning in Montana.

15

The Centenarian

SONJA JUMPED OUT OF the car and raced to the jeep on display in front of the Montana Military Museum. Fort Harrison usually had some type of war vehicle parked on the lawn. The volunteer on duty was quite proud of the fact that they were able to have one to exhibit. He began explaining all the interesting historical facts and background to Sonja, who eagerly listened. Bill studied an odd looking vehicle under a portable shade. "Is that an old Weasel?"

"It sure is. It's one of three we've got, but this one doesn't run yet."

"You mean you have some that work?"

"Sure do."

Sonja interrupted, "What's a Weasel?"

"It's a small amphibious tractor that was developed for the First Special Service Force – the Devil's Brigade. You know, the joint Canadian-American commando unit that fought in the Aleutians, Italy, and France in World War Two."

"I've read about them. Dad says they made a movie about them."

The old soldier's expression changed. "Hmm...yes, well we don't talk about that here. It wasn't terribly accurate – just a bunch of Hollywood nonsense."

Sonja was unperturbed. "So is the Weasel like a DUKW?"

"No, the DUKW could swim like a Weasel, but it was bigger and based on a deuce and a half."

"You mean a World War Two Army two-and-a-half-ton truck," Sonja beamed.

"Well you sure know your vehicles."

"I should; we own a 1947 Willys CJ2a jeep with a 1945 MB Go Devil engine."

The elderly veteran chuckled and smiled, "Then you'll love the Weasel. It isn't much bigger than a jeep, but it can swim a river and climb a mountain full of snow with its tracks."

Sonja looked at Bill and said, "Dad, can we get one of these?"

"I doubt it, Honey. They're about as rare as hen's teeth and just as useful to us. I think we'd better stick with the jeep and summer driving."

While the three continued chatting, I decided to venture indoors and look at the uniforms, tools, and weapons under the glass display cabinets that spanned over 150 years of Montana military history. Upon entering the museum I was confronted by racks of memorabilia and books they sold to help offset their operating costs. One book in particular caught my eye. It was propped up on a stand by itself. The cover jacket featured a black and white photo of a man in a parka with a fully packed snow sled and dogs. The title read: *Camp Rimini and Beyond: WWII Memoirs,* authored by David Armstrong. It looked like an interesting book and I made a mental note to peruse it before leaving the museum.

I heard familiar chatter behind me and saw Bill and Sonja coming through the door. Sandy was now working part-time, and I was still adjusting to the fact that our family outings wouldn't always include her anymore. Bill went down one corridor of exhibits, but Sonja joined me and we took a different hallway. We stopped at a display of old medical instruments. Since Sonja wanted to be a nurse, she found it particularly interesting. "Mom, look at this." I leaned in and started reading all about the medics and what they carried in their triage bags. We saw Carlisle dressings and triangular bandages, safety pins, emergency medical tags for identification of the wounded soldiers, scissors, adhesive tape, a thermometer, iodine swabs, tourniquets, and aromatic spirits.

"Honey Girl, that isn't much to work with. One wonders how they managed."

Sonja somberly shook her head. "I don't know either."

Sensing this was disturbing her, I discussed the war art from that period that was on display. Some of the posters were beautifully executed, with very patriotic themes. I remembered seeing a small selection of these prints hanging in my doctor's office back at the old Walter Reed Army Medical Center.

Sonja and I continued around the corner and found a display of toy sled dogs and yards of cotton representing snow covered mounds. An actual sled sat on a table, its well-worn leather harnesses mute, but no doubt full of stories of adventure, hardship, and danger. *If only they could talk.* I read the placard next to the displays. "Look, Sonja; these dogs were amazing. They were trained nearby in Rimini by the Army. They were taught to rescue people and find the remains of soldiers so they could be brought home to their families. You really have to commend the men in uniform for such dedication. You know how brutal and unforgiving the mountains can be, especially in winter. I saw a book about this subject at the front desk. Can you imagine what it was like to travel into the most remote areas of the world by sled with a team of dogs?"

By now Bill had arrived and we continued our discussion of the rescue work. He then wandered down another maze of corridors while I indulged myself in thoughts of imagination. Looking at the display I could almost feel the cold, and I wondered about the discomfort and hardship of the missions, the isolation, risk of frostbite or injury, and having to be physically and emotionally strong enough to perform a rescue. *I think the dogs had an easier time—impervious to the cold. The sled dogs seem to thrive no matter what the weather.* My own experiences with our dog, Kobi, reinforced my beliefs.

Voices nearby brought me back to the present. An elderly man and a woman about my age were chatting a few feet from me. They too were interested in the exhibit. The old gentleman smiled at me and announced, "It's my birthday today and I'm a hundred years old!"

"Well, happy birthday! What a wonderful way to celebrate, a day at the museum."

His companion laughed and replied, "You aren't a hundred years old today and it's not your birthday."

My new friend was indignant. "Oh, yes I am! I was born in 1922."

"That makes you 97, not 100."

He turned to me and said, "You do the math. Tell her, go on; tell her."

Quickly making a mental calculation, I decided not to get involved in this argument and instead changed the conversation to the exhibit in front of us. Things were beginning to click in my mind, like small puzzle pieces that were snapping into place. I extended my hand to the elderly gentleman. "I'm Nancy Quinn."

He looked delighted. "I'm Dave," he replied, taking my hand, "and I'm always happy to meet pretty ladies."

Such a charmer!

"I trained these dogs a long time ago." He extended his arms and swept them across the display."

Suddenly I made the connection. "Are you David Armstrong, the author of the book about training dogs at Rimini?"

"Yes, yes, I am."

"How wonderful to meet you!"

"I'm Kathy," his companion offered. "Dave is being honored tonight at a dinner, so we thought we would stop in and see the museum."

"Congratulations."

I noticed a slight concern in Kathy's expression. She pointed to a nearby chair. "Dave, why don't you have a seat while we talk?"

I turned to Sonja. "Stay here and don't let them leave. I'm going to buy his book and have him sign it." I stepped around the corner and purchased one of the paperbacks. When I returned I asked, "Dave, I have a copy of your book. Would you honor me with your signature?"

He looked a little startled, but complied with a smile growing wider by the moment. I know I saw a twinkle in his eye.

"I was also hoping for a photo of us all together. Would you mind?"

"Posing with girls? How could I say no?"

After taking the pictures I sent Sonja to find her father. She quickly returned with Bill in tow.

"There's somebody here I think you'd really like to meet." I made the introductions. Dave was enjoying all the attention as he described to Bill how, after setting up the school and training the dog handlers, he was later sent to Europe to locate and recover the bodies of airmen who had crashed in the Alps during the war. Some of them had been up there for almost two years.

"It was the hardest thing I ever had to do," he said, tears forming in his eyes. "But over the years I received letters from many families. They thanked me for bringing their sons, their husbands, their brothers back from the war. It made me…it made me…feel…proud."

We took a few more photos on my phone, but I could see all this attention was beginning to tire Dave. He sat quietly on the bench and I leaned down to speak to him, placing my hand on his shoulder. "Before we leave I just wanted to say how much I appreciate what you have done for your fellow servicemen and for your country. Thank you, Dave."

When I returned home, I opened Dave's book and began reading chapter one. It described his early life and the dog training experience he had gained before entering the Army. It went on to discuss how Camp Rimini was set up, why particular dogs were chosen and trained, and listed the different types of missions they accomplished. I soon turned to a page that contained a copy of a letter Dave had received from the War Department in 1943. It commended him and his sled dog teams for their efforts. Upon further research I discovered that in 1944 Rimini was the only U.S. Army training center of its kind in the United States. Dog sled teams that trained there were sent to northern countries worldwide for use by the Allies. Most of the dogs were purchased by the Army or loaned to them by their owners. Some were bred and trained in the camp from puppyhood to the time of their maturity. The breeds included Samoyeds, Malamutes, and Siberian Huskies. They ate both raw meat and prepared dog food, and were well cared for by their trainers. Teams consisted of eleven dogs and one man. Each soldier carried his own equipment on his sled, including a sleeping bag and Army mountain rations. Their clothing was often a mix of Army issue and other items the soldiers themselves brought from home. They were given parkas, sweaters, wool lined trousers, rubber-bottomed shoes, ski mittens, sheep-skinned caps, and sun goggles. Many of the men wore Mukluks, a seal skin boot made by the Eskimos. These were not Army issue, but the soldiers said it was ideal footwear for sled dog drivers. As I perused the photos I recognized Dave as a young man all those years ago. Even in a black-and-white picture I saw that distinctive twinkle in his eye that I had noticed when we first met, a confident, yet playful look that said "I can, I will, I did." I felt so honored that I had met such a courageous leader of men and canines. His book will always be a treasure to me, along with the memory of meeting an exceptional veteran of our United States Army. I hope he does reach his hundredth birthday.

16

The Code of the West

I AWOKE FROM MY slumber to the sound of crows cawing. My eyes still closed, I listened to their chatter. It always amazed me how a sound can seemingly throw one back in time. For the next few moments I was a child of eight standing in the woods behind my house. At the edge of the glade there was an enormous tree I liked to climb. From the top of the branches where I would perch myself, I could see mounds of purple periwinkles below and hear the cackling of the large black crows swooping above my head. I was incredibly fortunate that our house in the suburbs of Detroit had acres of undeveloped woods behind it where Brian and I could play every day. I assumed that was where my love of the wilderness originated. But the memory was fleeting. The woods are gone and I'm no longer a child, just a middle-aged woman who does not wish to rise and meet the day until every kink in my body has unkinked itself. But since there isn't that much time left in the universe, I must face reality and curse the crows who brought it to my attention.

I eased myself up; kink number one had to be dealt with. I rubbed my back gently. I found the floor with my toes and stood up; kink number two now awaited dispatch. I balanced myself against the bed while flexing my legs. So far, so good. Now to reach for my robe – whoops, there went kink number one again. More back rubs were called for. I eased myself erect and moved forward a foot. If only I could reach my robe. I donned it, but what about my fuzzy socks? They were on the floor, a million miles away. If I sat back down on the bed I might be able to lift them by curling my toes. That worked. Now to put them on. I had to risk kink number three and allow one leg to turn and rest over my knee. That hurt, but at least my feet would be warm. I repeated the gymnastics for my other foot. Finally, I could move. I shuffled to the balcony window and raised the shade. The view below me took precedence over my mortal coil and I forgot my morning aches for a moment. The waterfall was turned off, so the song birds were happily bathing in its basin pool. Some of their kinfolk were above them, eagerly vying for a position at the lone birdfeeder suspended beneath a tall shepherd's hook near the top of the waterfall. The less aggressive members were on the ground below, picking through the seeds they spilled. Chipmunks and ground squirrels darted in and out, stealing whatever seeds they could before scurrying back into their dens or up the mighty fir that shaded the patio, basin pool, and waterfall. It was business as usual.

The morning ritual continued with our horses neighing and whinnying for breakfast. I glanced down at Penny, still resting in her bed. "My, they are demanding." Penny yawned, sneezed, and rose to perform the Penny stretch. *Now shake it out and trot over to greet Mommy.* She stood on her hind legs and rested her forepaws on my knees. "Well hello to you too. Have you had your breakfast already?" Penny acted coyly, as though not understanding my question. But I knew better. She'd already been up once, had breakfast, and returned to bed in hopes I might feed her as well. It's a game that has never worked, yet she does not tire of playing it.

I went into the bathroom to brush my teeth and begin my ritual of grooming. It's the same every day, and like each day, I am grateful for clean hot water and indoor plumbing. I know the local critters find drinking and bathing in our manmade ponds and fountains to be the envy of all other woodland creatures who must settle for rainwater runoff or drinking from the creek, but I'm just relieved I don't have to do either.

Today the sun was shining brightly through my rear bedroom window. It cheered me to see it as I dressed. Penny and I walked onto the loft and I paused to peer out the front windows at the panorama that always awaited me. Penny jumped up, balancing her front paws on the windowsill so she could search the yard for rodents while her tail spun wildly. A cheerful voice beckoned me from below.

"Good morning!" called Bill.

"Good morning," I replied as I descended to the bottom of the stairs. In our morning ritual we hug, kiss, and say "I love you." It began the day we married, and no day is complete without it.

This morning Bill was cooking omelets in the frying pan. In a single sniff I detected the scent of bacon, sausage, onions, mushrooms, peppers, and cheese. It was a proper Western omelet. Penny smelled it too. She waited anxiously by Bill's feet, hoping a piece would jump out of the pan and head for the floor in a swan dive. It's not an unreasonable idea; a sausage once rolled off the counter and popped her on the head. We had a bit of a tug-of-war over that piece of meat. I was afraid she might choke on it, so she settled for half. Now I was worried grease might splatter from the pan, or worse, Bill might trip over the dog.

I commanded, "Penny, go sit in your bed." Penny's ears drooped and she reluctantly slinked to her bed in the dining room and plopped down with a loud grunt of dissatisfaction.

I turned to Bill. "Is Sonja coming down to eat?"

"No, she was up early and already had breakfast."

"The weather is perfect for haying. The other day Chase was explaining to me in detail how they use the beaver slide to form the stacks. I would like to get some photos of the process."

"I thought you had some already. You constructed one out of plastic straws for the top of that haying cake you made a few years back."

For an instant I felt a pang of sorrow over the loss of Gail's friendship. Out of awkwardness and a fear of rejection I stopped baking her family an annual cake. "True, I know how to build one, but I would like to film it in action. Everyone uses a bailer these days. The old way of stacking hay is nearly gone. I know Chase doesn't use horses to work the pulleys, but it's still living history. I think it's fascinating. In the future the practice may be a lost art."

Many of the Old West traditions have been fading as cattle ranching techniques modernize and join the 21st century. I often see cowboys herding cows on four-wheelers instead of horseback, and rows of square and round bales are methodically produced by automated equipment rather than by forming haystacks using beaver slides.

"Chase explained to me, while stacking hay is more labor intensive, the hay can remain fresh for years beneath the surface. This isn't the case with bales. They can rot quickly when exposed to weather. Baled hay has to be kept under some kind of shelter. He said some of the hay at the bottom of the stacks is a decade old and still edible."

"Speaking of edible, your omelet is ready, Nancy."

For some reason I felt the need to tell Bill everything I'd learned about haying, as if failing to pass this knowledge along meant it will be lost to posterity. Bill listened patiently to me, but I suspected he'd heard much of it before. Perhaps he was only humoring me. I didn't care, so I continued to talk as I ate. "The big haystacks are an insurance policy in case of a poor summer grass harvest. Chase confided in me that he loves haying. He enjoys the fresh air, the heat of the sun, and the challenge of pitting his strength against the natural elements. He said, 'At the end of a long day I feel like I've really accomplished something.'"

I thought about his words as I remembered the rows of cut green grass laid out on the fields of the long valley. They had been there for a few days, and I marveled at all the shades of green that shone in the daylight. The rows stretched for miles and almost had an artistic design to them. The cut vegetation would dry in the sun. Soon Chase would gather the grass with a buck rake. It was fitted to the tractor and scooped up the hay into a large open bucket. It was then carried to the beaver slide for stacking.

When viewed from the side a beaver slide resembles a large triangle. It's around thirty feet in height and was invented in 1910 in western

Montana It can be moved to wherever the hay needs to be stacked. The hay is placed in a large hay basket which is pulled up the inclined surface by means of a pulley system. As it reaches the opening at the top of the slide, the grass drops through the opening and is piled into a stack. It's dangerous work and I made it a point never to distract anyone while performing this time-consuming job.

I've been respectful of the old traditions of the West and the cowboys who still herd their cattle through wind and rain, feed them in the bitter cold, and nurse them through their injuries. They calve all through the cold nights and protect the newborns from wolves, coyotes, cougars, bears, and eagles.

The small family ranches and the cowboys who work them are a dying breed, even in rural Montana. By recording some of these fading traditions, even if only in words, I too felt some satisfaction knowing, in some small way, I was a part of the living history that is the old traditional code of the West.

Beaver slide. (Courtesy of USDA Natural Resources Conservation Service)

17

A Sign of the Times

SUMMER WAS IN FULL swing, so it was time for Bill's annual complaint that we had never made an entrance sign for Cimarron. He'd long ago drawn a picture of what he intended it to look like, a large wooden plaque with massive lettering that reminded me of Coca Cola font. The capital C sprawled across the bottom of the word, encapsulating it. The only problem was how to make the sign. We could not find a decent piece of wood large enough for the enterprise without spending a huge amount of money, so this year we finally settled on a different approach. We decided to use a half dozen pressure-treated 4x4 cedar posts, each eight foot in length and staggered atop one another. Each post was secured to the one below by massive spikes, so that the final product was a single integrated sign. Two more posts were bolted to the back of the sign to form the legs which would be buried in the ground. On the face of the sign we outlined the word "Cimarron", then carefully routed it. For the final touch I selected a yellow-gold outdoor paint to fill in the lettering. This nicely complemented the red color of the cedar posts. The project took two days, and once the sign was complete, all that remained was to emplace it at the entrance. This presented a new challenge, for the final product weighed about four hundred pounds and we were a quarter mile from the entrance. Even with all four of us trying to ease the sign onto the back of the truck, the task proved to be a Herculean effort beyond our mere mortal abilities. Twice we nearly dropped it before ending this attempt. We had no flatbed trailer, so towing it was out of the question, and dragging it would only damage the sign. One option was left to us; use the tractor. Even with the power of the rear bucket, we could not safely lift the sign high enough to place it in the bed of the truck. Instead, we crisscrossed the sign with padded chains and tie-down straps which we hooked over the rear bucket before lifting it into the air. Our pioneer spirit had prevailed, but it was a long, slow, bumpy drive to the front entrance, and the sign began to swing precariously. Bill stopped driving after a few yards and signaled us to come over.

"Each of you will have to hold a corner of the sign and walk along with it," he yelled over the noise of the diesel engine. The three of us cautiously took our positions and began the long march down the hill and toward the front cattle guard. To minimize swinging, Bill drove at near idle speed. We were able to maintain this pace and enjoy the scenery while chatting along the way.

We had chosen the perfect spot for it on a knoll just above and behind the front cattle guard. Bill mounted the backhoe and swung the sign as far onto the hill as he could before gently unlimbering it to the ground. We removed the straps while he used a tape measure to determine exactly where to place the holes. Bill marked each spot with a posthole digger. At first the work went quickly, but soon he encountered rock and hardened clay. When he broke through them and finished the holes, he collapsed in exhaustion. Between gasps of air I heard him spout, "Well, Babe, I guess I'm not the he-man you married."

"Just rest a bit and you'll be fine."

He sat up and shook his head, "No can do, *kemosabe*; I've got to go back for the concrete and water."

"But you're exhausted."

"Once more unto the breach."

"The battle can wait. You'll injure yourself if you push your body too hard."

"Though I be wounded, I am not slain. I'll lie me down to bleed a while, then I'll rise and fight again."

"More Shakespeare?"

"No, Andrew Barton, a Scottish privateer."

"Well, Captain Drake, I still think you should rest some more."

He shook his head and staggered to his feet. "I'll take the tractor; I can rest while I drive."

We waited by the hillside for his return. It was a beautiful autumn day and I decided to enjoy the sunshine and the warmth of the afternoon. Within ten minutes I heard the sound of our pickup truck approaching. Time to go back to work. Bill stacked the bags of concrete cement by the post holes, then brought up two five gallon jugs of water. "This should do."

With our help he dragged the sign close to the hole and oriented it so that the legs were ready to be lifted into place. "I can't get this upright by myself, so I need everybody to join in and help me."

We tried, but collectively we could not do it. The sign was simply too heavy. I sighed, "So close and yet so far." Now I was becoming philosophical. "I wish Chase was here. Maybe we should have asked him to help us."

"No, he's busy hauling rock for his roadbed. I don't want to bother him." Bill stood up, dusted off his gloves, and motioned us all to try again. We stood in our designated places and attempted to lift the sign. This time we almost got it upright before running out of strength. We had to set it to the ground once more. Bill waxed eloquently in words that made the girls blush. I wondered at this moment if he wasn't regretting his desire only to have daughters.

I raised my head and felt a light breeze, and with it came a familiar sound. "Listen, Bill. I hear a truck coming."

We all looked to see Chase's dump truck slowly rounding the corner and crossing the cattle guard. He couldn't proceed because our pickup was blocking the road. I looked at Bill and smiled, "The cavalry has arrived."

"And in the nick of time."

Chase called out as he jumped down from the truck, "What are you doing here?" After explaining our predicament, Chase laughed, "I can lift this myself, no problem."

Oh, to be young again, I thought.

"C'mon Bill, we can do this."

Chase began to heave the massive sign from the center while Bill scrambled to lift one side. The sign began to precariously sway and fall onto Chase. "Chase, wait!" Bill called out loud.

The sign hung for a moment in the air, like a dramatic slow motion scene in a movie. It then fell back into the grass with a thud, almost crushing Chase under its heft.

"I didn't think it was that heavy!" Chase cried out.

After a more coordinated effort, the sign was placed into the post holes, leveled, and filled in with concrete and dirt. It now had a permanent home. I retrieved five solar powered spotlights from our truck and placed them in the soil in front of the sign. I then stepped back to look at our efforts.

"It really looks great, Nancy, and it's large enough," Chase teased. "Whenever I round the corner I'll know exactly where I am."

"It's Montana-sized, but it represents more than just a home to me." It was true; I had always been in search of a home. From my childhood days to well into my adult life I had wanted a place to belong. Although I remained a fish out of water and still was not fully accepted by most of my neighbors, I belonged to this tiny spot of rough and rugged land that I called my own. The sign reassured me of this with its size, its resilience, and its permanence.

We all thanked Chase for coming to our rescue, but I did tease him that he didn't have a choice with our truck blocking the road. I suggested he stop by the next day and pick up his payment, a batch of cookies of his choice. Although Chase had arrived wearing a baseball cap and driving a dump truck, instead of wearing a white hat and riding a big stallion, his timing could not have been better. The cowboy had saved the day after all. You can't get more western than this.

Cimarron

18

It's a Jungle out There

I STEPPED THROUGH THE door into my greenhouse. The crunch of gravel under my feet and the gentle sounds of water misting from the spray nozzles overhead combined to form their own unique style of music. I hoped the plants appreciated it. This was our first year having a bumper crop of vegetables. I was completely thrilled that our decade of effort was finally showing some success. The broccoli contained huge, dense heads; the carrots had bright green tops; and two varieties of lettuce so greatly overflowed their boxes that they encompassed half the interior space. Onions and mint were flourishing; cauliflower and Brussel sprouts were well on their way to maturing; and little cherry tomatoes numbered in the hundreds. I thanked the ancient Aztec Indians for having discovered and first cultivated these little jewel-like fruits (vegetables?).

With the exception of corn, tomatoes had long been the bane of my horticultural experience. I knew Florida produced the most tomatoes in the country, but even when we lived there I couldn't keep a tomato plant alive. In Montana, with its short cool growing season, the challenge was compounded. I experimented with a variety of tomatoes, searching for one that could survive the scourge of weather, bugs, disease, and anything that tried to gain access into my vegetable fortress. At last I had succeeded. Tomato vines extended in all directions and spilled over their raised box. I had to set up a small ladder in order to reach the ones now brushing the ceiling. It had become such a tangled mass of leaves that I had to lean over precariously and engage in a treasure hunt for the little red gems. As I searched, my mind conjured up interesting facts about the history of the tomato. The age-old question still remained. Is the tomato a vegetable or a fruit? Botanically it is a fruit, but the government classified it as a vegetable in the late 1800s because they wanted to impose a tariff on it. Perhaps that is where the great debate began. At least the issue of their toxicity had long been laid to rest. As I pondered, I held a colander in one hand and gently picked through the vines with the other. It was a balancing act to lean forward without falling, while trying not to disturb the delicate vegetation. I quickly filled my container with a mound of bright red marbles. This was painstaking work, but all previous attempts to grow larger beef tomatoes had failed. Their long growing season was always interrupted by a killer frost which destroyed most of them before they could bear fruit. The smaller varieties ripened much faster and had the added advantage of being sweeter and tastier. Regardless of the effort involved, I found harvesting any vegetables a satisfying experience. There is an earthy quality to smelling rich soil, handling soft leaves, snipping chives, uprooting green onions, and feeling the nourishing connection to nature. It's a peaceful time, almost meditative. My thoughts were interrupted by the creak of the screen door. Sonja entered, carrying another colander.

"I thought you might need this; we have so much to harvest this year."

"Great idea, thanks, Honey Girl."

Sonja looked into her favorite bin. "Are the cauliflowers ready yet?"

"You tell me? Take a look."

Sonja took a few steps to the rear of the greenhouse.

"Stop! Don't move!" I called out.

"What! Snake? Bee? What!" Sonja began to look around wildly.

"Lettuce!"

"Lettuce?"

"Yes, on the ground. I found it a few minutes ago growing out of the gravel. Don't step on it."

"That's funny, Mom." Sonja stooped over to study the tender green leaves. "How did that happen?"

"I can't imagine. Perhaps someone spilled some seeds during planting, right?"

"I suppose that would be me," Sonja replied.

"I'm not angry. Besides, it doesn't matter where it grows, it's still edible as long as it doesn't have a boot mark on it! Why don't you pick those leaves so they're no longer underfoot? I'll concentrate on the tomatoes." As I plucked away, a humorous thought came to mind. "These huge plants remind me of a movie comedy called *Attack of the Killer Tomatoes.* Giant tomatoes attempt to take over a town and the National Guard is called out to stop them."

"Never seen it. What happens?"

"The tomatoes get squashed in the end."

"Very funny, Mom. I'll try not to laugh. I'm just glad we didn't plant limas."

"Why's that?"

"If you'd found any growing through the floor you might have accused me of spilling the beans."

"Well aren't you clever?"

Sonja nodded in vigorous agreement. We then focused on our task and soon had two colanders brimming with tomatoes. I pulled up a half dozen green onions and threw them on top of the pile, then picked a few chocolate mint leaves for our tea. "That's enough for now. I'm ready to go in."

"Me too. What are we having for supper?"

"Well, we could have fresh stir fry vegetables with brown rice, or I could make a fresh tomato sauce for homemade pizza, or -"

"Pizza!" Sonja injected with enthusiasm.

"I would never have guessed. I'd better get started on a quick rise crust or we won't be eating till midnight."

"Hey, whatever's easiest for you, Mom." Sonja surveyed the greenhouse. "This is our best year ever, don't you think?"

"Yes, it's really doing fabulous! I can't wait to see what else we can harvest this year. Finally, we have a real garden."

"Betty Crocker would be proud."

"Betty Crocker isn't real. She's an advertising character for recipes and brands of food."

"How about Ma Ingalls?"

"Close enough, Honey Girl."

19

A Falling Star

I PULLED THE SHADE to prevent the glare of the sun from reflecting on my computer screen. I was answering questions from readers through my social media accounts when an equine photograph captured my attention. The horse reminded me of Wilson; he was white with a few specks, but had black stockings on his legs. His left hip appeared distorted, and the hind leg drooped to the ground. *Poor fellow, what happened to you?* I read the caption and was surprised to learn he belonged to Linda, the trainer who taught my girls to ride in their younger days. She had been instrumental in helping us find Wilson and Whiskey, the perfect horses for our family.

My curiosity was peaked, so I continued reading the short description under the photo. Linda was seeking a home for this horse. He also needed medical care and special nutrition, neither of which Linda could afford for him. By now the wheels were turning in my mind. ***Nancy, you don't need another horse to look after****...But, this poor fellow needs help and we have room for him...****Nancy Quinn, this is going to be expensive and you don't even know if he is docile or mean****...Just look at that sad face; he must be a fallen angle...****He may not get along with Wilson and Whiskey, and they are your first priority****...But he looks so lost and helpless...****There are a lot of questions to be answered such as***

how Bill will feel about this. *Maybe we—I mean I—should call and get some information, no commitment or anything, just the facts.* ***What if someone has already spoken for him?*** *In Montana, really?* ***This is ranching country, no room for sentimentality.*** *I don't care; I need to find out for myself or it won't stop bothering me.*

Logic having lost the argument with sentimentality, I picked up the phone and dialed Linda's number. *Maybe this is a mistake.* Linda answered quickly. *Too late now.*

"Hi Nancy, what's going on; how are you?"

I forgot she has caller ID. We exchanged a few pleasantries before she asked me why I called.

"It's about the injured horse you have, the white one that you're trying to find a home for."

There was a moment of silence before her voice burst out with hope and exuberance. "Yes! The white Arabian. He's a very nice horse." She began telling me the heart wrenching story of how this poor gelding had been seriously abused, beaten, and starved by his owner, a middle-aged woman who lived on a ranchette in the valley. The situation peaked one night when a neighbor overheard what he thought was a domestic dispute. The woman was screaming threats of murder, so he called the Sheriff to the rural residence. When the Sheriff arrived he found the woman was not threatening another person, but her horse. She was overwrought with anger and was violently throwing rocks at the frightened fellow. She screamed she would no longer feed him, then tried to shoot him with a shotgun. The sheriff managed to subdue and disarm her, after which he called Linda and requested she come pick up the animal. Otherwise, he feared the beast would not survive the night.

"I was scared when I arrived. That lady was off her rocker. I told the sheriff I had no legal authority to take him, but he just said 'She doesn't know that.' So I haltered the horse and he limped into my trailer, dragging his leg."

"What's wrong with his leg?"

"I think his stifle joint is swollen, but he's dragging his leg because his hip is injured. It's protruding upward. I think he may have been beaten there and it never healed properly. But he's a really nice guy—honest."

"I believe you. What's his name?"

"Star."

"Do you think he would get along with Wilson and Whiskey? I can't have anyone beating up my boys. Sometimes abused horses are mean just out of fear."

"Are you thinking of taking him? That would be great!"

The magical question—am I thinking of taking him?

She continued. "He is sweet; I don't think you would have a problem. Do you want to meet him?"

Do I want to meet him? The idea banged around in my head. "Let me think this over and talk to Bill. If we decide to see him, I'll give you a call and set something up."

I thought I detected some disappointment in Linda's voice, but we said our goodbyes and I hung up the phone. Now all I had to do was convince Bill that Star was worth a look. We really didn't need a third horse, but for some reason I couldn't just abandon this poor fellow without at least meeting him. As I walked over to Bill's shop I felt a sense of Deja vu. This was exactly how I had approached him the last time I went horse shopping.

Bill listened patiently to my recital of the recent drama without interrupting me. This was uncharacteristic of him and I feared it was a bad omen. When I was finished he casually remarked, "If you want to see him, we can go tomorrow."

I was stunned, no argument, no debate. Now I was having second thoughts again. *I suppose it wouldn't hurt to just go meet him, not making any promises, just to see for myself.* Then I blurted out, "I'll call Linda right now and set up a time. Sonja can come, but Sandy will be at work."

Linda was thrilled to have us come by, and she wasted little time taking us into a muddy corral where Star hid in one far corner behind another horse. He looked at us but did not approach. Linda placed a halter on him and tried to bring him to the center of the corral, but he wouldn't budge from his corner of the enclosure.

I called to Linda, "Let's see if he'll come to us without any prodding."

Linda returned to huddle with us and discuss his history. "He's very shy, probably because of his injuries. He can't lie down because of his hip, so he always sleeps standing. If he ever did lie down, I don't think he'd be able to get up again."

As we chatted I spied Star out of the corner of my eye and was pleased to see him inching cautiously toward us. As he did I saw him drag his left hind leg through the mud. At last he had the courage to stand close enough to us for me to examine his leg. His feet were in terrible condition. They were dry and overgrown, with cracks and splits. The front tip of the hoof on his injured hindquarter was worn down from dragging and the nail was curled under. *Has he ever had his hooves trimmed? Is he in pain?* I didn't acknowledge him as he stepped forward again, closing the gap between us. I simply observed his behavior and body language. Within a few minutes I felt him gently sniffing about me. "You can come closer," I coaxed.

Linda beamed, "I told you he was friendly." She reached out and patted him. I waited to see if he would acknowledge me and draw even closer. His natural curiosity overcame his fear and I soon felt his hot breath near my face. I usually don't allow an unknown horse so close to me, but a little voice inside told me this time it was necessary. I slowly turned to him and spoke in a reassuring tone.

"Hello big fella," I murmured. He seemed smaller than Wilson, but he stooped so that I could not judge his actual size. He was painfully thin and gaunt. His hip bone protruded awkwardly and it made me wonder how much pain he was in. Star stood still and waited for me to reach out to touch his neck. As I did, he remained perfectly still. We continued to chat as though nothing had changed. Star moved over to Sonja and sniffed her hair. Sonja needed no more acceptance than that, and she swiftly patted his neck, then enthusiastically rubbed his chest.

After several minutes of getting to know Sonja, Star approached the only man in the group.

Bill smiled at him and rubbed his forehead. "He's such a nice boy, but so sad," he said, turning to me. We continued talking and watching Star greet each of us again. It seemed that no matter who I was talking to, or what direction I was turned, I found his face near my own, first on my right side and then on my left, gently nosing my shoulders.

"He likes us!" Sonja blurted out. "We can help him, Mom; I know we can."

Bill added, "If you want him, I'm fine with it."

I felt torn. Everyone looked at me, including Star. I approached Star again and rested both my hands on his shoulder. *What do you have to tell me?* His emotions were on the surface. They flowed through my palms and fingertips. I could feel them. It was a tactile sensation, like the physical warmth of his body. His thoughts and feelings emitted off of him and poured into my hands. I had no trouble recognizing them. He wasn't bitter or angry. He was simply frightened, alone, and unloved, so much so that he was willing to overcome his apprehension and take one last chance at human bonding. What he wanted most was a touch of kind companionship. He was clearly, desperately, and unabashedly in need of it. I scolded myself. *What are you waiting for, Nancy, what's bothering you?*

Linda interrupted my thoughts. "Don't feel obligated; I can give him to my sister. She'll put him in her pasture if you can't take him, but I do really want you to take him home. I know you guys will take great care of him. But he can stay at my sister's if you don't feel comfortable about it."

Removing my hands from Star, I smiled at Linda, trying to break the tension. "I need to sleep on this and think it over. Can I call you tomorrow?"

"Of course, I'm not trying to pressure you. I want him to go to a good home, and he would have the best home with you guys. I know you would love him and give him everything he needs."

I knew what Linda was saying was true, but at what emotional cost?

What about his health? Would he be able to recover or would he remain a hopeless cripple? It was a lot to consider, and I needed time alone to think about it, for I knew I would be the one nursing and training him. Was I even up to the task? I dared not look into those pitiful eyes or I would have broken down and cried right there.

20

A Star on the Horizon

WE RETURNED HOME WITH Sonja chattering the whole way about Star. She knew we could cure all his ails and give him a loving home. She promised me she was fully capable of helping me take care of him and was willing to take on the extra work. I listened and nodded, not saying much one way or another. When she got out of the car, she dashed inside to call a friend and tell her all about Star. Bill took advantage of the respite and turned to me. "What's bugging you, Quinn? You've been awfully quiet, so something is weighing heavily on your mind."

"Taking on the physical and emotional care of another living soul is serious business. You know that if Star is here I won't just turn him out. I will make a full commitment to him. He needs help physically and emotionally. I have to be sure in my mind and heart that we're doing the right thing…that I'm doing the right thing."

"I think you already know the answer, but I won't push you into anything. I understand you're gun-shy. Sometimes our best efforts don't work out. You think about it and take your time. No one is going to take that horse. I mean he won't get scooped up if you need a day or two to be sure."

He sensed I needed time alone to think and headed to his shop. I knew I had to face my fears. The loss of my dogs Luna and Kobi still weighed heavily on me. I felt I had failed them. And poor Cookie, she became so depressed at not having any pack members that we were forced to find her a new home, gratefully a happy one with another Newfoundland like she. These remained painful memories. Then I reminded myself we had saved them, along with two horses and our little Penny. Kobi had been with us for nearly twelve years, and Cookie now had Fred, who had been grieving the loss of his partner. We'd saved Wilson, whose feet had been in worse shape than Star's when we got him, and we'd given a renewed purpose in life to Whiskey after he'd been alone for a year with no more children to provide therapy to. So what was I to do? Walk away from this dear boy to spare myself from further grief? *That's not you, Nancy. You'd never forgive yourself if there was the slightest chance you could have helped him, but didn't.* No, I couldn't hide anymore. I had a life to save, at least I had to try.

I walked into the shop and announced, "I've decided to adopt Star. I know having another mouth to feed and vet care will be expensive. I don't know if we can ever ride him. Time will tell, but I'm guessing we most likely can't, but we can ground train him and give him some peace and happiness. He may turn out to be a good companion for Wilson and Whiskey. I mean, Whiskey isn't getting any younger, and when his time comes I don't want Wilson to be alone. He'll panic. Bill, I can't walk away from this. Linda's sister won't be able to provide him the medical care and love he needs. I simply must try to save him."

Bill looked at me from across his workbench. "I always knew we'd have three horses someday. We need to rename our place Cripple Horse Ranch instead of Cimarron."

"You're really okay with this?"

"Honey," he said, looking me in the eyes, "I never doubted what you'd decide for a minute."

I turned to leave. "I'll call Linda right now." As I walked back to the house I thought about how much more work I was taking on, but Star's warm breath on my shoulder was still fresh in my memory. I picked up my stride and marched inside the house with confidence in my new purpose. When I told Sonja, I thought her eyes would pop.

"We're adopting Star!" she blurted. "Mom, that's great. I really hoped you would!"

I apologized to Linda on the phone. "I didn't mean to put you off; I just had to think things through. It's a huge commitment. I needed some time to consider all the issues. My main concern is if he will get along with Wilson and Whiskey. We have a calm and peaceful barn life that's safe for the whole family. I don't want to upset that applecart. I know I said I would call you in the morning, but I've made my decision. I've decided that we would love to have Star join our family, so we want to adopt him."

Linda was elated. "I thought for sure you were going to tell me you weren't going to take him. I'm so happy you will! I'll make you a deal. If Star is too disruptive and you can't handle him, I'll take him to my sister's place."

"That sounds fair to me. I plan to have the vet out right away, and the farrier too. His feet are in bad shape, but I think it'll work out. We're happy to help him any way we can."

"Nancy, that's great. The first thing I have to do is get his ownership papers cleared up. I'll get started on that, but it may take a while. I'm going to be in Texas for about a month, so I doubt I'll have everything squared away before I leave. I'll deliver him when I return. Is that okay?"

"Sure, it gives us time to prepare for him."

This time, when Linda hung up the phone, I could hear the relief in her voice. I immediately began to make a list of all the things we needed for Star. I still had my pink sparkle bucket, a few new brushes, and some hoof picks that I had purchased several years earlier when I thought I'd be getting my own horse, but that deal had fallen through. We'd need a new hitching post and latch, also some more corral panels so we could increase the size of our paddock. Then there was specialty feed and supplements for weight building. I'd have it all ready for him when Star came home. Home, what a nice word.

Sonja and I went down to the corral to take some measurements and break the news to Wilson and Whiskey. The Cimarron herd was expanding and a feeling of hope was once again in the air.

21

Mountain Girl Meets the City

WE WERE SO PROUD of Sandy; she had started college two years early and completed her associate degree by age eighteen. Our family celebrated the event with lunch at a Mediterranean themed restaurant. It had become a favorite dining location of hers due to her maturing tastes. No longer did pepperoni pizza reign supreme. Today she was dining on spanakopita, tortellini, and orzo. I chose shrimp kabobs, tender grilled seasonal vegetables with basmati rice, and red lentil soup, all served with focaccia bread. I was careful not to eat too much because I planned to indulge in a slice of crème brûlée cheesecake. The girls opted for chocolate cake, and surprisingly, Bill ordered the same delight. The others quickly finished their confections before I had hardly begun nibbling at mine.

"Need help with that, Quinn?" Bill's fork hovered menacingly over my plate, then dove like an osprey about to snatch its prey. It quickly rose again, absconding with a mouthful. The girls laughed as I protested.

"Hey, that's my dessert. Eat your own."

"Already have. It's the quick and the dead; you snooze, you lose; he who hesitates is lost."

I sighed, "Would anyone else care to sample my dessert, or are you both too full?" Suddenly forks and spoons came at me from three directions. It was a feeding frenzy.

For a moment Sonja held back. "Are you sure, Mom?"

"Go ahead. Honestly, I don't mind; I'm finished."

With no leftovers to deal with, we began the leisurely stroll back to our car. At times like these I felt sad that our family milestones were celebrated with only the four of us. I often wondered if my girls were missing out because we didn't have family nearby. There were no living grandparents, and their closest relatives were fifteen hundred miles away. But each time I asked the girls about it, they seemed just fine with their lives the way they were. I was even more isolated than my girls when I was growing up, but for different reasons. The isolation had been psychological rather than physical. It was a relief to know my daughters were content and excited with the knowledge that their futures were just opening up for them. Sandy wanted to move to the city, have all kinds of grand adventures, and work in the travel industry. She loved the hustle and bustle and the feeling of energy that comes with the constant motion and activity. Plus, in the city one could always find a good bakery and plenty of coffee houses. Sonja's interests were more diverse. She was currently torn between raising horses, rebuilding old cars, or becoming an Air Force nurse.

As we drove back across the mountain pass toward our home, I set aside my wandering thoughts and focused on the moment. The beauty was all around me, there to be appreciated if one took the time to notice it. Today was a stunner; the pale blue sky was marbled by lacy cloud patterns. The wind twisted and curled the formations which seemed to race past us as we topped the pass. Although the drive could feel achingly long in inclement weather, on days like this it was far too short. We parted the highway and turned onto the dusty gravel trail that meandered up to our home. A quarter of the way there we were greeted by another of nature's surprises, Lady Moose and her new calf. She spent her life around the vicinity of our property, moving from pasture to pasture as the mood struck her. Last summer's visit had included a special surprise, a set of twins. No matter the number, I always treated her rare appearances as omens of good luck.

The horses greeted us with whinnies as we pulled into the garage, and when I emerged from the car I could hear the single chirp of our Downey Woodpecker. She had become a regular visitor. The celebration over, everyone went their separate way, Bill to his shop, the girls to their rooms, and I to my loft desk to check my emails. Penny, ever happy to see us, greeted me with sneezes and wags before settling into her pillow under my desk where she quickly curled into a ball and fell asleep.

I groaned when I opened my laptop and saw all the new entries. I scanned the messages and methodically began deleting those that I could, while preserving the rest. As I was responding to my fourth or fifth query, I found it difficult to type and read the screen. My hands began shaking, as did my computer. Was this a seizure? An uncontrollable tremor had suddenly overtaken my body. It was more like a vibration which continued to grow. I gripped the side of the desk to balance myself and realized it wasn't vertigo, but an earthquake! The sound and fury continued to escalate to that of a freight train, forcing me to shout in vain to my girls. I could not stand or move; I could only hang on for dear life and pray. As suddenly as it started, it was over. I waited for an aftershock…nothing. I glanced down in amazement at little Penny still curled in a ball near my feet, fast asleep.

Sonja rushed from her room and exclaimed, "Wow! Did you feel that? I thought we were going to get another big one!" Her eyes were wide with excitement.

"I wasn't sure myself." I touched her hand. "Are you sure you're okay?"

"I'm fine. We haven't had one in a while."

"Actually, we have. I often feel them at night. The bed vibrates a little, then it's over. Anytime I hear a slight ticking sound from my lamp, I know one is coming."

Sonja looked surprised. "I feel them too; I thought it was just airplanes flying over us."

"Nope," I replied, shaking my head. "Earthquake. We actually have seven to ten micro quakes every day somewhere in the state. Many of them are so small you don't notice them; 2.8 is the average."

"That was a bad one, Mom. I hope we don't ever have another."

"I agree with you, Honey Girl. Funny, no one ever mentioned it when we were looking for property out here—until we had one! You were too young to remember, but the day we agreed to purchase this land we had a 5.4 quake that very same evening. I was taking a shower in our hotel room and didn't even notice it. When your Dad told me, I thought it was a bad omen, but he said it was just Montana welcoming us."

"I remember you telling me that story."

I looked up and spied Sandy standing silently and pale in the hallway. I smiled at her and she nervously spoke. "I remember that too. I hope earthquakes aren't this bad in the city. What's the worst we've ever had?"

"The biggest one on record was 8.5."

"Wow!" replied both girls.

Our reminiscing was interrupted by Bill returning from his shop. "What are you guys talking about?"

"The earthquake, didn't you feel it?"

"What earthquake?"

Now I knew how he felt the night I spoke these exact same words to him in our hotel room. Sometimes history does repeat itself, though this time it was with a twist (and a shake).

22

A Star is Reborn

MY HANDS AND FEET were a little restless as I stood outside waiting for the horse trailer to arrive. The air was electric with anticipation. Star would be here at any moment, and I strained to see down the road, willing the vehicle to appear around the bend. I suppose the delay was fortuitous. My brother, Brian, and his wife, Cara, were visiting from Florida, and they were anxious to meet our new family member too, so they joined Bill, Sandy, and Sonja on the gravel parking area and waited with anticipation. Finally I heard the low throaty sound of a diesel engine. The white Dodge pickup slowly lumbered up the last 200 yard rise to our house and stopped in our turnaround with the horse trailer doors facing our little group. A lean, leathered cowboy emerged from the cab and approached us.

I offered a hello as I walked up to meet him. "We're the official welcoming committee. I'm Nancy, and this is my family." I introduced everyone by name.

"I'm Nick Harper. Nice to meet you all," the cowboy replied. He looked at the assembled group and added, "You'd think this horse is some kind of celebrity."

"Well, he is a Star," I laughed.

Nick grinned. "Linda couldn't come, so she sent me to deliver Star.

It's so great of you to take him. I thought he was going to have to go to the kill buyers."

Those words sent a shiver down my spine. Many horses are brought to the loose pen sales and often end up in the slaughter houses. Our own Wilson was a horse rescued from the loose pens. Our Whiskey might have suffered the same fate had we not bought him.

"Star is safe now. He has a family and we'll do our best for him."

Nick looked around the place and said, "Lucky fellow. It's beautiful here. Well, let's get him out. I had a hard time catching him. He didn't want to leave his buddy."

"I didn't know he had a companion."

"Yep, a mustang Linda took in for training. They got along well. Probably the only friend he's ever known."

"Well, he'll have lots of friends here."

"I reckon he will." Nick flung open the doors and I saw Star's wild reaction. Fear was in his eyes and he began flinging his head, stepping from side to side. I felt sorry for him even though I knew his fears were unwarranted. Nick stepped into the trailer unperturbed and tried to sooth Star as he untied his halter. "This fellow has had a pretty rough time. Do you really think you can help him? Look at that hip." He pointed to the bony protrusion under the skin, and the sunken leg.

"I've got the vet and farrier coming out soon to look at him. I'll know more then. But even if they can't do much, he'll be safe here. He deserves a good life."

"That's kind of you folks."

Star followed Nick out of the trailer. When he saw Whiskey and Wilson, he started to whinny frantically across the fenced-in field where I had them enclosed. My boys returned his call and began to pace behind the corral.

"Take him down to the round pen, Nick. I have water and food there. We'll keep him separated from the other horses and let them get to know each other slowly. I don't want anyone getting injured."

"That's a good idea." Nick began leading Star down the hill and across the pasture. We all fell in behind and followed them through the meadow. Sonja raced ahead to open the corral gate and round pen gate. Star entered both without objection and immediately went to the feeding trough for hay. As he munched, the sound of dinosaurs pierced the air. Whiskey and Wilson were beside themselves. They rushed to the round pen and strained to get a closer look at Star through the panels. It was not a friendly welcome. They demonstrated their dominance by squealing, stomping, and thrusting their heads at the interloper. *Who is this upstart in our round pen? He's eating our hay!*

Star looked up, his eyes widened, and he stopped chewing for a moment. Once he realized they could not touch him, he calmly returned to eating. He was careful to avoid the edges of the round pen to prevent any nipping. I had purposely placed the food and water troughs near the center of the pen so he could eat and drink without being molested. The theatrics died down, so I allowed the boys back into the corral. Wilson was the first to extend an olive branch. He paced outside the round pen, then stopped and sniffed in Star's direction before extending his head. Star gingerly stepped toward Wilson and their noses met. Wilson gave Star a little nibble and Star screamed out loud. All of us watched with anticipation. Nick was the first to speak. "They'll just have to work it all out between them. Horses are like that. Give 'em time." He removed his hat and surveyed our place. "Say, how long have you folks lived out here?"

Surprisingly, Brian answered for me, and he and Nick struck up a lively conversation about ranching and trucks. We continued to watch the spectacle of "getting to know you" when an idea popped into my head. "Nick, I have Star's vaccines; would you mind injecting him for me before you leave?"

"Sure, no problem."

It took Nick a few tries to hook a lead rope on Star's halter because he wanted to play "catch me if you can." I stepped into the round pen and walked up close to Star. I began speaking gently to him and he soon calmed down. As he stood quietly, Nick showed me a triangular area on his neck and explained how to place the needle into the muscle. I handed him the syringes containing the West Nile and Flu vaccines.

Nick's technique differed from the way local ranchers injected their animals. Instead of slapping the horse repeatedly on the neck with the flat of his hand while jabbing the needle quickly in, Nick gently pushed the needle to the hilt into Star's neck, then slowly backed it out. Star remained quiet and still.

"I'm surprised it didn't upset him," I marveled.

"I've been doing it this way for years."

I promised myself to tell Chase about this technique. Maybe he would use it on our horses in the future. We finished our work and left Star in the round pen. Although still separated by the panels, the horses once again began sizing each other up and commenting vocally.

"I guess I should be on my way," Nick remarked. "How long will you keep them separate?"

"A few days. Perhaps it will make the real introductions easier in the future."

"Good idea. I hope you can help him." He turned to give him one last look. "I really like Star. He never deserved any of this. He's a good horse."

"I'll let Linda know what the vet says. She can pass the word to you."

"I would like to know, thanks."

We all said our goodbyes, and soon the horse trailer turned the corner in a flurry of rock and dust, leaving Star to begin his new life.

The afternoon wore on, and Cara and I were sitting in the family room talking when I jumped up from my seat. "Do you hear that?"

"No, what?"

"It's Star!"

I looked out the picture window to see Star screaming and racing furiously in circles, dragging his leg, and desperately trying to jump the corral panels. He would throw his front feet up and fall into the side of the enclosure. "Wilson and Whiskey are nowhere in sight. They must be in the side pasture. Star can't see them and now he's all alone and in full panic mode. I have to get down there before he injures himself." I hit the intercom button on my way out the front door and yelled, "Sonja, come to the barn immediately!"

I moved down the hill as fast as I dared, calling Star's name along the way. He turned to the sound of my voice, but continued his frenzy. "You are not alone, Star," I called out. Cara was trailing me, but Sonja raced by both of us. As she entered the corral he began to calm down. When we reached the round pen he was still breathing heavily. His sides were heaving and he looked rather sick to me. "Sonja, find the boys and call them home. Star can't be left alone."

"On it!" Sonja disappeared around the corner and I heard her calling, "Wilson! Whiskey! Star needs you; come home now!" Within moments the two equines came trotting from the Aspen trees, completely unaware of the chaos they had inadvertently caused. As they entered the corral I instructed Sonja to close the gate and keep them in the paddock. The round pen kept them separated from Star, but at least he could see them and they couldn't wander away.

"Sonja, give the boys some hay as a reward for coming home. We'll stay with them for a while to make sure everyone remains calm."

Cara had collapsed into a chair under the shade of the only tree in the corral, casually smoking a cigarette. "I'm glad to hear that. I'm exhausted from running down here."

"I'm sorry; I forgot you aren't used to the altitude."

"I'll survive, but I do need to rest a while." She took a long drag on her Marlboro and exhaled it up into the air with force.

"Me too." My heart was still racing. We remained with the horses for a half hour before heading back to the house. My excitement meter had pegged for one day. "I could sure use a hot cup of tea."

Sonja replied, "I want a pop."

Cara added, "I need whiskey—and I don't mean the horse!"

23

A Rising Star

TWO DAYS PASSED BEFORE I introduced the boys to Star without a physical barrier between them. Normally I would bring the horses into opposite sides of a field and allow them to migrate toward each other. With Star's injuries I knew this approach would not be my best option, so I decided they would meet in the more enclosed space of the corral. Even though our boys were good natured fellows, I was tense, fearing their natural instinct to challenge any new member of the herd. Often when new horses are introduced to each other they are bullied, bitten, or cast out, depending upon the personalities of the individual equines. A hierarchy must be established for reasons of health, safety, and survival. Injured or sick horses in particular are driven out and must trail far behind the rest of the group. Star was fragile. Not only did his injury leave him lame, but he was emaciated and very weak. I didn't want him to come to any additional harm, but the time had arrived for him to begin to bond as a functioning herd member. If it came to a fight, I knew it would be dangerous for us to break it up, so Bill and Sonja led Wilson and Whiskey to opposite sides of the corral, far from the round pen. I then opened the round pen gate and let Star out. I joined Bill and Sonja in the middle of the corral. Star approached us and milled about.

Whiskey and Wilson eyed him but did not approach. Star wandered over to the horse water fountain and sniffed the unit. He was curious about his new surroundings. In a flash Whiskey bolted from his corner and flew at Star, screaming. He tried to bite him and kicked at him with his feet. I had never seen Whiskey so vicious, and I was afraid he would hurt Star. Whiskey attacked again and Star retreated. I stepped in front of my little Morgan and commanded him, "No, Whiskey. Step back!" I put my hands out in front of me like a policeman directing traffic.

Whiskey tried to move around me, but I was quicker and blocked his path. "No," I repeated, "Go back to your corner." Whiskey retreated, but Star seemed unaffected and decided to approach Wilson, who was taking advantage of the opportunity by stuffing himself at the hay trough. Wilson laid his ears back, and that quickly changed Star's mind. He stopped in his tracks and waited.

"Why is Whiskey so angry?" Sonja asked.

"He is just protecting himself and Wilson. He sees Star as a threat. They'll be fine; you'll see. Whiskey will come around."

Whiskey continued to glare at Star, but Wilson, having satisfied his belly, now approached him. Star and Wilson nuzzled and investigated each other. Several grunts, squeals, and false nips were exchanged, but otherwise they seemed to have worked out their differences for the moment. Whiskey would have none of it and kept his distance, muttering to himself.

"That's enough for today," I said. "Let's separate them for tonight, and tomorrow we'll try again. It didn't go as well as I had hoped, but it's still encouraging. I don't want to have to keep them apart for eternity."

We gave the horses their supper and walked up the hill toward home for our own dinner. Maybe tomorrow would be better.

It was a cold and drizzly morning as I watched the farrier's Chevy pickup truck drive down to the barn. We had long since learned that seasons were little more than suggestions and rarely representative of what most people expected. I pulled up the hood of my new dark plum Carhartt jacket. This was the brand Gail wore and highly recommended to me. They were expensive, but durable and long-lasting. No real rancher was ever without one. Until now I had soldiered through with an assortment of inexpensive coats and secondhand jackets, but Bill found the real McCoy on sale at Higgin's Ranch Supply in Helena and decided to make it an early birthday present. The new color options appealed to my sense of style, hence the choice of plum over the ubiquitous tan version.

We had a new farrier this year, Brant. He was soft-spoken, polite, knew his horses, and was all cowboy. Born and raised in Montana, he grew up on a local ranch like so many of my other neighbors. He had agreed to make a special trip to look at Star's feet. After he heard Star's story from me and Bill, he examined him all over before going to work.

I fretted. "His feet are in bad shape; I hope he doesn't need corrective shoes. I'm worried that one foot is permanently damaged from dragging his toe."

Star was reluctant to have his feet handled. He kept pulling them away, but Brant was undaunted. "Oh, I've handled much worse than this. Star is just being a pill."

"He may be afraid," I offered, "or maybe he can't put weight on that hip."

Brant shrugged. "Could be, but I think he's testing me. A horse can stand on three legs temporarily."

I put my hand on Star's neck. "You must stop this; we are trying to help you."

He must have believed me because he ceased fussing and let Brant look at his front foot. Brant began cutting away the nail and examining the frog and underpart of the hoof. "His feet actually look pretty good, Nancy, better than I expected." It was another story when Brant reached for the damaged leg. Star pulled back and began to dance around on the lead rope. I couldn't calm him.

"Can I try?" Brant reached out his hand and I placed the lead rope on his palm.

"He's injured, but don't let him take advantage of that fact." Brant backed him up and began to give him a lesson in manners. He made him sidestep, then walked him, and finally pushed him back into a proper position at his shoulder. He refused to allow Star to run away or intimidate him. When Star tried, Brant quickly pushed him backwards. "He needs to learn some manners."

"I should have warned you; I haven't had a chance to work with him."

"That's okay," Brant replied as he placed the rope back into my hand. "He should be more cooperative now. He's a good horse, nice fellow really; he just needs to know what you expect of him. He's clearly been abused though. You saw how he tried to rush past me when he got spooked. Now for that foot."

Star had some trouble balancing, but did allow Brant to look at his injured foot. The rain continued to spit and drizzle, and the cold wind began to whip across my cheeks. Despite the warmth of my Carhartt, my face and hands were turning numb. Brant seemed unaffected and looked up at me, still holding Star's hoof in his hand. "I have good news for you. He won't need special shoeing, especially since he'll be here living on this pasture. It's got soft soil. I'll cut away the overgrowth, but nothing's reached the soft tissue."

I felt a great relief. "That is just grand!" At that moment I didn't feel the cold or notice the ankle deep mud I was standing in. Star was going to recover – mostly anyway. I still had the integration problem to deal with so I asked Brant for advice. "I'm trying to integrate Star into the family, but the boys are giving him a hard time and I'm afraid he might get hurt."

"Your horses are not near as mean as mine. I think they'll be okay. If you want, we'll put them together and give it a try. I have a few minutes. If I have to break up a fight, I will, so I won't let Star get hurt."

"I'm so grateful. Let's do that."

"You guys stand back out of the way. They may chase each other around the corral. I don't want anyone getting trampled."

We opened one of the corral gates and guided all three horses into the pasture. At first they milled around each other. Nothing much happened and they were tolerating each other. Suddenly, Wilson made a beeline for Star and began nipping at him. Whiskey joined in and they started chasing Star across the field. For an injured horse, Star proved to be surprisingly agile and quick. Brant grinned and reassured me all would be well. "You see how tough he is, Nancy? Your boys won't hurt him. They aren't that aggressive; they're just showing him who's boss around here."

Star ran through the meadow with surprising alacrity, despite his gimpy leg and protruding hip. It gave him an unusual gait, three legs moving in close synchronization, while the fourth produced a strange sort of hop. He occasionally stumbled, but managed to navigate the field well on his own. I watched him intently. *At least he can get away from predators.* Wilson and Whiskey followed at a more leisurely pace and pushed him around the pasture, but now it was looking more like a game of tag rather than pure pursuit. They still fussed a little as they ordered Star about, nipping at his face and laying back their ears. But Star now realized he could easily outdistance and outmaneuver them if he tried.

Bill laughed, "I think he's found his mojo again."

I nodded in agreement. "He does seem to be enjoying it."

Within a few minutes everyone had stopped running and had begun casually grazing together on the new grass. My heart soared.

Brant called out to me from the field, "They're just fine; they worked it out. I didn't even have to break up a fight." As if an omen, the sun began filtering through the clouds and I knew my stiff, half-frozen fingers would soon begin to thaw. As Brant packed up his tools, all three horses came to say goodbye. They hung their heads over the fence and looked curiously at him.

"They look like The Three Amigos, or maybe The Three Stooges," I joked.

Brant smirked, "No need to worry about them. I wouldn't keep them apart any longer. They don't need any supervision." He waved as he departed. I could just imagine my little herd pondering what force of nature had brought them together in harmony. *Who was that unmasked man? Why that was the lone farrier! Hidey ho, Silverado, and away.*

Sonja and I spent the rest of the afternoon on the porch enjoying the sun, watching all three horses nap on newly dried grass. "I love it Mom; seeing them all together makes me so happy. I'm really glad you agreed to adopt Star."

I was feeling content myself. My fingers gently fondled a round foil object in my coat pocket. "I have something for you, Sonja. I already gave one to your sister, but now it's your turn."

"What is it?"

I pulled out a sweet surprise covered in a gold aluminum wrapper and handed it to her. "A chocolate covered cherry!" Sonja's face lit up. "Like the ones you got from your Dad when you were a child."

"Yes, that's right, my dear." I felt a great satisfaction in carrying on such a loving gesture. Perhaps one day she would continue this family tradition. For now I was content in knowing it had turned into a perfect day after all.

24

Nancy's Hair Salon

MY EYES OPENED THE moment I heard the first sound. The gentle wave reached my ears and I had to grin. It was still dark outside, just before daybreak, and the "hoo…hoo…hoo" called me to the window. The great horned owl was a talkative fellow, or perhaps it was a gal. I couldn't tell from where the calls were emanating, but they became louder and closer as each moment passed. This chatty communication lasted for nearly three minutes, and it started my day with a bit of magic. Often songbirds greeted me as I ate my breakfast, but I was thrilled to listen to the owl so early in the morning. I rose from my downy sleep and dressed for breakfast, after which I took a stroll down to the stable where the rest of the family was already gathered to assemble the new section of corral. The weather was finally starting to cooperate. Mercurial Montana had given us a clear cool morning, and I rejoiced in the fresh air. We all stood in the corral and looked on with amusement. It took the four of us to move the steel pipe panels into a new configuration. Bill and the girls did the heavy work while I determined where the two new panels and two additional gates should be placed. Normally such an effort would not require more than two people, but I had determined the entire corral setup needed some rearranging, so like a train into which one is inserting new boxcars, everything else had to move to accommodate the expansion. The uneven ground on one side of the corral also necessitated the movement of dirt and concrete blocks to level the panels. Bill had completed this preparatory operation and was now focused on filling a posthole with a new hitching post for Star. Sonja held the post in place while he filled the remainder of the hole with concrete cement.

Sandy had taken the horses into the field where they sniffed and snorted at the alterations being made to their accommodations. They engaged in a lively group discussion, most likely expressing disapproval at any change to their familiar environment. Even the newcomer, Star, appeared somewhat distressed. All three of them pranced back and forth outside the corral, stopping periodically to share notes from their joint investigation. Wilson was the first to speak. *What are they doing? I don't like it, not at all.*

Whiskey was undaunted. *Really, Wilson, don't get your tail in a knot. They know what they're doing.*

That's easy for you to say; nobody's messing with your favorite spot. Just look at it, look at it! The panel has been moved to the edge of the tack room. Where shall I stand now? I like standing in the middle with the tack room behind me and the panel to one side. Now I'll have to move to the edge of the tack room if I want to be near the panel. I'll likely get pelted with rain and snow and hail. Worrisome, worrisome I tell you; I don't understand it. We didn't ask for any remodeling. I'm not fond of change.

Star interjected his opinion. *I love it!*

Whiskey shook his head. *Star, you love everything.*

True, True. Oh look, I think I'm needed over there. Bye!

Wilson muttered to himself. *Newbie.*

Star offered to help us install the new panel and gate by the edge of the tack room. By this, I mean he kept darting through the opening before Bill and Sandy had completely attached it.

Bill barked, "Why does he have to help? Sonja, get him out of here!"

I laughed, "Because he's never had his own hitching post before! He's just excited. I'll move him away. Sonja, you just keep helping your Dad." I led Star out of the area toward the round pen. "Stay here, Star, while I round up your buddies." I knew he didn't want to be separated from them, so I lured the other two into the round pen with a few sweet treats. "There, now nobody will get hurt and nobody will interfere, right?" The neighing continued off and on until noon when the task was finally completed.

"Well that took a lot longer than I'd planned," Bill groused.

"Yes, but look how much more space they have in the corral, and it's finally level, and it's got a gate on all four sides. And the feeder is right in front of the hay bin so they can't get into the food, but the girls can easily feed them. And you've got room to back the truck in for offloading hay. And the hay is protected from deer by the mesh panels."

"Well I'm glad you're so pleased. Are we done here?"

"Yes, Bill, you can hurry back to your manhole and tinker to your heart's content."

"It's what I do." With that said he pulled down his grey Air Force baseball cap, climbed into the tractor, and trudged back to the garage bay of my studio.

"I've got to get cleaned up; I have to be at the café in thirty minutes." Sandy did not wait for my reply before heading back up the path to the house.

"Well, that just leaves us, Sonja. Shall we try out the new hitching post and groom Star? The concrete should be pretty well set by now."

"I'll get the buckets," she snapped, then darted into the tack room. We haltered and tethered all three horses. Wilson and Whiskey were in their usual places. There was no point in upsetting their routines. Star was tied to the new post close to his friends. He was fussy. He began stomping his feet and pawing at the ground.

"Sonja, I think Star is having a 'horse tanty'; look at him."

"Looks like a temper tantrum to me."

I checked the breakaway latch on the post. If a horse pulls hard enough, it will give way and free him. It's safer than tying them to a post. When they panic, regardless of the reason, they can snap a 4x4 post as if it were a matchstick, and flail it about like a shillelagh.

"Calm down, Star; it's time for your brushing." I ran my hands along his flanks and inspected his overall appearance. He was beginning to gain weight, but he was still too thin. He loved to eat and eagerly consumed his supplements. He munched his hay with relish and was thrilled with every bite. I knew the vet would be pleased when she met him, but I had warned her in advance of his prior status.

Star calmed down after I showed him the brush and curry comb, and I began to use them. His mane and tail needed a good deal of work, so I set Sonja to the task of unknotting his tail while I removed burs from his mane. His stifle joint was still quite swollen and he kept favoring his bad leg, but he seemed much more at ease and quite happy. I was finding it difficult to comb the top of his mane and around his ears. "Sonja, have you ever seen Star stand this tall? I had no idea he was this big! I can't reach the top of his head. I knew he was larger than Wilson, but not like this."

"He must be at least 16 hands, Mom. I better get the stepstool."

It was a stunning revelation. Star was so broken when he arrived that he always cowered and kept his head lowered, so I had no trouble touching his ears. Now I couldn't reach them because he was standing tall and proud. The wind blew through his mane, causing it to flow, and he looked like one of those proud stallions you see in the movies. His head was up and he raised his tail in the style of a true Arabian. He was magnificent. Star had regained his dignity. The tears began to well up in my eyes. "I can't believe it," I whispered to him. "You are so deserving. I can't change what happened to you, but we will do all we can to help you heal and become whole again. You're well on the way, my friend. Welcome home."

Sonja returned with the plastic steps she had used to mount horses when she was smaller. "Mom, are you okay? I thought you said something."

"I'm fine, just talking to Star. He's looking better every day. Why don't you brush Wilson?" When I was finished with Star I moved over to Whiskey. Our old man was looking a little tired. I was concerned for him. Before Star had arrived I noticed he wasn't eating as much as usual. He always left some of his food in the bowl. I wasn't too concerned, given he'd just turned thirty-two, but I promised him when the vet came out for Star, he would get a checkup as well. I wanted Whiskey to live at least as long as "Old Billy" had. He was a horse in England who was documented to have lived to the age of sixty-two years before he died in 1822. *Only thirty more years to go.* I removed the tangles from Whiskey's copper hair. His mane remained wavy, with golden highlights threaded into it. I had to marvel at all the beautiful colors woven in his long locks. I knew many women who would pay a king's ransom to have such hair. I loved touching his glorious locks and seeing the sun glint on this thick, copper-colored, tangled mass. Whiskey enjoyed the attention and rested in the sunshine that was warming the day. I could only describe it as idyllic.

"Mom." Sonja's gentle voice pulled me out of my musings. "I'm having trouble getting these burs out of Wilson; they're everywhere."

She was right; I didn't know how he always managed it, but he was once again full of them, and not just in the mane and tail, but stuck to his legs and shoulders as well. I frowned. "He's covered in them. I'm finished with Whiskey. I'll help you out." We both gently pulled at the burs that were stuck to Wilson like Velcro, but half of them ended up clinging to our clothes, and within minutes we were both laughing, trying to pull them off ourselves. "Don't let them get back on Wilson; they have a mind of their own. I'm Sticky Fingers Quinn!" I showed Sonja my cotton glove, coated with burs. It was nearly a futile effort, but after a while we were rewarded with a clean white horse.

"Thanks, Mom, I'll finish him now."

"Okay, I'll clean the water tank and start getting their food ready."

When I had finished my chores, Sonja was still working on Wilson. I decided to take advantage of the situation and pull a chair from the tack room to relax under the old fir tree. I was exhausted, so I rested and watched the scene about me. The shiny new red corral panels contrasted with the older dull green and red panels, some of which were badly dented. *I'll have to replace some of those soon. Better not mention it to Bill for a while.* Sonja hummed quietly to herself and the birds chirped happily. I stretched out my legs and looked at my pretty pink boots. When I purchased them ten years earlier I had been a bit self-conscious, fearing they might be too ostentatious, but now I wore them proudly. They represented a milestone for me. I was a high heels and nylons girl when I arrived, and still am when the rare occasion allows it, but just because a sturdy pair of boots is more practical most days doesn't mean they can't be stylish as well.

Sonja had her own concept of style where horses are concerned. To appease her tastes, we had purchased four different colors of horse glitter, each specially formulated not to harm their skin and easily removable with water. I watched her as she applied them to Wilson with studied seriousness until she at last announced, "Done!"

I walked over to see. "He looks fabulous!" Wilson was the most glamorous horse I had ever seen. Sonja had swirled pink horse glitter on one hip, and braided his silver mane with colored bands and feathers. His hooves shined from a coat of clear polish and his long tail twinkled in the sunlight with pink and blue streaks of glitter. Wilson seemed indifferent and was more interested in a snack. "You should give him a treat for being such a patient boy."

"I want to take his picture and put it in a frame," Sonja replied. "You don't think he cares that he's wearing pink, do you?"

"I don't think he's embarrassed, if that's what you mean. Wilson trusts you. Un-halter these fellows so we can feed them. I'm hoping Whiskey eats a little more tonight."

Sonja released the horses. Star and Whiskey immediately began prancing and grumbling, complaining that their supper was late because of Wilson's beauty treatments. I expected the same behavior from Wilson. Instead of thrusting his head in the tack room as usual, he looked around, headed for the nearest wet grass outside the corral, flopped down into a mud puddle, and began to roll.

"My feathers!" Sonja was aghast. I watched with a mix of dismay and amusement. Wilson completed his rolling about, then returned to us, caked in mud that nearly obscured his pink and blue body art. The gorgeous colored feathers in his mane were now filthy and drooping. "I might as well clean him up now," Sonja groaned. "I didn't get my photograph either."

"Perhaps he wanted a mud and clay body wash; I hear they're all the rage these days." I put my arm around Sonja and continued my feeble attempt to cheer her up. "Don't worry, the mud will dry out and you'll get that photo. We have plenty of time."

The sun was low on the skyline. Another day was coming to an end. We chatted as we walked up the hill toward home. Another experience, another moment of joy, it was something to look back on years from now when all this would be but a pleasant memory.

Our handsome, happy Star.

25

Tie One On!

MY CONCERN FOR WHISKEY was growing. He wasn't eating much. This problem had been manifesting itself for approximately a month. He had lost some weight, but was not dangerously thin. I had tried all my usual supplements and treats, but he would have none of it. I still got the impression he was hungry, although after consuming a few bites he would stop eating and walk away. I had called my usual vet, Jeannie, but she was on vacation, so I scheduled an appointment with her partner, Hillary.

I was disappointed when she came out for the examination. Without inspecting his mouth she decided Whiskey had an abscessed tooth. When I asked her to confirm this she refused, citing a previous bad experience with another horse. She gave him a shot of antibiotics, told me to drive out to their office in a week, pick up a syringe, and give him another injection myself. I called the vet's office a few days later and explained Whiskey was getting worse. The office manager said the vet had no time to see Whiskey again, so I was instructed to wait for my regular vet to return in two weeks. I didn't know if Whiskey would survive that long, but the office manager insisted there was nothing else to do. It was frustrating and disconcerting.

By now we had fallen into a pattern of having the girls measure the amount of food Whiskey ate each morning and afternoon. They would report their findings to me and we'd tally his intake for the day. "How much did he eat?" I would ask with trepidation. The reply from Sandy or Sonja ranged between nothing and a couple of pounds. I would manage a weak smile that looked more like a frown, and assure them he would do better at the next meal. After four days of this I headed down to the barn to feed Whiskey myself. As soon as I closed the house door I heard a whinny from Star, beckoning me to come for a visit and rejoin the herd. It was his new ritual to call whenever he saw or heard someone step outside.

As I arrived, Star was the first to greet me with a friendly attitude and the hope that a treat was in his near future. He had become a consistent source of joy to me and would often stand by my side for no other reason than to appreciate my company.

"How is my happy boy today?"

Do you have a treat for me? He bobbed his head gently.

"I usually do; come with me and I'll give you a snack."

Star followed me to the tack room door. Whiskey was fast approaching and I could hear his snorts and mumbles. Wilson would not be left behind, and soon all three horses were jockeying for a position by the tack room entrance.

Star's head thrust through the doorway, a "no-no" in my book. "Star, for shame. Back up now! Has Wilson been teaching you his ill manners?"

Not me. Wilson's face was angelically innocent. *It was all his idea.*

I moved my impatient horses away from the door with a wave of my hand. They stood in a line, awaiting their respective turns. Each horse recognized his own bowl, so I called them by name and fed them in a separate area of the corral. There was no point in encouraging competition over food. I placed Whiskey's bowl in the round pen enclosure so he could eat in peace, then pulled up a chair next to him and sat down. He eagerly ate a few mouthfuls and began to chew his senior feed, dropping a few morsels on the ground. Within five minutes he ceased eating and turned his head to me.

"Whiskey, what is wrong? I need you to eat." He remained mute; I couldn't even feel what he was saying to me.

"How about a little music with your supper?" I rubbed his face and began to softly sing to him the Gordon Lightfoot ballad *If You Could Read My Mind.* He relaxed and began eating again, munching away to my serenade. I didn't want him to stop, so I continued with *Canadian Railroad Trilogy*, followed by Carole King's *You've Got a Friend.* By the time Whiskey finished eating, I'd nearly performed an entire concert of their collected works.

I have been told I worry too much about my animals and treat them like people. I suppose that is true, but I believe they have feelings and emotions. They know love, fear, rejection, joy, and companionship, perhaps not in the same way as humans, but in a way a person can appreciate. I know I can't save them all, but I can help save a few, and that makes all the difference in the world to me. There is something magical about the connection formed between humans and animals, so if I have to sing until I'm hoarse in order to help my horse, I will and I did. I confess that doing so proved to have a calming effect on me, so maybe by helping him I was helping myself.

By now there was very little food left in Whiskey's dish. He had eaten more than he had in days. Until I could diagnose and remedy his problem, I was more than willing to sing for his supper. Wilson and Star were unimpressed. They had long ago finished eating, and now they hung their heads over the round pen panels like twin vultures, eyeing the little bit of grain left in Whiskey's dish and thinking the same thought. *You gonna eat that?*

I divided the food that remained between them before heading up the hill toward home. Hearing a distant rumble, I turned to see its source. Chase was coming down the logging road with his dump truck, no doubt carrying a load of loose granite from their gravel pit higher up the mountain. He stopped to chat for a moment.

"Hey, Nancy, how are you doing? How's Whiskey?"

I explained the problem and recounted my experience with the vet. Chase shook his head in disgust. "What's a vet doing around these parts if she won't treat a sick horse? I'll take a look in his mouth. I can tell you if he has a problem with his tooth or not." He hopped out of the truck and left the engine running. We walked over to Whiskey, and Chase firmly clasped his upper and lower jaw. He attempted to open them, but Whiskey refused. "He's strong for an old fellow." Whiskey finally relented. Chase looked inside and felt around his tongue. "No abscess here. You'd see it, feel it, and smell it. His teeth are fine; he just doesn't have too many of them. His gums are nice and pink. The problem isn't in his mouth."

"He did eat a little better today. I don't know, Chase; one day he eats a little, then the next day he won't touch a bite."

"He may come out of it. He does look great for his age. Those concentrates you give him are miracle workers. You know I would never have thought it would work, but I bought some of the supplements you recommended. Man, does it help! My mare is really improving. Still hard to believe, I thought they were a waste of money. Gotta bolt; I have to get this gravel unloaded."

"Thanks, Chase, I'll let you know what the vet says when she comes to see Whiskey." I waved and turned toward home. Somehow my feet felt lighter and it wasn't so much of a trek as it had been in the past. I went inside to find Bill sitting at the dinner table with an ice cold beer and chatting with the girls.

"Well this is a rare event, you drinking a beer."

"I was thirsty and felt the need for one. How'd things go at the corral?'

I told him about my success singing to Whiskey.

"Maybe you should have offered him a beer instead."

"Like the Toby Keith song, *Beer for my Horses*," I replied.

"Do horses really drink beer?" Sandy inquired.

"I bet they wouldn't turn one down!" Bill responded.

"Not my Wilson! He wouldn't drink," Sonja interjected. "I remember when Sandy and I had a sip out of Dad's glass; we didn't like it."

"Did Old West cowboys ever give beer to their horses?" Sandy mused.

"Nope, too expensive," Bill retorted as he took a swig.

"Dad's right. Drinks were costly in the Old West. However, there was such a thing as a free lunch. Can you believe it?"

"Warning kids, I feel another historical factoid coming from your Mom."

"Humph. As I was saying before I was rudely interrupted, the saloons offered some nice meals with a purchase of beer or liquor. Smaller saloons served sandwiches or soups. The idea was to draw you in and keep you drinking after you finished eating. In fact, have you ever heard the expression 'Tie one on'?"

Sonja and Sandy nodded; Bill raised his bottle.

Supposedly it came from the idea that cowboys would tie up their horses and go drinking all night in the saloons."

"That doesn't make any sense," Sonja remarked.

"Welcome to Montana," Bill smirked.

The days passed uneventfully. I had just finished a pleasant lunch on the back patio by the water fountain. The gurgling sounds of water continually spilling forth had masked all other noises. Now the sunbeams filtering through white billowing clouds were bathing the midday sky in a soft yellow hue as I began my afternoon walk. For once the air was warm and lightly scented, and I detected a subtle hint of wildflowers in the light breeze. Surveying the beauty of the mountains was a tranquil experience which compensated greatly for the brutality of winter. The sunshine was icing on the cake of this glorious day. Despite the perfect weather, my endurance was not what it used to be and I had to pace myself carefully. *Not too far from the house, Quinn. Not too high up the hill.*

I turned to head home, my walking staff supporting me on the awkward slope. From up here I could clearly see the far green fields of our neighbors, the little stream that meandered toward the highway below, and two of our horses in the pasture directly beneath me. Whiskey stood alone and unperturbed, his head lowered, and no doubt slumbering in dreamland. Thirty yards away Wilson was busily mowing the grass in a manner that would make a landscaper proud. But where was our new boy, Star? Systematically, I scanned the field around the boys, but to no avail. I continued my search, looking further afield until I spotted a large, white, motionless lump on the ground. My heart jumped as I remembered Linda's warning when we first took him in. *Star can't lay down. If he does, something must be wrong. He won't be able to get back up.* I started running down the hill toward him. I saw Bill approaching from the house. He must have noticed the problem as well. We met at the bottom of the pasture. As we came near, Star lifted his head, looked at us, and let out a huge sigh before flopping his head back down to the ground.

"Star, are you alright?" I looked at his abdomen for signs of breathing. His eyes were closed, but I saw his rib cage rise and fall. *So far, so good, but how do we get him up if he hasn't the strength to do it himself?* Star appeared exhausted and either unwilling or unable to rise.

"Bill, either he's the happiest, most contented horse in the world, or the worst has happened."

Bill crouched down next to Star's back. "Let's try to get him up."

I knelt next to Star's face and gently stroked his head. He opened his eyes. "Buddy, I need you to stand up. I must know you are okay. Are you feeling alright?"

Star rested his head in my lap for a moment. We encouraged him to get up. I lifted his head and Bill pushed on his hind quarter. Star began to roll.

"That's a good sign," Bill said hopefully.

"I'll feel better when he's back on his feet."

We coaxed Star to rise. He tried a couple of times but fell back to his supine position. It was hard to see him struggling, but we kept up the pressure. He almost made it on the third try, but he rolled over on his other side instead. He then rolled back with greater momentum. Now his feet were under him and he rose awkwardly, shakily, until he was standing again on all four legs. To the sound of our cheers and praise, Star shook off the loose grass that clung to his coat and snorted, tossing his head up.

"He did it. He got up on his own. Oh Star, you really had me scared for a moment." Star snorted even louder. I was elated. "He has his mojo back—again! I think he just wanted to enjoy this beautiful day by sunbathing. It's probably the first time he's stretched out and relaxed in who knows how long." I was near tears with joy. "What a relief. I'm so happy for him! I never thought we would see it after what Linda said. Wait till I tell the girls!"

Bill replied, "You go ahead and spread the good news. I was only coming down to fix the horse waterer when I saw him. The heat tape isn't working properly and I want to repair it before we get another cold snap."

"I know, even in summer it can snow."

Bill just nodded and went about his chore. I returned to the house and shared the good fortune with the girls. This was really turning into a grand day. The afternoon wore on and I headed back down to the barn to feed the horses their supper. Bill was still there, muttering invectives to himself. The horse fountain casing was on the ground and he was trying to remove some parts that were difficult to reach. "Who designed this thing anyway?" he yelled out loud. "The parts are so close together I can't get my hand inside to disconnect the bolts. And what is this extra wire for?" Bill's frustration had grown to the point that he had called the manufacturer from the stable, but nobody he spoke with could help him until he emailed them photos of the inner workings of the fountain. "It's an older model they don't make anymore, so they can't advise me until they see what's wrong."

"You're not going not leave it like that are you? The horses need to drink."

"I'll put it back together after I take the photos and send them. I just asked Sonja to bring down the camera."

I heard the familiar thump of my young daughter racing down the hill, camera in hand. Bill grunted and struggled to crawl back under the waterer to take the pictures. We then returned to the house to email them and await the company's response. An hour later Bill heard from them. "The bad news is they have to send us some replacement parts. The good news is it's still under warranty. We should have them in a week. The only problem they could see in the photos was that extra wire; it's not supposed to be there. They want me double-check it and find out where it goes."

"You mean they don't know?"

Bill nodded and shrugged. "I'll get the waterer back together. It'll work as long as the weather doesn't drop below freezing."

We went to the barn together and I watched him work. Perhaps because he knew I was present, his epithets were quite demure. "Well, this should do for now," Bill remarked as he gathered up his tools. "I'm going back to the shop. Are you coming with me?"

"No, the vet is due today, remember? Send Sonja down, please."

Bill glanced at his watch. "It's nearly five. Is she running behind schedule?"

"No, she told me it would be late afternoon." I looked up at the sun. We still had several hours of daylight left. "I guess this qualifies."

The vet arrived within the hour and soon we were crowding around her for a report. I was very glad to see Jeannie looking so well and rested from her trip to Ireland. She was in her typically good spirit as she opened Whiskey's mouth and examined inside. "Not much to see here. I can file one tooth down to make him a bit more comfortable, but this wouldn't cause his sporadic eating problem." She stepped back and faced me squarely, looking uncomfortable.

"You know he is an older fellow." She hesitated. "He may have a problem in his stomach, or cancer in the digestive tract. At his age sometimes horses start to shut down. But all and all he really doesn't look sick to me. I'm puzzled. I want to start him on medication for ulcers. Perhaps that's the problem. I must warn you it's expensive, so I'll start him with a week's worth and we'll see if it helps. If it doesn't, then I have done all I can do."

Jeannie tried to comfort me by reminding me that I had given Whiskey the best life anyone could. I listened politely, but it fell on deaf ears. I simply was not ready to give up on him.

"Call me in a week and tell me if he is eating normally. This one is a pickle."

I agreed and thanked her for coming out to Cimarron. After Jeannie's departure, I gave Whiskey a thorough brushing and told him how special and important he was to our family, that we had more rides to take, and many conversations to enjoy in our future. I told him I loved him and that I would see him the next day. But inside I pondered nervously; what would the future bring us?

Splendor in the grass.

26

Barnyard Rhapsody

Two weeks had passed and the new medication didn't seem to have any effect on Whiskey's appetite. I felt rather deflated as I watched him walk away from his dish after a few bites of food. I couldn't understand it, so I decided to retrieve my chair from the tack room and serenade him acapella. I placed it under the old fir tree in the center of the corral and put Star and Wilson in the round pen. Then I called Whiskey to my side. As I sang to him I heard Bill approaching on foot. When he entered the corral I noticed the large tool bag he was carrying.

Those parts finally came in; I think I can fix the waterer. Is our old man eating any better?"

"Don't call him old man. You know how sensitive he is."

"Sorry." Bill dropped his bag near the stable and kneeled down to take the waterer apart.

I continued, "No, I'm afraid he's still not eating well. I think I'll change his feed again and see if that makes a difference. He does seem hungry."

"You'll figure it out, Quinny. Right now I have to replace this heat tape. The techs at the company said they don't know what that extra wire on the pump is for, or what it attaches to. Maybe it's for an older unit. They have a new design now, so they're assembled differently. Let's see what we have here."

Bill laid on his side so he could see under the unit. I turned my attention back to Whiskey and his bowl of uneaten food. I patted his head and told him we would try again later. He was due for another dose of medicine in a few hours.

Wilson and Star hung their heads over the round pen panels and begged for the leftovers. Their ears were perked up to the sky and the noses on their white faces wiggled in unison.

Wilson spoke first. *Are you gonna eat that? If not, I'll take it.*

Star nearly panicked. *No, I want it!*

I asked first.

You'll waste it; give it to me.

I was here first!

It's mine; go away!

I divided the uneaten grain into two small pans and placed them under the tree before opening the round pen gate. The two boys made a beeline for the bowls. Wilson wolfed down his portion in a few moments, then pushed Star away. Before Star could respond, Wilson shoved his face in Star's pan and took a large mouthful.

"Wilson!" I stepped over to him and removed the pan from the ground. I scolded Wilson and placed the pan beside Star. "Bill, have you ever seen such a display? They eat like tomorrow will be a day late." I no sooner said this, when three Columbian ground squirrels (aka gophers) scurried across the paddock and joined the horses at their feed dishes. "And look at this—our herd is expanding."

"I'm a little busy, Nancy. Can it wait?"

"But there are gophers everywhere. They're getting so bold that they're eating out of feed bowls while the horses are standing here. Shoo!" As I spoke, our three resident gophers, Moe, Larry, and Curly darted under Whiskey's feet to steal what little grain had fallen on the ground beneath him. Not to be left out, a robin took his place alongside of them and picked up small bits of supplement that had dropped from Whiskey's mouth.

Bill just shook his head and continued working. "I think I fixed it, but there's a wire left over. I'm going to take it out and have a look—

if I can just get this bolt loose."

I watched him become more irritated as he fumbled with one hand at the very back of the unit.

"I got it!" He sounded triumphant. "I can send the company a photo and then the mystery will be solved."

As he withdrew his hand and inspected his source of frustration, he began to laugh out loud. "Nancy, you won't believe this!"

I listened halfheartedly; my focus was still on the invaders who were stealing my horse's feed literally from under his feet.

"It's not a wire, it's a worm! It must have crawled up here and got caught inside. It was stretched from the top to the bottom of the heat tape. Wait till the manufacturer hears about this."

I came over and glanced down at the long, thin, corpse. "Was it electrocuted?"

"I think he got in there to keep warm and got roasted for his effort. Oh well, at least the mystery is solved. The unit should start heating water again when the next cold snap hits. Now what was it you wanted me to see?"

I had returned my gaze to the interlopers and finally snapped. "The dining room is closed!" I yelled, then I ran toward them waiving my walking stick in the air. But my uninvited guests didn't listen. They ignored me, although Larry looked a little uneasy. "Goodnight all!" I picked up the food dish and headed back to the tack room. The Three Stooges stood up on their hind legs, shocked and aghast that I had taken their dessert dish. The robin had no opinion. He figured the show was over and simply hopped a few feet away. The stooges followed me back to the tack room, and the only way I kept them out was by poking at them with my staff. I was surprised by how close they would come to me, the little devils. Each time the staff got a bit close to one, he'd jump back a foot, but not run away. The robin watched from a safe distance, curious as to what was going on. After closing the tack room, I opened the pasture gate to let the horses out for a few hours of grazing. The stooges scurried about the corral, but the robin followed the horses on foot, hopping across the ground. Now it was my turn to watch in amusement. He continued to walk and "graze" with the horses, looking for bugs and other edibles in the grass. He was very close to Whiskey's nose and sometimes his feet, but the feathered friend was not concerned. He stayed near Whiskey and continued his search for food. I checked my watch. I had just enough time to make a phone call to the vet. Jeannie often worked long afternoons and I wanted to talk to her about Whiskey's lack of progress.

I returned to the house and dialed the vet's number. A cheerful voice answered the call. "So, is he any better?" I explained our disappointment and we discussed our options. "Nancy, other than changing his feed, I don't have any way of helping him. I don't have specialized equipment for endoscopy procedures. We talked about this before. Whiskey is really getting up there in years and you have to think about what is best for him."

"Do you think he is in pain?"

"I think he may have some stomach discomfort, but I don't think he's in terrible pain, no."

"Then I want to give him more time. I'll try some different feed and treats. He still enjoys horse cookies. Perhaps I can get him eating before winter sets in." There was silence on the line. I was hoping Jeannie would say something. "Don't worry, Jeannie; I won't let him slowly starve. That would be cruel, but I'm not ready to give up yet. I believe I can save him. I just have to figure out how."

"I hope it all works out."

"I'll keep you posted. Thanks, Jeannie." I hung up the phone and knew I had sounded much more positive than I actually felt. One day I would have to make a decision, but today was not that day. I still believed we had more time with our elderly gentleman.

I stood at the window and watched the horses grazing in the field. Whiskey nibbled the grass and looked rather content. I noticed his bird friend was still at his side. *Mr. Robin, please encourage your faithful herd member to eat.*

I had seen him there for weeks, this plump, colorful robin who enjoyed loitering around our barn. I didn't think much of it at first, but

Sonja kept pointing him out to me, and commenting on his presence. I had wondered if it was the same one who bathed every evening in the basin of the waterfall near my balcony. Now the robin was a constant companion for Whiskey and it warmed me to know he was never completely alone. If only he could get Whiskey to eat more.

27

Queen of the Hill

I WATCHED MY ELDERLY FRIEND dip his head into his bowl and happily ingest the senior feed without interruption. The round pen now permanently served as Whiskey's own private dining room where he could eat all his meals and supplements in peace. This was a necessity rather than a luxury. Wilson and Star had developed the chronic habit of stealing his food at every opportunity. It was unbecoming of them, but it was the natural thing to do, for nature overrides nurture in the adult animal kingdom. Horses are no different in this regard. The strong weed out the weak. But I was having none of it. My rules trumped nature, if only in my corral. Whiskey did not have to defend his food from the other herd members.

Not be left out, I always provided the envious Wilson and Star with a handful of feed in bowls of their own. It kept them distracted while we set up Whiskey's feed pan and sent him into the round pen. They fell for the trick every time.

I settled into my chair next to Whiskey and monitored his intake. He was eating much better now, so I was praying the danger had passed. I knew that when the weather turned colder I would miss our meal times together. As granules of enriched oats fell from his mouth, I glanced up to see Moe, Larry, and Curly race in from the field to assume their usual positions below Whiskey's feed bowl. However, this time they were not alone. Several smaller versions of the furry critters raced in behind them and filled the empty spots around the bowl. They all sat on their haunches and stuffed their faces as if they were a family at the supper table. How did they multiply so quickly? Perhaps Moe was really a Maureen!

They paid no attention to me, and one of the youngsters was only a few inches from my boot. I looked down at Moe-reen and chided the little devil. "Now you've brought your entire family to the buffet? Whiskey won't share his food with the horses, so why would he offer to feed your clan?" Stomping my foot on the ground, I ordered them to leave. They just ignored me and continued chewing, their cheeks puffed out. "I'm serious! Go home! Scoot your buns! Be on your way! Run along now! Go! Scram!" I stood up and began swinging at them with my walking staff. This got their attention and the now rotund rodents turned to run away with their young in tow. I watched as they raced under the corral panels and jumped into the nearest holes.

I called to Sonja, "I closed the chow hall to all uninvited guests. Let's go ahead and groom Star and Wilson while Whiskey finishes eating."

"Mom, I saw them run. Did you give them a royal command?"

"I did, and I used my royal scepter." I held up my staff. "I'm queen of the ground squirrels?"

Sonja just laughed as she carried the buckets of grooming supplies from the tack room. The sun was now glaring down on us, so I suggested we groom our two goofballs in the shade under the fir tree in the corral. We began with Star. Sonja held the lead rope and I started brushing his body with the curry comb. He was behaving much better with each grooming session. His fears of being haltered and touched were disappearing. He seemed to enjoy the attention and decided to relax. I heard him blow loudly as he snorted air through his flaring nostrils. This was a good sign. I inspected his protruding hip and gently felt along the stifle and upper thigh of his leg. The swelling seemed to have changed into a hard lump like cement. Even when I pushed and gently prodded it, I saw no indications of pain.

Sonja and I chatted and joked as I continued to brush and she pulled burs out of Star's hair. When I reached down to pull a different brush from out of the bucket, Star pushed his nose in it, picked up a pink comb, and held it in his mouth.

"Mom, Star wants you to use the pretty one."

"I can tell. I didn't know he had a preference. It matches his pink nose. That must be why he likes it. Who knew Star had such a sense of style?"

I removed the comb that Star was now chewing on. "It's a little slobbery. I think Wilson is teaching him bad habits. I keep seeing them nose to nose, discussing current events. They've become the best of friends."

"Star has to be near Wilson all the time now, Mom. He's like his shadow."

It didn't take long to get Star clean and shiny. We released him, haltered Star's "older brother", and brought him to the hitching post. We had taught Wilson a technique called ground tying. When we drop his lead rope to the ground, he understands he must remain where he is. We can walk away and he will not follow us or leave his spot, although he often shuffles his feet in frustration.

Sonja dropped the red lead rope to the ground and before we could get started, Star stepped to Wilson's side and rested his nose on his companion's back near his hind end.

We laughed. "Look at Star, Mom. Why is he doing that?"

"I think he's offering his reassurance. If you listen and watch closely, you'll understand what they're thinking."

Star's face said it all. *Don't worry, Wilson; the halter won't hurt you. They just want to brush you and tell you how great you are. Everything will be all right. If you get scared, I'm here. Don't worry. You are safe with me. I'll stay beside you.*

Star continued to offer his assistance to Wilson, and I had to lift Star's head in order to brush Wilson's back, then lower his face back onto Wilson's rump. Star would not leave his friend in his perceived perilous situation. For horses, any confinement is difficult until a trust is established and they are acquainted with the routine. Wilson didn't mind and was quite tolerant of Star. He stood quietly while we brushed out the dark mud stains in his white coat. He appeared to be dozing now. I listened for the sounds of snoring. Wilson often fell sound asleep on his feet during grooming sessions and we worked to his rhythmic sounds. His head began to drop toward the ground, a sure sign he was sleeping. He had us just where he wanted us, at ease and unsuspecting. While Sonja was preoccupied with her grooming, he opened his eyes, reached forward, and snatched the cowboy hat off her head, flailing it up and down as he bobbed his head. *Look what I can do? Look what I've got!*

"Wilson, give that back!" Sonja snapped. "He does this all the time. It's his new game."

"He's quite good at it. Practice makes perfect."

Sonja calmed down immediately when she saw Wilson's face. He stopped flinging the hat and stood solemnly, looking unappreciated.

"It's okay, Wilson," Sonja said as she retrieved her favorite hat. "It's kind of funny, really. I just don't want you to damage the pin Mom gave me."

Sonja inspected her hat. I had given her one of my coat pins from my wildlife art jewelry collection. It was a three inch ornate turkey feather design, cast in bronze. She used it to pin up one side of her brim in Australian slouch hat fashion. It made quite a statement.

"It's fine," she said, inspecting her treasure. "At least it wasn't my straw hat; this one is more durable."

"And not edible."

We finished our tasks and Star finally raised his nose from Wilson's back. I gave them each a treat, even though our two boys were now prone to thievery.

Finally done with our chores, we headed back home. We found Bill on his hands and knees in the front patio, looking in the garden pond. He had arranged the two fountain pumps to spray water from the pond into the garden. This proved to be the easiest way to drain the pond in preparation for winter. The water flew in a wide arc in the air and

Wilson with his new chapeaux.

some of it gently sprinkled him. He did not seem to mind, for he was focused on something at the bottom in the green sludge left behind. He stood up as we approached and called out to us. "Look what I found! I've been looking for these."

When we stepped onto the flagstones, Bill showed me a pair of reading glasses. "Where did you find them?"

"In the pond!"

Sonja spoke up, "I remember those. Dad lost them a long time ago when we were installing the fountains."

Bill was pleased. "I'm going to clean them up and see if I can use them."

Unfortunately, his efforts were in vain, the repeated hard freezes and thaws had damaged the lenses, but at least the forgotten mystery

Wilson: Horse thief.

was solved. Later that evening we all gathered on the front patio. I had my camera in hand, anticipating another beautiful sunset. I wasn't disappointed and I snapped several photos to share with everyone who couldn't be with us that night. I anxiously awaited each evening for this moment when the sky became one vast watercolor painting. As I stood there, I was impressed by all I surveyed. I could see for nearly twenty miles from our perch on the mountain. I often wondered what the wildlife did at nightfall, prepare for bed or search for supper? The latter thought gave me a chill, for to me it seemed these twilight moments should have a more serene purpose, but such is the way of nature. It filled me with a profound sense of appreciation, as well as responsibility. I was steward of this land. It was a gift and a privilege. The darkness drew around me like a cloak; colors of blue, peach, pink, and purple began to emerge; and the last shimmers of light kissed the edges of the clouds before disappearing into darkness. It was inspiring to watch the Grand Master at work as another painting faded into starlight. The twinkle of the night sky served to remind me of the promise of the coming tomorrow.

Western Gothic.

28

Gopher Madness

IT WAS BECOMING ABSURD and unlike anything I had ever seen before in all the years we had lived on the mountain. Whenever we approached the barn, a flurry of activity would ensue. The gophers would begin to assemble on the perimeter of Whiskey's private dining room. They came in all shapes, sizes, and ages. The news of the generous folks who set out a twice daily buffet had spread throughout the county. Some were bold and took a place in line near Whiskey's feet, while others waited until we left before joining the crowd. Upon my return to the house I would look out the window and see a sight that made my skin crawl. I would count at least a dozen or more rodents in the round pen. It was a gopher convention/feeding frenzy that was producing some of the fattest ground squirrels I'd ever seen. Their bloated bellies bounced across the ground as they dragged themselves away. The younger ones were brave enough to jump in and out of Whiskey's bowl while he ate. The amount of food they were stealing was appalling, but Whiskey did not seem to mind. I, on the other hand, was livid. Not all rodents engendered abject fear in me. Had they been mice or rats, I would have been petrified. But squirrels and their close kin have no effect on me, although I now held a certain loathing for them.

I finally had enough. "Bill, we have to do something about this rodent infestation. We need to find a way to discourage them from dining in the round pen."

"I can start shooting them with a .22, but not when they're near Whiskey. Or we can toss poison down their holes, but there are an awful lot of those around the pasture. Maybe Chase would be interested in trapping them."

A slew of images danced in my head with each recommendation, but I found them all distasteful. "We can't poison them. It's a slow death and other animals that eat them might get sick or die. I know Chase traps animals, but I don't want that either. They'll suffer too much."

"You're not leaving me much choice, Quinny." Bill sounded exasperated. "I can start popping them tomorrow." He raised his arms and aimed an imaginary rifle in the air. "That's what Alfred Wheeler once recommended to me, if I recall correctly."

I winced at the thought. "You, the king of the misses, sniping ground squirrels?"

"Columbian ground squirrel, my dear. That's the richest kind."

Suddenly I had a flashback to the old Folger's mountain grown coffee commercials with Mrs. Olson extolling the brand in similar fashion. Only now I saw her face on the head of a squirrel as it was caught in the crosshairs of deadeye Bill. I smirked, "Do we have that much ammunition?"

"Oh, funny. We have to do something about the critters."

I knew he was right, but finding the proper method of disposal or discouragement was the problem. I took little comfort in the idea that they were basically rats who lived underground, but something had to be done.

By now Whiskey had finished eating, and Sonja and I went to the paddock to let him out of the round pen. As he walked out, Wilson walked in with Star trailing close behind—shift change at the cafeteria. They each looked for morsels on the ground that whiskey dropped, but they were competing with the gopher community. When one of them got too close to Wilson's tail he would swat them with it. The gophers were not intimidated and just accepted the challenge as part of the game. They simply moved a few inches over and tried again. Wilson followed them around and pushed them along with his nose while competing for the bits of feed on the ground. I watched with fascination and giggled at the sight. When the food was gone, Wilson and Star returned to the corral. The gopher clan began their trek homeward, waddling across the field as always. *Pretty soon you'll be too large to get your fat bottoms down the hole.*

Sonja and I retrieved the pans and immediately noticed how many furry interlopers had relieved themselves in them. I wrinkled my nose. "Oh, this is disgusting. Now we have to scrub these bowls—no telling what kind of diseases they carry."

As Sonja approached the tack room door, she picked up the broom in the doorway and jumped in with both feet, swinging it wildly. "I'll get him, Mom!" She began swatting and poking the broom on the concrete floor near the closed feed bin. "He's in here; I see him. Get out!" she yelled with every determined swing of her broom.

Oh, no, it must be a Fat Rat relative, or a mouse. With one last whack of the broom, a young gopher jumped out the door, ran over my foot, and dashed across the yard with Sonja in hot pursuit. He darted under the corral panels and disappeared down a gopher hole. Sonja stood by the edge of the corral with broom in hand and shook it vigorously. She turned around to face me with her arms straight down by her sides, gripping the broom tightly. "Oooh, they make me so mad. They can't be in here!" She stomped her foot so hard that I feared she might sprain it.

"My hero, Sonja, vanquisher of rodents.'"

"It's the least I can do for our Montana Queen." Her expression changed to exasperation as we walked back to the tack room. "Really, Mom, we have to find a way to stop them."

"I agree, Honey Girl. I wish we had some flying monkeys to catch them. The eagles sure aren't doing their job." I paused to survey the damage in the tack room. "Just look at the mess one of them made in the tack room, then eating our horse feed, using Whisky's feed bowl as a toilet, and running over my foot!"

"That's a capital offense by itself."

When we returned to the house, I slowly climbed the stairs and flopped into my rocking chair, defeated.

"You look beat," Bill said.

I recounted our misadventure and he tried not to laugh. Bill offered solace by making our supper. I heard him downstairs clanging away in the kitchen. I knew we were in for a treat. It didn't take long before he called us down. I was still getting used to having one less daughter at the table as we seated ourselves. Bill offered us each a spoon but no plates or forks. I presumed this was to be a Bohemian dinner. I was expecting a cheese platter with cold salmon or perhaps some other kind of finger food, but the single spoon puzzled me. Maybe it was stew.

Bill came out of the kitchen and placed a huge banana split in the middle of the table. It was loaded with ice cream, whipped cream, chocolate syrup, fudge, and almond slivers, all surrounded by a sliced banana and topped with a cherry. Small amounts of cherry juice drizzled down the mounds of whipped cream and filled the tiny nooks and crannies of the bowl. Sonja spoke first, "Wow, this is dinner?"

Bill was so pleased with himself. "I had to use the rest of the ice cream before it expired. There are three kinds in here, including chocolate, vanilla, and strawberry."

Although it wasn't the nutritious meal I was expecting, it was definitely comfort food. Penny was pleased too. I watched her stumble out of the kitchen with the empty ice cream carton on her head. It was her new toy, and she was having a grand time with it, sticky head and all.

Did having ice cream for supper make me a bad mother? I decided not this time, but I promised myself I would not make a habit of it. Besides, I had other fish to fry, or in this case, rodents.

Licking the bucket!

29

The Theory of Relativity

ONE QUESTION I OFTEN get asked by people who do not know us is how we are able to handle primitive living without all the modern conveniences. I always laugh while explaining we live pretty much the same way as everyone else and lack for nothing. Yet after more than a decade here I was still occasionally flummoxed when members of our family visited us for the first time. But nothing quite prepared me for the shock I was to receive when one of Bill's nephews, Malloy, came for a visit. We had not seen him since he was in grade school, but now he was a senior in college and arriving on an afternoon flight from the east coast. He shared our interest in horses and was intrigued by all things western. We were delighted at the prospect of showing him our rural way of life, knowing it would be quite different from anything he had experienced in warm and sunny Orlando, Florida. The only problem was that his flight landed in Missoula instead of Helena, adding an hour to our commute. It was a long drive, but we arrived on time and had no problem spotting Malloy as he came through the airport arrival gate. He was tall, with a shock of red hair and bright blue eyes. We greeted him as an old friend and ushered him to our car after retrieving his bags. He was surprisingly quiet for the first few minutes during the drive home, but then I heard an unfamiliar voice. "Did you say something, Malloy?"

"No, Ma'am, I was just on the phone. I'm telling my friends I'm here in Montana and won't be dispatching on my regular schedule. I put in a request for leave time. I know your cell service is sketchy."

His comment puzzled me and it took a moment to digest this information. I knew Malloy was intensely interested in becoming a police officer, but I was unaware he had a job requiring leave notice. "Do you have to request leave from your job? I thought you were a fulltime student and only worked part-time."

"That's right. I work at Chuck E. Cheese Pizza in the evening after school. No, the leave is from my dispatching duties. I'm a sergeant you know."

Now I was completely confused. "Tell me about it."

The phone never left his ear. Something held his interest and it wasn't our conversation. I could see in his eyes he was distracted. He moved the phone close to his lips and released a string of codes before turning his attention to me. "It's an online club I'm in; we even have real police officers in it. They provide us realistic scenarios that we have to respond to online or over the phone. It's a popular game."

I sat back in my seat and thought about how much things had changed since I was in conservation law enforcement. We didn't have cell phones or internet, and all the "scenarios" were real and often dangerous. In our off time we might watch a police drama on television, but usually we ended up dissecting their police procedures and pointing out the flaws. It was part of the fun, but to anyone outside the law enforcement community it could sometimes prove exasperating. I decided Malloy was just playing a game, so I changed the subject and focused on the real world, here and now. "Malloy, how would you like to do some horseback riding while you're here?"

"Sure, I'd like that – 4260, respond to a signal 20 at 357 Gladstone Street. Acknowledge, please."

"Are you hungry?" Bill asked, unaware that Malloy was busy posting assignments. However, it did have the desired effect.

"Uncle Bill, I'm always hungry. I eat a lot."

"Hmm," Bill muttered, "It must run in the family."

I remained mute on the subject, and just chuckled inwardly. I was prepared for this. I had asked Bill's sister about Malloy's diet and food preferences, and had purchased a large assortment of his favorite cuisine. I'd even cooked some meals in advance, but I thought he might not be able to hold out that long. "It'll be a while before we reach Cimarron. Would you like to stop and eat in Missoula first?"

"No, I can wait. I really want to see the scenery and your place."

"Well, there's a lot to see, and when we get home I've got some of your favorite foods prepared. We're even planning a barbeque later."

"I love good barbeque."

"Maybe next time you should fly into Helena. It's closer to us."

"Planes don't come to Helena," Malloy replied.

Bill glanced at him in the rearview mirror. "They come there all the time; it's the state capitol."

"Oh, that's not what I was told—4240, I need a radio check." Malloy was back in his game world. This routine repeated itself throughout the entire drive. After a while I could see it was getting on Bill's nerves. His grip tightened on the wheel and the speed increased slightly. We were only a few miles from home when Malloy lowered his phone, gawked out the window, and excitedly yelled, "Train! You have trains! I love trains! This is great." His eyes remained fixed on the railcars until they rolled out of sight and we could no longer hear the whistle or the rhythmic thumping along the tracks. Surprisingly, Malloy abruptly changed the subject. "Uncle Bill, I was hoping to help thatch your roof; I really want to learn how to do it. When can we get started?"

Bill looked into the rearview mirror again, incredulous, and said, "What did you want to do?"

"Help thatch your roof."

He contained his laughter and replied, "I'm sorry to disappoint you. We have a metal roof. It doesn't require any maintenance."

"Oh, I was hoping I could learn how to thatch. Mom said you had a thatch roof. Where do you get your electricity and plumbing? Do you use a generator?"

Bill kept his eyes on the road ahead, but now he was smirking. "No, we just wait for an electrical storm to appear and run up a kite."

Malloy did not hear him; his phone was to his ear again. "4260, have you delivered that signal 20 to the mental ward yet?"

🐎 🐎 🐎

Despite family and friends having visited us over the years, some people back east still expressed concern about our ready access to electricity, sanitation, and medical care. Their impression has been that we live off the grid somewhere in the wilderness and are at the mercy of a generator or solar panels. While internet and cell phone service may be less than ideal, everything else has been the same as one would enjoy in any urban setting. How Malloy came to the conclusion that our house was a glorified medieval cottage was a mystery to me. His own sister had spent a week with us the previous summer, so he should have had some inkling that we were well ensconced in 21st century living.

🐎 🐎 🐎

I knew Malloy would be tired the next day, so I wasn't surprised when he slept late into the morning. Sonja, Bill, and I greeted him warmly when he finally arose. We had prepared a hearty breakfast at Malloy's request, but he ended up not eating nearly as much as I had anticipated. I chalked it up to jet lag and altitude change, so rather than broach the subject, we discussed the day's plan.

"What would you like to do today?" Bill asked his nephew.

"I thought we could work on your forge and make some tools." Malloy's voice was full of anticipation and his face was sincerely hopeful.

Bill's reaction was sardonic. "Sorry, Malloy, I buy all my tools at the hardware store."

"So I don't get to work the forge?"

"I don't have a forge. I have a lathe and a milling machine."

"But no forge?"

"No forge. How about a jeep ride around the property instead? We can take the old Willys up the mountain. There's quite a view up there."

"Okay, that sounds fun, but I also want to see the town and get a cowboy hat while I'm here."

My ears perked up at the idea of shopping. "We'll have to take you to Higgin's – that's our local ranch supply store. It has a huge selection of Stetsons. We found my brother a great cowboy hat and boots during his last visit."

We firmed up our plans for the next couple of days as we cleaned the kitchen. Sonja was particularly excited about the jeep ride, so she worked with unusual vigor to get the kitchen sparkling. Her love of all things jeep relate bordered on an obsession. Bill had been teaching her how to drive the Willys, and Uncle Max had sent her a collection of repair manuals and history books which she devoured.

Always willing to forgo an opportunity to experience a bone-jarring ride along dusty trails, I opted instead for the comfort of my art studio. I knew I would have about an hour to myself and I wanted to make productive use of it by working on a new project. I soon became absorbed in my task and lost track of time. It was only when I saw Bill approaching up the driveway on foot that I realized two hours had passed and something had to be wrong.

"Where's the jeep?"

"Down by the highway with Sonja and Malloy. It stalled and I can't get it started. I think the starter's out. I came back for the truck."

"You plan to tow it up here?"

"Well, I can't leave it there," he replied, tired and exasperated.

"Do you need my help?"

"No, Sonja can steer it while I tow. I'll have Malloy watching her."

Another half hour passed before the vehicles came crawling back up the hill toward the garage. Malloy was in the truck bed and Sonja sat behind the wheel of the jeep. When they stopped by the studio, she got out and I saw her eyes were welled up with tears. "What's wrong, Honey Bear?"

She turned and walked away. Bill climbed down from the truck cab and approached me. He pointed to the front bumper of the jeep, which was folded into a V shape. The tow chain now hung limply in the center of the V.

"What happened?"

"With all the dips in the road, Sonja had trouble keeping constant tension on the tow chain. She got too close and hit the brake. I couldn't feel the slack in the tow chain, so I kept going. When the chain went taut again, I was moving and she wasn't. Something had to give, and it was the bumper. Now she's upset and blames herself. I blame the weak bumper."

Sonja had composed herself and now walked up to me. "Mom, are you angry with me? I'm so angry with myself. I've ruined my jeep!"

"No, of course not; it was an accident and you did the best you could. It could have been worse. You might have smacked right into the truck and hurt yourself, and caused even more damage to the jeep."

Malloy echoed my sentiment. "Sonja, it really wasn't your fault."

Bill pitched in. "It was really my fault. I should have used a tow bar."

"Dad, we don't own a tow bar."

I couldn't console her, not even with the offer of a root beer float. Bill and Malloy, however, were up for it, so we sat down at the dining room table with them and focused on our plan for the next day. "What are we doing first tomorrow?"

"I want to buy a cowboy hat," Malloy injected.

"I have to get up with my mechanic about repairing the jeep. If he can't make it out here, I'll have to rent a trailer and take it into town."

"Sonja, what about you? Would you like to go to Higgin's? They have your favorite Breyer horses there."

"I guess so," she replied gloomily, "but I don't deserve one after damaging the jeep." She turned to her father and added, "If it will help, you can take the money out of my savings account to pay for the repair."

Bill smiled and shook his head. "No, Honey, I told you it wasn't your fault. Don't worry, once we get it fixed it'll be better than before."

Sonja wasn't accepting it. I knew it would take some time for her to feel better. I believed a day away from the mountain was just what she needed.

"Try this one on," I remarked as I handed Malloy a hat. It was tan colored with a brown embroidered band and wide curved brim. I thought it would look good with his red hair. It nearly dropped over his eyebrows. "It's a little big. Do you know your hat size?" I continued to muse over the different styles.

"No, Aunt Nancy, I just try them on till I find one that fits."

Bill picked out a soft brown felt hat. "How about this one?"

"No, the brim's too small. I want something bigger." Malloy cupped his hands a foot from each ear to indicate the brim width.

We kept searching. Nothing seemed to suit Malloy until he tried on a black hat that local ranchers often wore. He looked in the mirror and was pleased with it. Our search was over. As I placed the other hats back where they belonged, I was startled by a furry tail that waved at me from the shelf. "What's this? Oh you scared me! How are you today?" Higgin's resident store cat flipped his tail and fell onto his side, requesting a rub. I didn't know the cat's name, but he had been living in the store for years. He was a stray that appeared there one day and adopted the place as his home. He roamed the different departments of the expansive store, but his favorite perch seemed to be in the home décor area where I often saw him napping. The employees took good care of him, the customers accepted his presence, and he always acted with aplomb.

"I need a scarf."

I turned to Malloy, perplexed. "What?"

"I need a scarf to go with my hat, Aunt Nancy."

"You mean a bandana."

"Yeah, like the ones the cowboys wear in the movies. Here they are."

"Those are okay, but real ranchers prefer silk. Silk is nice and light and doesn't chafe the neck."

My drawing of Higgin's resident cat.

If it made Malloy look like a cowboy, he wanted it, so I began sifting through all the different options.

"How about this one?" He held up a colorful paisley style.

Oh dear, no. "That's actually a ladies scarf; I'm not sure how it got mixed in with these." *I can't send him home wearing that!*

Malloy wanted to be a policeman, so blue was his favorite color. I found him one in a vibrant solid hue, square, bandana sized. Best of all, it complimented his hat and his complexion.

Satisfied with his two prized possessions, we went in search of Sonja in the toy isle, then headed to the car. Malloy unboxed his hat and placed it on his head, then tied his bandana around his neck in a bow. "I want to wear this during lunch. How do I look?"

I had to blink a couple of times. "Hmm…let me help you with it." I removed the price tag hanging from the bandana. "The cowboys wear them like this." I untied the scarf and looped it once without a bow, gently patting my finished effort. "If you want folks to think you're a Westerner, this is how it should look."

"Okay, thanks, Aunt Nancy."

Once in the restaurant, we placed our order. As I suspected, Malloy chose a king-sized meal. He was sure he could eat every bite and more. "I eat a lot! I can finish all of it, plus dessert."

I watched him as he ate, but soon had to ask, "Do you need a box, Malloy?"

"I might; I guess I'm not as hungry as I thought."

The next day we took him on a tour of various museums, starting with the old territorial prison and the antique car display. After spending two hours in these locations, we headed across the street to visit a period log cabin, general store, saloon, school house, and livery stable. As I read the placard on the log cabin, I failed to notice Malloy drifting away to the sound of metal pinging on metal. He had discovered a blacksmith hard at work. Bill tapped me on the shoulder. "It appears Malloy has found his forge."

"Oh dear, we'll never get him away from there."

"You guys go ahead and shop at the old prison store. I'll stay with Malloy and meet you there later."

Sonja and I spent the next forty-five minutes leisurely touring the shop where craftsmen from the current prison system sold their artistic creations. Many of the items were handmade leather goods, but what most intrigued me were the bridles, hat bands, and key chains woven from dyed horse hair and then intricately braided. When Bill and Malloy finally showed up, Bill quietly related to me what had transpired while Malloy wandered the shop. "He was completely captivated and spent the whole time pestering that poor blacksmith with one question after another. The old boy was pretty good natured. I think he appreciated the sincere interest Malloy was taking in his work, but I swear he couldn't get anything done."

"How did you pry him away?"

"With the offer of food."

"Well I wasn't planning to eat here. We have so much food at home."

"I know. I told him we'd stop at the Outback Bakery and get some pastries to go."

Malloy ran up to us, excited. He was holding a pair of handmade boots and shared his epiphany with us. "I want a pair of cowboy boots!"

"Not custom handmade ones, these cost a fortune." I glanced at the price tag of $3,000.

"Aunt Nancy, can we go back to Higgin's and get me a pair of boots?"

Since I'm not one to complain about shopping, we scheduled a trip back to Helena the next day. So far Malloy had enjoyed a truly western experience that included historical sightseeing, archery, knife throwing, shooting, and horseback riding. He didn't get to thatch a roof, but he helped Bill assemble our new BBQ grill. He didn't get to use a forge, but he did get to see a forge in operation. He didn't get to exercise by climbing our mountain, but Bill did allow him to drag fifty 200 pound railway ties to the shop for landscaping. Fortunately, Bill and Sonja helped, and even Chase showed up to assist and "encourage" Malloy whenever he felt faint. For this, everyone was rewarded with donuts and bear claws we had bought at the Outback Bakery. And now he was getting his first pair of western boots. This would be both a cherished memory and practical footwear – well in Montana, in Florida maybe not so much.

"My feet hurt," Malloy complained. Bill and I turned from the shelves of boots we were searching and looked over our shoulders at Malloy.

I asked, "Because of the new boots you just tried on?"

"No, it's my feet; they're blistered. These shoes I've been wearing are too small."

"Didn't you bring any shoes that fit?"

Malloy shrugged, "I've had 'em a long time."

I offered him another pair of boots. "Try these on."

Bill looked at Malloy's old shoes. "I'll find you a size larger than these."

"The same size is fine," Malloy insisted.

Bill was adamant Malloy needed a larger size, and when we convinced him to try the next shoe size up, Malloy smiled and gushed, "These feel great."

Now he was completely outfitted and looked like a real cowboy.

Upon our return home, and during the days that followed, he never took his hat off indoors. I noticed one morning his beloved hat had a bend in the brim.

"Malloy, what happened to your hat? Let me see it; I might be able to reshape it."

He looked a little sheepish, and it suddenly dawned on me why.

"Malloy, have you been sleeping in your hat?"

"Well, yes, a time or two."

"I know you love it, but I would rethink that idea. You can't really sleep in it; it'll ruin the hat. Just curious, are you wearing your boots to bed?"

"Sometimes, Ma'am."

"I recommend you not do that either. It must be uncomfortable, and your feet need the fresh air."

"Okay."

"I know you think being prepared all the time was how the West was won, but put your cowboy attire away for the night, get a hot shower, and sleep in pajamas. Trust me, you'll feel better the next day and be ready to take on new adventures."

Malloy thought about it a moment and replied, "Life is different here, but not that different. You don't live anything like I heard about or imagined. I'm really glad I came for a visit."

"We love having you here. Now you can see how we blend the best of modern life with the Wild West—indoor plumbing included at no extra charge."

Two days later we said our goodbyes as we put Malloy on a plane back to Florida. When we returned from Missoula I went into the guest room to clean it for our next visitor. As I stepped through the doorway my nose wrinkled at some malodorous odor. Yes, a young cowboy had definitely been staying here and had probably worn his barn boots to bed. I removed the sheets and began the process of washing, spraying, and scrubbing. When I got to the bathroom I feared the worst, but it only needed the normal sanitizing. I did smile at one thing. I noticed the head of our moose toilet paper holder was finally left uncovered. It was nice to know that someone appreciated my powder room décor.

30

Working Girl

"THIS HAIRSTYLE WILL BE perfect!" I announced as I wielded the scissors above Sandy's light brown hair. Like my own, it had continued to darken as the years passed, so that she was no longer blonde, but now light brunette. I had always been the family's stylist. All I needed was a photograph to inspire me. It started when Bill didn't have time to schedule haircuts at the Pentagon. He was required to keep his hair short, but after September 11th, he didn't have two minutes to spare, and there were no barbers open at 2:00 a.m. when he got home from his shift. As a result, he asked me to cut his hair, and from that day on he never went back to a barber. He also enjoyed the thought of all the money we saved through the years by my being his barber.

Sandy fidgeted and felt nervous as I trimmed her hair. She was about to go on her first real corporate job interview. A national hotel chain was opening in Helena and was accepting applications. Sandy now held an associate degree and had applied for a position as a front desk clerk. She was interested in the hospitality industry and thought this would be a good place to start. She needed to look the part, so first on our list was a new hairstyle. Like any good barber or cosmetologist, I chatted away as I snipped her silky locks. "Did I tell you about the gal I correspond with in Washington state?"

"No," she replied, distracted.

"Her chicken laid eggs in the dead of winter, and when they hatched she brought the new chicks inside because she was afraid they would freeze to death. She named one of them Tumbleweed. She was the cutest thing and made friends with the cat. Can you believe it? Maggie sent pictures of them sitting together."

"I guess so." Sandy's mind was far away and she skittishly wrung her hands. It was a nervous affliction she developed as a child. I pretended to ignore it for the moment, hoping my story would distract her.

"This is the funny part. The chick clung to her, as they have been known to do, and Maggie started taking Tumbleweed to church on Sundays. The chick would sit on the brim of her hat or on her shoulder, quiet as a church mouse. When the service was over, all the children gathered around to see her. Isn't that cute?"

Sandy's demeanor brightened. "Really? That's a nice story."

"Oh, there's more. Early one morning Maggie heard a loud crowing outside. Apparently Tumbleweed had turned into a rooster! All along we thought the chick would grow into a hen. Funny, right?"

Sandy's face broke into a grin and I knew I had succeeded in my mission. The haircut was finished and she looked at her reflection in the mirror over the bathroom sink. I'd shortened her hair to just above her shoulders and given it a few layers near the bottom. She looked like one of those chic European models in the fashion magazines, and she voiced her approval as I held a hand mirror behind her so she could see its reflection in the bathroom mirror.

I had her get out her gray skirted suit that she wore when she was a library intern two years prior. At eighteen, I knew Sandy's age was against her, even with a college degree, so she needed to look as mature as possible. I gave her my best pair of nylons and we chose some black pumps out of her closet.

"Try these on," I offered, "Let's see how you look, then we'll practice your interview."

Sandy was very polished in her suit, but something still wasn't quite right. "Take off the jacket." She complied and I commented with satisfaction, "That looks much better."

I carefully surveyed her svelte figure and clothes. The fuchsia pink blouse gave her maturity without appearing matronly, and it matched the thin pink threads in her plaid skirt. Overall, the skirt and blouse gave her a youthful, but polished presence. "Pretend I'm the person who will interview you. Stand over there. When I call you to the table, come and sit down."

Sandy approached me from across the room and sat in the chair. She crossed her legs appropriately as a lady would when wearing a dress, but she slouched at the shoulders. I cautioned her, "Sit up nice and straight and remember to smile. Pretend there's an egg on your head." She laughed nervously.

I started with the first few questions, but Sandy had a hard time getting into the spirit. She simply began to giggle uncontrollably. I decided to join in for a moment by asking, "What is so funny?"

"It's you, Mom. How can I take this seriously?"

"It's important you have your thoughts together. I'm sure your prospective employer will ask you some of these questions and you should have some intelligent answers."

We practiced for most of the afternoon, by which time Sandy was feeling more relaxed and prepared. The real interview was coming up the next day.

We got up bright and early the following morning and left in plenty of time so we would not feel rushed. As we pulled into the hotel parking lot I was impressed by how new and elegant it appeared, just the perfect place for my daughter to begin her career. Sandy asked me to go inside with her for moral support. I promised I would follow her in a few moments after she entered the lobby, but I would remain in the background. I had difficulty hearing the muffled conversation with the interviewer, but from the tone I could tell an issue had arisen. The discussion ended abruptly and Sandy brushed past me without saying a word, so I followed her out the front door. When we were safely out of earshot, she stopped, turned to me, and spoke. Her voice was distressed. "Mom, they said they didn't have any openings in the hotel and that Ellen, the lady who set up my interview, didn't work here!"

"Isn't this the address they gave you when they set up the interview?"

"They didn't give one; I just assumed this was it. They didn't know which hotel was hiring, so they told me to try the other two branches in town."

"Didn't they provide you some numbers to call?"

"No, they said they didn't know any; they don't work together."

Now I was getting irritated, but I glanced at my watch and said, "We'd better get going then."

In the car I explained the situation to Bill and we quickly headed across town to the next hotel in the chain. I was frustrated, but Sandy was becoming very nervous, fearful she would be late for her interview. I talked matters over with her and assured her we had plenty of time left to find the right hotel. She would not be late for her interview.

We entered the parking lot of the next closest hotel. It was more of a motel and not nearly as posh as the first one. Indeed, posh is not a word I would use to describe it. This time I went inside with Sandy and approached the front desk. There was no one about and we waited several precious minutes to no avail. I suggested Sandy step around the corner to the office and ask for some help while I perused a display of brochures. When a young woman emerged and Sandy began her inquiry, I felt dismay. For the second time I saw Sandy's crestfallen face and I knew we were again in the wrong place. As I approached, Sandy turned to me and said, "The job interview isn't here either."

Gratefully, the desk clerk was very helpful this time. "I think it's at the Old Grand that's being remodeled. I know it's confusing; a couple of other people have come here by mistake." She called the hotel to confirm Sandy's interview and concluded by saying, "I'll send her right over."

We hurried back to the car and I told Bill where to take us. He responded in irritation, "What's going on?"

I quickly explained the situation before Bill could begin lecturing

Sandy on the importance of doing good reconnaissance before embarking on a mission. The poor girl was already flustered. I knew any further criticism would not help her mindset and only make matters worse. Critiques would have to wait until after the interview was over.

Once again we got out of the car. "You can do this; just breathe for a few moments and gather your composure. I have faith in you."

I let Sandy go inside first and followed her a few moments later. I was actually a bit relieved when I saw all the improvements being added to the place. It was very nicely decorated and had a winding staircase that rivaled the one portrayed in the movie *Gone with the Wind.* It was planned to be even more glamorous than the first hotel we'd visited, and I knew the atmosphere would appeal to my daughter's sense of elegance.

I saw the front desk clerk motion to Sandy to sit in the dining area. I walked by with just enough of a glance in her direction to see her smile and give me a thumbs up sign. I offered her a reassuring return smile and a wink as I passed by. I returned to the car where Bill and Sonja had remained. "Now we wait."

We waited and waited and waited until finally Sandy walked out the front sliding doors and across the patio. I got out of the car to meet her. By the look on her face I could see she was elated. She got in and spoke rapidly. "He talked to me forever! He liked all my answers about why I wanted to work in hospitality, and said he had never heard a perspective like mine. I told him how and why I like to make people happy and comfortable when they're away from home. He was impressed that I already finished two years of college and worked at the library. He said those were great skills for the front desk. He also said I was their best dressed applicant. He did say I was a little young, but thought they could find something for me!"

"I'm so happy and proud! Good work, Honey. This calls for a celebratory lunch." The rest of the afternoon went smoothly and without any pressure. By late afternoon we returned home to find a message on the answering machine from the hotel. Sandy quickly returned the call and conversed for several minutes. When the conversation ended she turned to me, once more crestfallen. "They offered me a job as a housekeeping maid."

My heart sank. "That's not what you interviewed for. What happened?"

"That's all they're hiring right now. The front desk jobs are already filled."

"What? Then why on earth did they interview you for it?"

"I guess that's the only way they can get applicants."

"Well did you ask them if there's any way you can advance from housekeeping into management?"

Sandy shook her head, "They said no; they don't promote housekeeping staff to other jobs, and their pay is a lot lower. I guess I'd better take it. "

"No, Honey. We need to discuss this. This is not the kind of work you are looking for. You need to find something you are interested in pursuing as a potential career. You can't even keep your own room clean, so do you really want to clean hotel suites every day?"

My remark fell flat, so I tried a different approach. "If this job offered advancement opportunities, I would tell you to take it and work your way up the ladder to a better job, one that made you feel happy to go to work every day. But they were clear about there being no advancement out of the housekeeping section. You are not obligated to accept the first job you are offered. Let's keep looking. It's like finding the right horse; we must have a good match for your skills and interest."

Sandy agreed and called the housekeeping representative back to politely decline their offer. Our job search would have to continue.

31

Home Away from Home

I WAS PERUSING JOB LISTINGS online when I noticed an advertisement for a server in the dining room of an assisted living facility. I immediately recognized the place with its grand entrance and meticulously landscaped grounds. Many times we had driven by it and commented on its elegant décor. It seemed like a place where Sandy would feel comfortable, and after reviewing their pay scale, perks, and advancement opportunities, I suggested she apply for the job. Within two days of submitting her application she was offered an interview. I dressed her as before and took her to meet the facility's resource officer. This time I remained in the car and let her handle matters entirely on her own. The interview must have gone very smoothly for I watched her bounce out the glassed entrance looking exuberant as she walked back to us.

"Mom, it was great. It's so pretty and peaceful inside. The lady I spoke with really liked my clothes, and after talking awhile she thinks she will homeschool her own children."

"That's great, what about the job?"

"She said she wants me to come to an orientation they are having."

"So you got the job?"

"She said I could accept part-time or full-time."

"Did she tell you if you have been chosen for the job?"

"I think so…she didn't say exactly. When we finished our conversation, she printed out this letter and gave me these papers to read at home." Sandy handed the typewritten pages to me and waited patiently.

I scanned the letter addressed to Sandy. After reading a few comments, I saw the sentence, "Congratulations you have been hired."

"You got it! All the pre-hiring requirements are here. You will have to fill out some more information for a background check, and they require a drug test. You can do this. I'm so proud of you."

The orientation period went by quickly and Sandy discovered she enjoyed the work, but soon found out there was more to it than simply serving food. She had to learn about the dietary restrictions of different residents and make certain they were carefully followed. She also discovered that working with the elderly sometimes entailed helping those suffering from memory lapses or physical problems. She found herself having to cheer up those who were despondent or confused. On occasion a resident would collapse, which meant medical help had to be summoned quickly. She had to learn to cope with the sudden decline in health or death of a resident she had befriended. She turned out to be a much better listener than I would have expected. She developed friendships with many residents, some of whom were immigrants who delighted in teaching her words in German and French, and sharing childhood memories of their homelands. The experience was maturing her more quickly than most other jobs would. The only fly in the ointment now was commuting. Bill had to drive over the pass twice a day to drop her off and pick her up at work. Sandy needed a more convenient place to live and the means of getting to work on her own. Her part-time employment at the café had not provided enough of a nest egg to afford a down payment on a car and an apartment. It would be many months before she could save enough money for both.

At first we thought locating an apartment in Helena would be easy, but we were in for a shock. Not only were they few and far between, but the rental prices were obscenely high. We wanted someplace safe, close to where she worked, and affordable. It was a monumental task that proved impossible, and time was running out.

It was October and the winds of change were in the air. We considered purchasing a used car and letting her commute on her own, but we didn't want her traversing the mountain pass in the winter ice and snow. We busily searched for a suitable vehicle, but knew that finding a place to live was paramount. We decided to split the workload. Bill concentrated on finding a car while I searched for an apartment. For the car we enlisted the help of my brother, Brian. Anytime Bill found a prospective vehicle, Brian would run it through the Ford car checker program to determine its history of maintenance and damage. Within a week they found a good candidate, a used, all-wheel drive, 2012 Ford Fusion at a dealership in Butte. Armed with advice from Brian, who would also be standing by on the phone for consultation, we met with the sales rep and test-drove the car. Sandy loved it, and after some minor bickering and gnashing of teeth, we settled on a satisfactory price. The only stumbling block was arranging insurance through our longtime insurance company, USAA. We could not drive it off the lot without coverage, and Bill had encountered the USAA employee from Hell when he tried to establish a policy in Sandy's name. It took several hours, multiple phone calls, emails, and faxes, but finally he reached an agent who resolved the issue for us. I was greatly relieved because it would have been bad form to deliver Bill's cow in the waiting room.

Sandy drove the car back to our house with me riding shotgun. For her it was a thrilling experience. For me it was nice to again touch the green, green grass of home. One problem solved, one left to go. At least Sandy could drive herself to work until we found her a place to live or the weather worsened. The race against time and the elements was still on. I continued my search with renewed enthusiasm, but the frustration level was high. As much as I had long rejected the notion, I now was in fear of having a cow of my own.

Bill was helping me investigate rental options, but nothing was affordable, not even "crap houses" as Bill called them. Many of the apartments wanted a non-refundable fee just to fill out an application. Other rentals were unavailable at the present time, and a few, in our opinion, were unlivable. I was feeling the pressure and exasperation when I mentioned to Bill, "We've looked at so many places, and none of them are suitable. I've tried finding her a room with some people we know, but that didn't work out. I'm running out of ideas. I hate to say it, but I think we should seriously consider buying a condo and letting Sandy rent it from us."

"I've been thinking the same thing. We've talked about having a place in town where we could stay when the weather's bad or we're just too tired to come back over the pass."

"And in time Sonja will be in college and could stay there too."

"It could be a good investment as well."

"Let's start looking." So we did. We shifted our search to condos and houses for sale. It wasn't long before we dismissed houses; we didn't want to deal with yard maintenance and snow shoveling in winter. We soon found what we wanted, a comfortable two bedroom condo with an office loft and private balcony. Even better, there was an attached garage, so my fears of Sandy walking through dark parking lots was dispelled. It was in an older neighborhood, a true sleepy hollow with charming cherry blossoms that coated the private drive with their petals. Nearby one could hear the chime of church bells and the laughter of small children. It was an easy commute to work and Sandy loved the place. She was both excited and a little scared of all the sudden transitions, but felt better when she realized this was a second family home. I assured her we would be there often, and periodically I would live there too. I was eager to unleash the many interior design ideas I had bubbling in my head. Let the decorating begin!

32

The Gatekeeper

I FOLDED EACH DISH towel and placed it neatly in the drawer. As I handled the soft and colorful fabrics, I felt an odd sense of comfort at my somewhat worn collection. Since I had to accomplish the mundane chore of drying my favorite dishes after every meal, I believed it could be made more pleasant by using a different lovely cloth each day. Some had flowers printed on them; others had delft blue and white patterns. A few possessed comical phrases, feather designs, or wildlife species. My ever growing collection changed during the holidays, to include some pretty Christmas and autumn themed drying towels.

My task finished, I closed the drawer and simultaneously heard the front door shut with a thump. Sonja had returned from the barn and I braced myself for the "Whiskey report."

"Mom!" Sonja cried out, "Whiskey ate all his food!"

As the meaning of these words sank in, a great burden flew off my shoulders. "Every bite?"

"Yes, all of it, Mom. I think he's better!"

"I have to go see him. Let me get my boots."

As we approached the pasture I motioned for Sonja to stop. I pointed to Whiskey and Star in the side meadow. Star was resting on the ground, basking in the rays of the sun. He looked quite peaceful and content with the breeze gently kissing his damp mane. When it fluttered in the wind, glints of light reflected off the water trapped inside it. It was a touching sight, but something else made it a special moment in time. Whiskey was standing guard over Star. He looked confident and proud as he watched the surrounding hills and protected his new herd member and friend. I turned to Sonja. "Can this day get any better?"

The remainder of the afternoon passed quickly. We finished our chores at the barn and began our walk up the hill. The air had turned cooler and I felt the chill through my long sleeves. Once back in the house I turned my attention to the evening's plans. After supper we settled in for a board game, followed by some individual light reading. No sooner had Bill sat down in his recliner than Penny popped her head over the arm rest and gave him a stare. Bill tried to ignore her, so she resorted to jumps and low growls. When these failed, she dropped back down to the floor and began spinning in circles as if chasing her tail.

Bill audibly groaned. "You know what this means."

"That Penny has to go outside, and she believes that every time you sit down you are not otherwise engaged, and that it is the perfect time for her to ask you to take her out for any number of reasons, including hunting and sniffing?"

"Yes, that would be it." His voice was flat.

Penny was elated; she spun a few more times for good measure and followed Bill down the stairs in triumph, her tail in full propeller mode. Within a few moments Bill returned inside with Penny and called upstairs, "Ask Sonja to come outside; I need her help."

"What's wrong?"

"Penny and I were on the patio and I saw something rustling in the shrubbery. It was big and I thought it was a bear at first. But no, it was Whiskey, Wilson, and Star. I don't know how they got out."

"I have my suspicions," I replied.

"Sonja didn't latch the gate properly."

"No, Bill, not necessarily. This has happened before. I think Kobi taught Wilson a thing or two."

"I doubt it; it was Sonja not closing the gate tight."

"I'll turn on the barn lights for you. They'll follow you right in."

Penny and I watched the bobbing beam of Sonja and Bill's flashlight. I could see two figures moving in the night and three four-legged friends not far behind. They walked down the hill and were soon all in the paddock together.

By the time they returned and we had settled in again, the clock was chiming nine. Bill began to read aloud to me and the world faded away as we moved to another time and place in our minds. Our universe was safe for another evening.

I awoke bright and early to the sound of birds chirping outside. I felt an inner joy that I truly missed in the winter. When the sun beams blazed a trail through my window, and the gentle songs of nature drifted to me on the wind, I knew that the day held many surprises and blessings ahead. My super sniffer detected the scent of bacon, eggs, hash browns, and biscuits. It aroused me from my rest. After dressing, I headed for the stairs and instinctively peered out the front windows. I saw with satisfaction that the horses were out grazing. I joined the others for breakfast and talked about our plans for the day.

"Sonja, I noticed you let the boys out early this morning," I commented.

"What are you talking about?" Sonja remarked between forkfuls of hash brown potatoes.

"I saw them in the pasture."

"What! Not again!" Sonja abruptly put her fork down and ran to the window. Bill just looked irritated.

"I didn't let them out, Mom. See, Dad, I told you. Wilson opened the gate we closed last night and -"

Bill interjected, "And you fed them this morning. You must not have closed the latch properly. Horses can't open that gate. They can't lift the latch and push the gate open."

I had to say something, for Sonja's face was flushed with frustration.

"Belle could open the hay gate. She pulled the key pin out and nibbled at the wires, remember?"

"This is different," Bill responded.

I turned to Sonja and said, "When we're finished with breakfast we'll take them back in, but we'll have to adjust their free time today. The grass is pretty dry now. A couple of extra hours in the meadow won't hurt them."

As we were clearing the table, Sonja spied a package on the kitchen counter. "Did you buy some movies or TV shows?"

"We're waiting for some that Dad ordered."

"Can I open it?"

"Sure, go ahead." I rinsed the dishes at the sink and heard an exclamation of joy from Sonja. I said, "I presume it's the latest *Pirates of the Caribbean* movie you've been waiting for."

"Nope, even better!"

"What are those?"

"My rat traps!" She proudly displayed them for me. "These are the real big ones! Dad had to order them online. Fat Rat's relatives are living in the garage. They keep springing the smaller traps and chewing up the jeep. They ate one of the seat belts and tried to nest in the engine. This is war, Mom. No critters will harm my jeep. This will get them good!"

Sonja scampered out to the garage, only to return a moment later. She looked a little embarrassed as she sheepishly remarked, "In all the excitement I forgot to bait the traps with peanut butter."

I hugged her without a word and watched as my little soldier made her battle plan. She deployed her traps around and on the jeep, now properly baited with Skippy peanut butter (the preferred peanut butter of mice and men in our home). Then she waited. Each day she inspected the garage until finally, success! Sonja dutifully, but glumly informed me of her victory.

"What's wrong, Honey Bear? I thought you'd be happy you got your rat."

"I did, but it turned out to be a big mouse. He was causing all the trouble."

"The important thing is that you got him and he won't be chewing on the jeep anymore."

"I know, but there's no bragging rights in catching a mouse, even a big one like this." She held up the dead rodent, still crushed in the jaws of the trap. Normally I do not consider myself a squeamish person, but when it comes to some vermin, I freely admit I'd rather face a reptile."

"Sonja, dear, please take that thing outside and dispose of it in the bushes where Penny won't find it. Then wash your hands thoroughly. I don't want you getting the Hantavirus."

Sonja shrugged. "Sure, Mom. But I'm bummed about the mouse. I really wanted to trap a big rat and email a photo to my friends. Now I've got *butkus.*"

My bloodthirsty little warrior certainly was taking after her father. *Butkus? I'll have to have a chat with Bill later.*

33

Dead Man Talking

I USUALLY PLANNED SOME kind of activity or event for our first holiday of the season, Halloween. We often had a party with decorations and themed food. My "cake eyeballs" were a family favorite, as well as "witches' fingers" (a thin rolled cookie with an almond at the end of it resembling a fingernail). My creative impulses led me to construct meatloaves that looked like Frankenstein's head, long sandwiches that resembled snakes, chocolate cakes in the shape of spiders, and hot dogs that looked like mummies. "Blood Punch" sat in a bowl placed in a plastic caldron full of dry ice. I kept the punch cold by adding "ice hands" made by filling surgical gloves with water, securing the wrist openings with string, and freezing them. After stripping away the gloves, I floated the hand-shaped ice in the red punch concoction.

The evening was not complete unless I was in costume. I had donned several different outfits through the years, including Elvira (Bill's favorite), Cleopatra, a 1920's flapper, and Lily Munster. This particular year I chose not to do very much. Sandy was at her new job and Sonja was much older now, so I was contemplating some new ideas. Since it was late afternoon and all was quiet, I decided to relax for a little while as I mulled over my options. I settled into my glider and gazed out the loft picture windows. Propping my feet on the ottoman, I gently rocked back and forth and awaited the setting sun. Penny settled in beside me on one of her dog beds and watched me intently. The shadows grew and the sky began to change its hue. Colors blended and faded slowly, and no matter how many times I watched it, the sight always managed to enthrall me. It was better than bourbon, as Bill would say. My tranquility was interrupted by the sound of the doorbell. It gave me a start. Who could that be, the UPS man? I rose and walked to the window where I could see the driveway. A truck was parked below, but I did not recognize it.

"I'll get it," yelled Sonja as she raced past me down the stairs with Penny hot on her heels. I moved move slowly, being the tortoise to her hare. I heard the door open and the familiar voice of Alfred Wheeler.

"Happy Halloween, I come bearing gifts for the holiday."

Sonja yelled up the stairs as I descended, "Mom, it's Mr. Wheeler. Should I let him in?"

I cringed. "Of course, Dear."

"Well, I only asked because he has one of his pigs with him."

"I'll be right down." I tried not to moan. "I can't move as fast as you with this sore hip." I approached Alfred and greeted him with a cheerful smile. "Alfred, what a pleasant surprise. Who is this you have with you?" Sonja had wisely picked up Penny and was keeping Miss Wiggles away from the little pig despite her earnest protests.

"Oh, this is Hermione. She's my youngest piglet. I thought Penny would like to meet her."

I glanced at Penny, who was now whimpering and squirming to free herself from Sonja's strong grip. I wasn't sure if she wanted to meet her or eat her, so I took no chances. "Well, Alfred, Penny can be quite excitable around unfamiliar animals, so I wouldn't want to take a chance of either of them being accidentally harmed."

Hermione let out a loud squeal and Penny followed up with a throaty bark and a cry. I knew what she was saying. *Let me at 'em! Let me at 'em! I'll protect you from this hairy ham! I'm not afraid of a piglet!*

"Perhaps it would be best if we separated them for now," I continued. Alfred appeared a bit flummoxed, but he duly returned the pig to his truck. She continued to squeal and grunt through the partially lowered passenger window after he closed the door. Meanwhile, Sonja took Penny upstairs and allowed her to watch Hermione from the lower picture window. Her paws braced the windowsill, her body trembled, and her tail flailed wildly. A low growl and occasional bark erupted from her. *It's still here. I can see it. I have to investigate this. One good sniff and a lick and I'll know its intentions.*

Sonja seemed to understand and she barked her own command, "No, Penny! You stay!"

Penny looked up at her with pleading eyes. *You can't be serious! Good gravy, you are!* Deflated, she returned reluctantly to her bed by my glider, plopped down with a grunt, and proceeded to pout.

The crisis now passed, I invited Alfred into the living room and offered him a treat.

"Do you have any sun tea?" he asked.

"No, but I can make you a cup of Earl Grey."

"That will do nicely, thank you."

I retreated to the kitchen to boil a cup of water. "It will only take minute. Make yourself comfortable. Sonja, tell your father Mr. Wheeler is here."

Sonja dashed out the back door and ran to the shop before I could tell her to simply use the intercom. Alfred remained standing between the kitchen and living room, rocking on his heels with his hands deep inside his trouser pockets. He gazed about, studying the décor with a critical eye. "You've done the place up nicely for Halloween, Nancy. Expecting any trick-or-treaters?"

"No, not really. They never come up here." The water was boiling, so I dispensed it into the cup with a sachet of Earl Grey and left it to steep. "I think you'll like the tea; it's made by Harney Tea Company."

"Never heard of them."

The back door opened and Bill stepped in.

I glanced at him. "Where's Sonja?"

"She went to let the horses out. She'll be back in a minute." He turned to Alfred. "Hello Al, what's up?"

"Not much. I just brought Hermione over to meet your family."

"I didn't know your ex-wife was visiting."

Alfred frowned. "Hermione is my pig."

"Another sow?"

"Yes, I guess you could say she's the runt of the litter, but she's the smartest pig I've ever had. That's why I brought her by. She's very perceptive and has a sixth sense that can be quite useful this time of year."

"How so?" Bill inquired.

"She wards off poltergeists." Just then the front door flew open.

Bill didn't miss a beat. "Are you sure about that?"

The door slammed shut and Sonja romped into the room. "What did I miss?"

Alfred turned to her and repeated, "Poltergeist."

Sonja's face was a puzzle. "What's that?"

Alfred smiled, "A phantasm."

"Huh?"

"A doppelganger, an apparition, or a banshee."

Bill interrupted, "He means a spook—a ghost."

"Crudely put, but accurate," responded Alfred.

"I don't believe in ghosts," Sonja snapped firmly.

Alfred replied, "Neither did I until I moved here, 'but there are more things in heaven and Earth than are dreamt of in your philosophy.'"

"Well said, old mole," Bill quipped.

Alfred laughed. Sonja was puzzled. "What old mole?"

Bill smiled. "We're quoting Hamlet."

"Shakespeare's *Hamlet*?" she asked.

"I know of no other," Alfred answered. "The Bard of Avon knew his subject well. And while I do not beware the ides of March, I do beware All Hallows' Eve."

Sonja lowered her head and raised her eyebrows as she looked up at Alfred with suspicion. "You mean you believe in spooks?"

"Where I now live it is wise to respect the spirits of the past, for I have seen and heard ghostly apparitions where once there was a town that is no more."

I wasn't sure what Alfred meant by this, and his voice and mannerism made me somewhat uneasy. Was he being sincere or simply playing his own trick for our treat? "Where exactly do you live, Alfred?"

"On land that once was known as Fernwood."

I recognized the name. "The old mining community? I've read about it, but it disappeared a hundred years ago."

"Physically, yes, but the memories of that place are firmly embedded in its sediment."

Sonja became more inquisitive. "What have you seen?"

"Oh, I've not only seen, but I have heard, nay, witnessed events of the past, repeated as though they had just happened for the very first time right before my eyes – but only on Halloween night. The first such incident occurred the year I moved here. I was putting the pigs down for the evening, but they were restless this night and had decided to gather in mass at one end of their pen where it faced the barn. I had just managed to quiet them down when I heard the barn door open and close. At first I suspected the wind, but the wheels that suspend those old doors are too rusty to move by simple force of air. I took my flashlight and shotgun and went to investigate. The doors were firmly shut and latched together from the outside, so I knew nobody could be inside. Just to be certain, I slid the doors open enough to peer about with my light. All I could see was my tractor sitting idly in the middle of the barn. I could hear rats scurrying about in the rafters and even spied one with my light. He quickly scampered into a crevice to join his friends in the darkness. The only other sound was that of a barn owl perched in a nearby tree, no doubt warning me not to interfere with his dinner plans. I closed the door and latched it again. The owl seemed satisfied and no longer screeched.

"Puzzled as I was, I concluded there was nothing more to see here. Besides, the shadows were growing longer in the full moonlight, and even I must admit it added to the eeriness of that Halloween. I had no sooner reached my front door steps when I heard what sounded like laughter coming from the direction of the creek, behind the barn. Ha, I thought, some local ranch kids are having fun at my expense. Well, two can play that game, so I quietly crept down to the stream. There by the remnants of a broken sluice I saw the silhouettes of two young men. I approached them cautiously and raised my shotgun. 'What are you boys doing here?' I yelled, mustering all the bravado I could manage. They glanced at me and laughed some more, before returning to their work. I could then see by their period dress that they were miners panning for gold. I shook my head and stepped closer, but as I did, a cloud passed over the moon. I fumbled for my flashlight and shone it toward them, but they were gone. The Moon reappeared and I looked frantically all around. There was nothing there, not even footprints in the soft mud of the bank. They had simply vanished before my very eyes."

Sonja leaned forward intently. "What did you do then?"

"Well, my first thought was that I must be dreaming. Nothing like this could be true. I returned to the house and sat up the rest of the night, too fearful to sleep, and pondered how to make sense of it all. It was not until the sun rose the next morning that I ventured out once more to check the sluice. Again I found no sign that anyone save I had been there. Being a professor emeritus, I could ill afford to mention the events to my former colleagues, so I decided to do some scientific inquiry on my own. I researched the state archives online to learn as much as possible about the area where I now reside. This was when I first learned about the settlement of Fernwood. It had been an active mining community from the 1860s through the 1890s, starting with placer mining around the creeks and ending up with lode mining—what you might call hard rock mining—until it finally died out around 1911. During this 'golden' age of mining the little town saw lots of ups and downs – floods, fires, cave-ins, shootings, and hangings. There were enough bars and brothels to meet the needs of up to 5,000 rowdy miners and loggers. Now it's all gone; nothing's left but a few sticks and some stone rubble. Fire and wind took care of the rest."

By now even I was enthralled by Alfred's histrionics. "What happened after that? You said this was your first such encounter."

"True, it was only the beginning. After that experience I was a bit shaken, but as time passed I eventually shrugged it off as some wild hallucination…until the following Halloween."

"You mean the ghosts came back?" Bill remained skeptical.

"Not exactly. This time I was sitting on my front porch rocker listening once again to that old barn owl screech. He'd grown fat during the intervening year and my rat population had correspondingly shrunk. I'd gotten used to his nightly calls and even welcomed him as an old friend. This year we didn't have a full moon, but it made no difference. It must have been around 10 PM that the pigs became restless just as they had the previous Halloween. They again gathered at the corner of the pen nearest the barn. That's when I heard the first unnatural sound. It was the roar of a stage coach approaching fast. I could clearly hear the driver yell and snap his whip. The team stomped their feet in unison and the coach squeaked on its spring mounts, while the wheels ground dirt and pebbles into dust. Suddenly all was again silent. I would have sworn it had stopped behind my barn. Once more I grabbed my shotgun and flashlight and went to investigate. I wasn't as fearful as I was curious this time, but I was taking no chances. I couldn't see them but I could sure smell them."

"You mean the horses?" asked Sonja.

"Yes."

"And the passengers too I suspect," Bill quipped.

Alfred smirked and continued his story. "I peeked around the corner and what did I see but six horses standing there snorting and heaving, their breath frosting the night air. The whole scene was bathed in an eerie glow as the driver stepped down to check the harnesses. He was wearing a very broad brimmed flat hat and a long canvas duster. He never took notice of me even after I made a feeble attempt to call to him. 'Hey you, driver, where is this stage bound?' I asked. Without so much as a glance in my direction, he climbed back on the stage and yelled once as he snapped his whip lightly in the air. The horses sprang back into action and the coach rolled forward in a torrent of dust. I stepped into the cloud right after it passed, but none of it settled on me. Like the stagecoach itself, it all melted away into a vapor that quickly dissipated, leaving me completely baffled. What had I just seen?"

"More like what did you just drink?" Bill laughed.

"I don't blame you for doubting me, but I don't drink, use drugs, or take any medication stronger than aspirin. I promised myself after this episode that I would be better prepared next year when the apparitions appeared. In the meantime I did more research and learned a stage line had once passed through my property."

"So who'd you call, Ghostbusters?" Bill was on a roll.

"No, but I did purchase a camera, some sound equipment, and a rack of bright lights on a pedestal mount. I practiced filming at night to get the sound equipment and lighting just right. I also started training my pigs as sentry hogs. I taught them to alert me to any strange and unusual sights, smells, and sounds such as people and horses. I was ready for the next encounter."

By this time we were all seated at the dining room table listening intently to every word. Whether true or false, there was no denying Alfred's ability to spin a yarn. And so he continued.

"That third Halloween couldn't come soon enough for me. I was on pins and needles waiting for it. I had purchased extra lights and strung them around the barn because I didn't know where the next apparition might be. I had a portable set of lights mounted on my camera along with a directional microphone so I could zero in on any sound. I had positioned myself inside the barn, but with the front and rear barn doors open so I could see both the pig pen by my house and the creek. The pigs were huddled in the middle of their pen, but making no noise. We all waited silently as the time approached ten o'clock. Sure enough, the pigs alerted to something, but it wasn't near the barn or the creek, for I could not see the pigs anywhere near the fence. They had disappeared into the shadows of my house. All I knew for certain was that I was in the wrong location. I stumbled out of the barn with my bulky camera setup."

"Did you have your shotgun with you?" asked Sonja.

"Not this time. My hands were full of camera equipment. And what was I going to do with a shotgun anyway, shoot a phantasm with it? No, I just started moving toward the house, hoping I'd catch a glimpse of whatever it was and capture it on video. I knew the pigs would point me in the right direction, so I stopped at their pen first. This time I was really stumped. They were all crowding by the wall of my house."

I was aghast. "You mean it was in your house?" I shuddered.

Alfred nodded. "Yes, it had to be inside. And the wall the pigs were pressing against was my bedroom."

By now Sonja was holding Penny tightly in her arms and snuggling her close to her cheek. "You could take that old spook," she said confidently to our pup. Penny just squirmed. She was more interested in any table scraps from the cookie crumbs we'd left. Normally I would have scolded her for having the dog at the table, but I could see Alfred's story was starting to have an effect on her.

"I opened the screen door—it made an awful screech, then pushed my front door open. I absentmindedly let go of the screen and *whap*! It slapped me on the backside. I fumbled for the camera's power switch and began recording video in the darkness. I didn't dare turn on the lights, for I wasn't certain what effect it might have on the specter. My bedroom door was ajar and I could see a purple glow emanating around it. For the first time I could feel a presence rather than smell it or hear it. A sudden chill passed through me as if I'd just stepped into a walk-in freezer. I started to shake from the cold, but still I inched forward. I stood behind the door and moved the camera around the opening. I panned the room with it but I could see little but soft shadows on the viewing screen. I then peeped around the edge of the door and looked into my bedroom. There sat a woman on my bed, cradling a young baby in her arms. She was rocking gently and seemed to be singing to the child, but I heard no sound. I continued to film and she took no mind of me. I softly spoke to her, 'May I see your baby?' She just kept rocking softly, so I dared for once to reach out and touch the spirit. My hand entered the mist but touched nothing, yet it felt as cold as ice. I quickly withdrew it as the lady continued to rock. I didn't know what to do. Unlike the prior apparitions, this one seemed unwilling to depart. I didn't have the heart to shoo her away, but I couldn't very well go to bed with a ghost rocking on my pillow—"

"Sounds like you were stuck between a rock and heart place." We all groaned at Bill's pun. "So what did you do?"

"Well, I'd forgotten that my screen door was torn at the bottom, which was probably a good thing this night because just then one of my sows rushed into the room and squealed at the spirits. Much to my surprise, the lady looked up from her child and then down at the pig. She clutched the baby tightly in her arms and vanished in a swirl of mist. That's when I realized the pigs could do more than just sense the phantom's presence. The phantoms could sense them as well."

Suddenly I felt a tinge of shame at having enjoyed four strips of bacon at my breakfast that morning, but I said nothing to Alfred. He finished his story.

"Ever since that night I've kept one of my pigs on a leash with me at Halloween. The sow that dashed in that night is the mother of Hermione. She probably felt I was in some sort of danger and wanted to protect me because she actually broke down the stall gate to get out."

"What about the film you recorded?" asked Sonja.

Alfred shrugged, "Oh that, well when I played it back all I could see were shadows and blobs. There wasn't any sound to record except for pig grunts, so I was back to square one."

"So why did you bring over Hermamanywahah?" Bill inquired.

"Hermione. Just as some pigs can find truffles, mine can find poltergeists. I thought the girls would enjoy searching for them before the witching hour strikes."

"Sandy's working tonight."

"But I'd like to do it," Sonja exclaimed.

"I thought you didn't believe in ghosts," I replied.

"It's research, Mom."

"Okay, once around the house."

"And the barn?"

"And the barn."

I am happy to report no swine were harmed in the search for poltergeists, and no spirits were disturbed either, although we did find a truffle.

Penny and I watched from the loft window as Alfred Wheeler drove off. Hermione's head barely jutted from the passenger window and I could see she was nodding and squealing her goodbye. Penny's tail wagged fiercely and her front paws trembled on the windowsill. She was focused intently on the truck as it quickly disappeared into the setting sun. I knew what she was thinking. *Oh, how I'd like to give that truffle sniffer a piece of my mind.*

I returned to my glider and opened a book about Montana ghosts. Penny plopped down on her bed beside me and let out a short grunt of disapproval. I looked at the page I had marked and glanced up at my daughter. "Come sit with me, Sonja, and I'll tell you a true story of ghosts in the Old West. This will be the perfect night for it."

"Not anymore, Mom. Hermione chased away any spooks we might have had."

"Well, she may have done that, but this is a chilling tale of the past that's part of local history. Have you ever heard of the Brantley Mansion in Helena?" Sonja shook her head, so I continued. "It was built in 1887 when Helena was still fairly rough and tumble. Theodore Brantley had just moved there with his wife and children from back east."

Sonja chimed in, "Sort of like us, Mom."

"Yes, that's right. Brantley was a Montana Supreme Court justice. Like us, he was a fish out of water. He wanted to bring a bit of class and civility to this still feral environment, so he always dressed impeccably, displayed the finest manners in public, and did everything possible to ensure justice was administered with fairness and decorum. His desire to remain impartial had the unintended consequence of distancing him from his neighbors and coworkers. People mistook his reserved nature for aloofness. It didn't help that he was terse, that is he used words sparingly and only after carefully considered thought. This made him appear unaffectionate and serious. But despite these peculiarities, he was respected for diligently working toward his goal of ushering in a safer environment for the boisterous community.

"Almost as if a reflection of his outward persona and public status, he built his house high on a hill. It was a magnificently beautiful wooden structure, with hand carved opulent details both inside and out—Italian tiled ceilings, curved staircases, a marble entryway, Persian carpets, and the finest Victorian furniture. The family dined on imported English bone china dishes and sterling silver cutlery. Given their elevated social status and the presence of so many neighbors who were millionaires, it was accepted practice in the Victorian era to live ostentatiously."

"Ostentatiously?"

"It means conspicuously."

"They liked to show off, eh?"

"Um, yes, but not in a mean way. He simply lived as he had back east. Many wealthy ranchers and miners built mansions in Helena for their wives during this gilded age, and these ladies constantly sought the sort of refinement and culture that Justice Brantley and his wife represented."

"Where were their husbands?"

"They had cattle, mines, and logging operations to attend to, so they usually remained on the range much of the year."

"You mean they preferred whooping it up with the boys in the saloons to sitting in parlors holding teacups."

"Something like that. Anyway, where was I?"

"You were talking about how the women of Helena sought out the judge and his wife for social niceties."

"Right. Even though his courtesies and formal behavior were out of place, he continued to treat everyone with grace and style, and the people of Helena grew accustomed to his 'peculiar' behavior, and many began to mimic it. By the time Theodore Brantley died in 1922, the town was quite well established and was the capitol of Montana. He had achieved his goal of bringing a modicum of civility to Montana, though he was a largely forgotten historical figure by the 1950s. This started to change when in 1970 the Brantley family sold the house to new owners.

"Late one night, a few weeks after they moved in, the new family thought they heard the front door open and heavy footsteps creaking across the wood floor. The sound continued up the spiral staircase until it reached the second floor landing, then it went down the hall. The footsteps stopped at the first bedroom door, and the door gently swung open, only to softly close again. The footsteps resumed and stopped at the next door where the process repeated itself until every door had been opened and closed."

"Wow, that sounds scary."

"But wait, there's more! The parents and all three children heard the noises and searched the house from top to bottom, but no one else was in the home.

"Soon this ghostly routine began repeating itself, always late in the evening, night after night. Apparently, the family didn't feel threatened by the specter; they believed the ghost was checking on them, but why? They did some research on the deceased justice and learned that one of his habits had been to check on his children every night in their bedrooms as soon as he returned home from working late.

"I guess I can't blame him; your Dad did the same thing when you girls were very young. After September 11th, he worked fourteen- to eighteen-hour days, but he always made sure to come home to rest, even for just a few hours. But the first thing he always did when he entered the house was to quietly check on us while we slept.

"Well, anyway, let's get back to our story. After the family began renovations on the third floor of their house, the ghost moved to the attic and began to pace the floor in the middle of the night. It would last for hours and the family had trouble sleeping. It was only after they began renovation work that they discovered a secret stairway leading from the master bedroom below. It went straight to the attic room that the judge used as his private office. The next time the parents heard the creaking floor boards above them, they opened the hidden door to the secret staircase to inspect the attic. But as soon as the father took one step up, the sound of pacing footsteps above them ceased. They could finally sleep peacefully through the night.

"In their research the family discovered another aspect of Theodore Brantley's personality; he loved sweets. This ghost enjoyed pilfering confections from the candy dishes. As time passed, the family was filling the dishes twice a day! They never did figure out what he was doing with them." I stared down at Sonja and laughed, "Now when you get candy out of one of my dishes, don't try to blame it on a ghost."

"That's disappointing," she smirked.

I continued my story. "The Judge had other proclivities. He was fascinated by modern technology. The family often came home to find every television and radio turned on and blaring at full volume. As they turned them off they scolded the judge, but it had no effect. This new routine continued every time the family left the house and even after the house was sold to the next owners."

"Maybe the judge was hard of hearing," Bill interjected.

"Where did you come from?" I replied.

"The dark abyss, what you would call the master bath."

"Hmm. As I was saying, the new owners were made fully aware of the haunted stories before their purchase, but even they were in for a shock. As they were moving in their belongings, they were stunned to see one of their house plants hovering in the hallway. Then it fell to the ground, breaking the pot and scattering dirt onto the floor. As frightening as that was, the story gets even better, at least from my point of view, because the vacuum cleaner suddenly sprang to life and cleaned up the dirt and shards of pottery. I love that part!"

Sonja and Bill just chuckled.

"The old ghost never did break another potted plant, but continues to this day to steal candy and walk the floors."

"Well that was fun," Bill said as he stood up and stretched, "but I have to go make sure the shop windows are closed. We might be getting some snow tonight."

I winced at the thought as he left. Sonja made no comment, but retired to her room with Penny close on her heels. I sat there alone again with my thoughts. As each year passed I found it becoming more difficult for me to say goodbye to the sun and accept the knowledge of the long winter ahead. I feared it might snow tonight, but the darkened clouds so far had only brought a rain and sleet mix, and I heard a distant rumble of thunder, most unusual for this time of year. Perhaps the storm would pass us by. I thought about my horses. Had they gone into the safety of the stable to protect themselves from the weather? I got up from the glider and approached the large picture windows where I kept a pair of binoculars. I lifted them from their pouch and raised them to my face. Suddenly I felt a burning vicious pain shoot through my finger and into my hand. I instinctively threw down the glasses, which then bounced step by step onto the staircase landing. I thought I might have broken them, but at that moment I didn't care. All I could think about was the cramping stinging sensation that was moving quickly up to my wrist. It nearly brought tears to my eyes. I must have let out a loud cry, for Sonja rushed back into the room in a panic. "Mom, what happened?"

"Something bit me; I saw it out of the corner of my eye as I flung the binoculars. It was a spider."

Sonja's face paled. "Was is a brown recluse? Remember when the carpenters found one while finishing my bathroom? Those bites can be serious, even fatal."

"I don't think so, Honey. They're not supposed to be native to Montana. Anyway, I didn't get a good look at it—just a glance, but we better try to find it. I can't feel my hand. All my fingers are numb." I tried moving them but they had begun to swell and I could see the bite mark was now slightly inflamed.

Sonja looked down to the landing at the binoculars on the floor. She crept down the stairs and gingerly picked them up, speaking quietly. "I'm afraid to touch them."

"Keep your eyes open," I instructed. Penny now trotted over to see what all the commotion was about. I turned to her and added, "You're a good little insect catcher. Look for the spider, girl."

We studied the gentle light patterns in the carpet and searched the stair treads – nothing. Since I couldn't find my eight legged assailant, I turned my attention to identifying the culprit. I sat at my computer trying to type in the information, but it was proving difficult with a numb hand.

I did manage to peck the words "poisonous spiders" and "Montana". None of the photographs that filled the screen looked like the one that bit me. I was searching for a yellowish, cream colored body with some black markings on it. All the arachnids I saw were either too large, too small, or the wrong colors and patterns.

I was now beginning to feel a little weak, so I decided to suspend my search and give Bill a call on the intercom. I didn't think I needed to go to the hospital, but I wanted his opinion. From the tone of his voice I got the impression he felt it was much ado about nothing. I returned to my chair and gently rocked in a futile effort to calm myself. I felt a cold blast of wind as the back door opened. I heard the familiar stomping of feet before Bill trotted up the stairs. He bent down next to me and said, "Let's have a look, Quinny." Bill called me Quinny whenever he felt affection or concern. I was betting this time he was a little worried. "Your face is flush, but you aren't sweating. How's your pulse?"

I stopped rubbing my sore hand and checked my wrist. "A little fast, but not racing. I don't feel faint. I am a bit nauseas. The pain's beginning to fade, but my hand is numb. I think I'm okay." My thoughts swirled and I remembered a conversation I'd had a while back with a woman who worked at the print shop I frequented in town. She had shown me her finger which was missing its tip, and then recounted the story of a Black Widow spider that had bitten her as she was retrieving logs from her front porch. I knew I hadn't been bitten by a Black Widow, but whatever bit me had me worried because it remained a mystery.

"Do we need to go the ER?" Bill asked.

"I don't think so," I gasped. I was now having difficulty speaking. I needed to calm down or I would risk hyperventilating. I spoke in staccato bursts, "We should know soon…if I start to…have trouble breathing…or feel worse…we'll have…our answer."

I laid back in my chair and rested once again, willing myself to relax. Bill placed a cool cloth on my neck and forehead, and they had a calming effect. I was able to doze a bit, and after a half hour had passed I began to recover the feeling in my fingers and hand. The nausea too was passing and I was perking up in general. Bill and Sonja were relieved, and I felt I had to do something other than sit and think about a spider. I managed a weak joke. "I guess this Halloween I got the trick."

Bill smiled reassuringly. "And the spider got the treat."

By now it was nearly the witching hour, and I was completely drained physically. I said goodnight to Sonja and flopped down in the blue recliner by our bedroom window so I could stare at the night stars. The storm had missed us after all. Bill sat down next to me and I rested my head on his shoulder. He spoke gently into my ear, "How are you feeling? You seem to have recovered from your spider bite."

"I'm feeling better, but the symptoms and not knowing what kind of spider it was really frightened me. My fingers and hand are fine now." I wiggled them as I spoke to reassure myself all was well.

"I know you were scared, Nancy. Spider bites can be a nasty business, but the only poisonous spider we have is the Black Widow, and we know that wasn't what bit you. Most likely you had a mild allergic reaction. I guess it doesn't help knowing your own mother died on Halloween, but at least it wasn't from a spider bite."

Was it possible he was right? Was my reaction partly due to the anniversary of my mother's death? It had been over two decades, but it was true that for me Halloween was always marred by the memory of her passing. My expression turned to stone. Like that family in Helena, perhaps I was haunted as well, not by ghosts, but by unpleasant memories of the past. I was too tired to think any more of it. Tomorrow would be here soon enough and I could forget about ghosts for another year. So until then I reassured myself by softly whispering, "Boo!"

"What was that you said?"

"Nothing, Honey." I snuggled in close to my husband, feeling calm and safe. "Everything is fine now."

34

Where the Wild Things Are

I STOOD IN THE paddock and ran my hands over Star's body, feeling his ribs, protruding hip bone, and stifle area. Although he was walking and running well, the hard swollen mass in his thigh remained, despite treatment. I wished I could do more for him, but I had stopped dosing him with anti-inflammatory medication when he experienced an allergic reaction and a nose bleed. While the veterinarian didn't seem to think the prescription was the reason, I felt it was too much of a risk, and she agreed we could stop treatment if it was causing me concern. Star was gaining weight, but it was a painfully slow process. His coat was still very thin and I considered using a blanket to help him survive the first winter at Cimarron. Upon further reflection I decided against it unless he looked sickly. He wouldn't grow a heavy coat if he wore a blanket all winter, and that could be dangerous for him. Being an Arabian-Thoroughbred mix, I knew his ancestry would impede him from acquiring thick protective hair like Wilson and Whiskey enjoyed. Star would receive supplements and all the feed and hay he could eat so he would have enough calories to burn in order to stay warm in the frigid temperatures that loomed ahead of us.

I felt a strong need to be with the boys as much as possible this time of year. In the cold, any outdoor chores have to be accomplished quickly. We humans are not built for the extreme weather conditions we experience each winter. Mother Nature has her way of protecting the wildlife, but not us. All the native creatures were preparing for winter in one way or another. They were either storing food, building solid beaver dams, heading south, or adding on body fat. They each had a mission in this season of their lives. So did I; it was to ensure my boys had sufficient food, shelter, and warmth to survive the bitter cold ahead. I wasn't very concerned about Wilson and Whiskey. I had seen them play in the snow during subzero temperatures. They handled it very well. My job was to prepare Star as best I could before the heavy snows fell.

As I was heading home and only partway up the hill, a flurry of activity broke out in the paddock. All three horses scrambled toward the open gate and flew out into the pasture, nearly on top of one another. They abruptly stopped and stood, staring in the same direction, ears straight up, tails held high in anticipation.

What has frightened them so? I felt my own body tense. I often looked to my four-legged companions to alert me to threatening conditions. They usually sensed danger before me, and at this moment I wished for my old canine protector, Kobi. I froze and remained mute, trying to assess the situation. Clearly the horses were upset. I looked for any movement, but everything remained still other than some slight trembling of the leaves on the Aspen trees. Star began to stomp and blow air forcefully from his nostrils, and Whiskey joined him in a cacophony of utterances.

This can't be good; Whiskey never gets upset. I continued to focus in the area that held their attention, and without warning I saw a huge silhouette emerge from the tree line. A bull moose stepped out into the field, displaying all his power and confidence. His head was high and his mighty antlers were spread out, giving him an air of majesty, like he was wearing an unusually wide crown. The horses stopped calling and stared at him, and I did the same. The moose ignored all of us and

Majestic moose leaving the meadow.

strode across the pasture with firm determined steps. He was a moose on a mission and had no time to waste with lesser creatures. He looked awkward and graceful at the same time as he marched on without paying us the slightest heed. He stopped only once when he approached the fence. A moment later he easily cleared it with a single jump that revealed his true grace and strength. Then he sauntered back into the woods and down toward the creek below. We just stood there, processing what we had witnessed. Even though the surprising event was over, Whiskey began running in circles as if to avoid an unseen predator. I returned to the paddock and tried to calm him, but he would have none of it. Wilson was at ease, and surprisingly, so was Star, but my unflappable gentleman was having a horse tizzy. He had to release his anxiety, so he paced and trotted all through the round pen and the corrals, in and out of the gate, and finally he ventured into the pasture. It was nearly thirty minutes before he found a place to rest and stand at ease. Since our property was in a migratory path for local wildlife, it would not be the last of our unexpected visitors. The change of seasons was afoot, and the birds and animals were following their instincts for winter preparation. *If only I'd had my camera with me!*

I returned to the house, excited to relate our experience. Bill listened patiently to me, smiling the whole time. For some reason it irritated me, as if he didn't believe me or care. I finally had to ask, "What are you so smug about?"

"Honey, I got it all on film from the balcony." Now I too was smiling.

35

The Fear Factor

THE FIVE DICE SOFTLY rolled to a stop on the blue felt tablecloth and displayed matching black dots. Yahtzee! It was Sonja's second perfect score of the game and she laughed with delight. She was the Yahtzee queen in our family. I rarely beat her, which gave my few winnings special significance. I resigned myself to my usual fate of taking a complete drubbing. Bill had long ago quit challenging us. If Sonja didn't win, I usually did. He was a distant third. When he wasn't plowing, Bill spent his free time glued to the internet, headphones on, and blissfully indifferent to our presence six feet away. Either way, it allowed us girls a chance to engage in small talk about life, politics, philosophy, or any other subject that entered our heads. As she tallied up her final score, Sonja casually commented on Star's condition.

"Mom, Star was shivering this morning. I think he may be getting too cold at night."

"I'm sure he is. Last night it got down to fifty-one below zero on the pass and it snowed heavily here. That's why your Dad's out plowing right now. How are the other boys doing?"

"They're fine, but they have heavier coats."

"Speaking of coats, did you bundle up this morning before going to the barn?"

"Of course I did; I know how to dress in extreme weather. But I'm worried Star isn't staying warm enough."

"Did you give him sweet feed this morning? He needs extra calories to burn."

"Yes, and some extra hay too."

"That's good. Aren't the boys huddling together in the stable?"

"Sometimes, but by morning they're either waiting by the feeder or down in the Aspens trying to stay out of the wind. I did notice something odd."

"What is it?"

"I thought the hay looked disturbed; I think some of it's missing. I'm worried we won't have enough to get through winter."

"How much are you feeding them?"

"A half bale between them. Whiskey can't really eat it, but Star sure can. He's eating even more than Wilson."

"Well that might explain your missing hay. Maybe you need to cut back a little on their rations."

"I don't think that's it. I think something's getting into the hay."

"Deer maybe, or that elk from last year?"

"I don't know.

"Well, when you go down this afternoon, count the bales. If we're short, we may have to cut back until we can find some more hay. I also want you to supplement Star's feed with some of Whiskey's senior mix. If he doesn't huddle with the boys at night, we'll have to put a blanket on him."

"Do you think it's too cold for his Arabian blood? His hair's mighty short."

"Honey, he won't always be this way, but it's going to take time for him to recover from all the abuse he's endured. With proper nutrition he should be fine, but it may not be until next summer. We have to get him through this winter first."

I glanced out the front windows. *If only the sun would come out, that would be so helpful.* The grey clouds remained closely knitted together without a single ray of light penetrating through. I checked the wall clock. It had been an hour since Bill left to clear the road. I didn't expect him back for another hour. It always made me anxious when he was plowing. I couldn't really relax until he returned. I no sooner pondered this thought than I heard the door open, followed by the stamping of feet.

"Bill?"

"Yeah, Honey."

"I didn't hear you drive up." I was already halfway down the stairs when I said this.

"I got stuck again. The tractor slid off the road near the bottom and one wheel is dangling in the air. I really need Chase's help on this one. It's pretty dicey."

"Why didn't you call me?"

"I never got a chance to finish plowing. You wouldn't have had any place to turn the truck around, so I walked home."

"Nearly a mile in this cold? Bad judgment, Bill."

"I can do it; it was a little nippy though. I had my watch cap over my ears and my scarf over my face."

"Nippy? Nippy! What would have happened to you if you'd tripped and fell? You could be lying out there, freezing to death right now. I thought you were still safe and warm in the tractor."

"I didn't fall though."

"Accidents happen. It could have been a couple of hours before I realized something was wrong. If you insist on walking home, at least find a spot where you can get a cell signal and call me so I know what's going on."

"Okay, I'm fine. I promise next time I'll call you. Right now I need to call Chase."

I stood in the foyer glaring at him with concern. His next words didn't bring me any relief. "Besides, Quinny, it's worth the walk. You're so pretty when you're angry; I don't mind getting into trouble."

Chase had his own issues to deal with and so we were snowbound for over two days before he finally was able to come help us free the tractor, after which Bill finished his plowing. Meanwhile, the temperatures continued to rise and fall, creating ice, snow drifts, and general misery. I knew the coldest temperature ever recorded in Montana was on January 20, 1954. It plunged to seventy degrees below zero at Roger's Pass north of Helena. This was also a national record for the lower forty-eight states. Odd as it sounded, I was grateful we had only reached minus fifty-one.

By the third day our imprisonment had ended. The road down our mountain was again open, but the Pass remained a dicey proposition. Whiteout conditions still prevailed at these higher elevations, so we decided to forego any trip to Helena for another day or two. We settled in for the evening and I patiently waited for Sandy to get back to the condo. She normally left work around 7:30 PM, and though it was not a very long drive, the ice and snow could delay her return. I could not relax until I knew she was safely home, but I promised myself not to make my nightly phone call for at least a half hour. I anxiously watched the clock until the hands reached eight before placing my call. The moment I heard her trembling voice I knew something was wrong. She was crying.

"Mom?"

"Sandy, what's wrong? Where are you?"

She made no reply, only the sound of sobbing.

"Are you home?" She did not respond. All I heard was sobbing and panicked breathing. I tried to calm her down. "Breathe and relax, then tell me what has happened?"

The sobbing ceased and I heard her take a deep breath. "I was in an accident! I think I may have killed someone!"

"Are you alright? Where are you?"

"My legs hurt. It just happened a minute ago. I don't know if I can get out of the car."

"Where are you?" My last question fell on deaf ears. A different, much older female voice spoke on the phone.

"Don't cry, Honey."

"Who is this?"

"Your daughter ran a red light and hit me head on. We're both okay. She's just shook up. I don't plan to sue you for everything you own. We can work it out. No, I won't sue you this time."

"Who is this?" I demanded. "Give the phone back to my daughter!"

The woman kept repeating herself as though she didn't hear me, then the phone went dead. A wave of nausea overcame me as I nervously redialed Sandy's number. There was no answer. "If I can't reach Sandy this time, I'm calling the police."

Bill shook his head. "You try to reach her; I'll call 911 on the business line. Find out where she is."

Sandy answered the phone on my third attempt. Her voice was trembling, but she had regained her composure. "Mom, I was waiting to make a left turn at the light. I didn't see any headlights, so I started my turn, and that's when I collided with her. I never saw her until the last moment."

"Have you called the police?"

"Yes, they're on the way. I also just called my supervisor, Mindy. She only lives a few blocks from here and she said she'd come right over."

Bill had hung up his phone and was now checking the weather. There was heavy snow and ice on the pass. I desperately wanted to be there to help, but one accident this evening was already too many. I felt helpless, like I was abandoning my daughter in her greatest hour of need. Bill picked up an extension and made the decision for us. "Sandy, let us know when Mindy gets there. She'll have to help you. We can't get over the pass tonight; it's too dangerous. Are the police there yet?"

"Yes, a police car just arrived. I need to talk with them."

"Call us back when Mindy gets there."

It was only a few minutes, but the waiting was interminable. So many thoughts raced through my mind. I didn't think Sandy was injured, but I presumed the rescue service would check her out just to be sure. Bill was back on the business line talking to his mechanic about where to tow the car. *Her car, that poor little car that Sandy loved so much and only had for less than two months. No, don't think about the car. What's important is Sandy is okay. What was that about not suing? Who was that woman? What really happened?*

The phone rang again and I immediately picked it up. This time Sandy's voice was calm and professional. "The officer said a tow truck is on the way. I need to tell him where to take it."

"Your Dad's working on that right now. How are you doing?"

"I'm better. Mindy's here now."

The initial shock and confusion was over. Having to answer questions and being assigned tasks to accomplish can have that effect on people. "You sound better. Sometimes excitement and adrenalin can mask the pain, so don't be surprised if you feel tired and sore later."

"Well, my legs hurt, but not too badly."

By now Bill had determined which garage to take the car to and I asked Sandy to let me speak with the responding officer. I gave him the name of the repair shop, then asked him what happened.

"Your daughter was attempting to make a left turn into traffic at a stop light. She said the light was green and that she saw no oncoming vehicle. The other driver claims the light was red and that your daughter turned anyway. I cited your daughter for failure to yield the right-of-way."

I was still processing the information when the officer left to speak to the tow driver. Sandy came back on the phone. "Mom, what am I supposed to do about my car and the ticket?"

"Nothing tonight, Honey. Just make sure you have your purse. We'll deal with it tomorrow. When Mindy gets you home, I want to speak with both of you, okay?"

"Okay."

As I waited for the next call, I tried to run the scenario over and over again in my mind. Something didn't make sense. *Why didn't Sandy see the headlights of the oncoming car? Why did the woman claim the light was red? If it had been red she should have stopped instead of plowing through the intersection. Wouldn't that mean she was partly to blame? Why did the officer only cite Sandy?*

It was practically a relief when the phone rang the last time. There was frustration and anger in Sandy's voice. "Mom, I swear I never saw any headlights. I wouldn't have made that turn if I had. I don't think she had them on."

"I believe you, Sandy. Can I speak with Mindy?"

A familiar gravelly voice said, "Hello Nancy. I guess this has been a wild night, eh!"

"I really appreciate you stepping in and helping out. You've done us a tremendous favor I can't repay."

"Don't worry about it. I try to look after all my girls, and Sandy is my favorite."

"So what do you think happened?"

"I'll tell you what happened. That police officer is a rookie and he screwed up. He took one look at Sandy, saw how young she was, then saw the other driver was much older, and assumed Sandy was at fault. While he was writing up the citation, I went and had a chat with the other driver, and the first thing I noticed was alcohol on her breath. I thought to myself, now why didn't he catch that? So I went back over to him and told him what I'd learned. I knew he wasn't going to tear up the ticket, but I figured he'd better check her out."

"Did he?"

"Well, as we were leaving I saw him giving her a sobriety test."

"Now it makes sense. I thought her behavior on the phone was kind of strange. So Sandy wasn't at fault!"

"Well, Honey, that's up to a judge to decide, but I suspect it qualifies as mitigating circumstances. Personally, I suspect the woman was speeding and didn't have her lights on, but how do you prove it?"

Sandy came back on the phone. "I told the policeman that I didn't see her headlights at all. I waited for all the cars to pass, and when it looked dark again, I started to make the turn, then WHAM! She came out of nowhere. I think she was speeding and driving without her headlights."

"Did you tell that to the policeman?"

"I tried too, but I think his mind was made up. He talked to the other lady first. Mom, when Mindy detected alcohol on that woman's breath, she had to run to the policeman's car because he was getting ready to leave."

Now I was furious. How could a police officer, even a new one, not notice the signs of alcohol? How could he be so incompetent? Bill could see I was fuming and told me to wait until we had more facts. *Who needs more facts? Some drunk tries to kill my baby and some idiot blames my daughter for it!*

"Mom, my new car is ruined, and I only had it six weeks. I feel terrible."

That brought me out of my growing rage. "Don't. You're safe and sound and that's all that matters. A car can be replaced; you can't." We talked at length, and when I was satisfied Sandy could sleep, we said our goodnights. Mindy drove Sandy to work the next morning, and for a couple of days afterwards, until the insurance company could arrange for a rental car. Bill visited the collision shop to retrieve the items Sandy left behind, a few CDs, her lucky charms (i.e., several Disney *Cars* plush toys), and some emergency equipment. The car was a complete write-off, which meant having to negotiate with the insurance company on a settlement. Bill took several photos of the damage and showed them to me later. I grew cold as I viewed the crumpled metal and bent right axle that had been a cute little Ford Fusion. It reminded me too much of pictures I'd seen of my father's car after his fatal accident. I began to physically shake. When I saw the red stains on the interior upholstery, I had to remind myself they were not blood, but only tomato sauce from the spaghetti she had been bringing home from work. Sandy had survived, and that was all that mattered.

Since Sandy's car could not be repaired, the next step was to settle with the insurance company and find a new car as soon as possible. The rental car was only good for thirty days. Once more the clock was ticking, but despite the fears and frustrations, something good came of it all. Much to our delight, our insurance company, USAA, valued the car at more than we had paid for it. This was a godsend because all the comparable cars we looked at cost considerably more than the Fusion had. Eventually we found her a nice Toyota Camry which was newer and had lower mileage than the Ford. As always, my brother Brian was invaluable in this search. He even set aside his usual Ford bias and admitted the Camry was a fine automobile.

Sandy too was getting over the shock, anger, and bitterness of the accident, and I was proud of her for overcoming her fears. Bill went with her to the traffic court. He explained the mitigating circumstances to the judge, but the judge replied the only options available were to admit guilt or demand a trial. The latter option would have been time consuming and expensive, with no guarantee of a positive outcome. The alternative was a one-day driver safety class and six months of citation-free driving, and she would receive a clean driving record. Bill encouraged her to opt for the latter. Sandy reluctantly agreed. She had just received her first real-life civics lesson.

Sandy remained apprehensive about driving, but the cowboy saying has merit. Once you are bucked out of the saddle, you have to get back on your horse. This applies to horsepower as well, so Bill and I rode with Sandy periodically to help restore her confidence. We did experience a bit of *schadenfroh* when we found out that the other driver in the accident was arrested for DUI, and it was not her first offense. Since there was no way to prove she was speeding or driving without headlights, we did not pursue the matter in court. However, we made USAA aware of her arrest. This may or may not have influenced them, but in the end Sandy was granted a one-time exemption, so her insurance rates did not rise. Most importantly of all, Sandy was unharmed other than some bruising on her legs, a miracle in itself, and we decided to focus on that blessing. Truly all's well that ends well, and this story ended well.

36

The Little Engine That Could

DUE TO A STEADILY increasing number of complaints, I began making heavier meals during the winter months. My usual preference for stir fry suppers, salads, and other lighter fare lacked the protein and carbohydrate requirements needed by Bill and Sonja to sustain them when working in the freezing cold. At least that's what they told me. Sonja's preferences for pizza, chips, cheese, and hamburger seemed somewhat suspect to me because she tended to indulge in these four food groups the year round—at least she would if I had let her. Bill was somewhat less demanding, though I often heard him complain how leaves, tofu, and rice might sustain a person living in a California climate, but such a diet would starve a Montanan. It was a gross exaggeration of my meal planning efforts, but I took the hint. Tonight we'd dine on beef stroganoff, Greek salad, and garlic toast. I began dinner preparations early so I could clean the kitchen before the Lowe's delivery truck arrived. They were installing a new stove in my art studio. There was no old stove to remove, for the studio had gone all these years without one. This had prevented me from hosting any parties there, not that I was much of a party maker, but I wanted to keep my options open for the future.

The stroganoff was in the oven, the salad was in the refrigerator, and the kitchen was sparkling again. All that was left was the garlic toast. It could wait till later. I wanted to check on my resident fox. He often came by the house about this time. The tracks he left in the snow on the patio were a pleasant reminder that hunting was still good around our place. I interpreted this to mean he was doing a good job of keeping the rodent population in check. School was finished for the day, so I reminded Sonja she needed to set the table.

"What's for supper?"

"Beef stroganoff," I beamed.

She frowned and reached into the cabinet for the dishes.

"What's wrong with stroganoff?"

"Nothing I guess. I prefer hamburger."

"Well, it contains beef and noodles. I think you'll like it."

Her reply was a muffled grunt. So much for my hearty meal, I felt like telling her that poor children were starving in China, but the world had changed a lot since my youth, and I needed another country to use as an example. I decided to let it go. Maybe when she tasted it she would change her opinion.

I kept my eye peeled out the front window for the truck. Sonja noticed me and asked, "Whatcha looking for, Mom?"

"My new oven." I glanced at the clock on the wall. "Lowe's should have been here by now. With the time change, it'll be dark soon."

"They're delivering it in this mess?"

"Yes, Honey Bear. I was surprised when the salesman assured me it would be delivered within the week. I hope they didn't get stuck. Your Dad's been plowing, but the road's still dicey."

Penny joined our conversation by raising her head from her day bed, then dashing to the window where I stood. She propped her front paws on the sill and spun her propeller tail. "What is it, girl?" I too heard the noise and strained my eyes to see its source. Penny wiggled from head to toe in excitement. A slight movement caught my eye. I glanced to the left at the horses standing in the field below us. They were frozen still and staring in the same direction toward the first bend in the road.

The sound of a diesel engine was unmistakable, like that of our tractor. The delivery truck lumbered slowly round the bend. It was a large box truck, and it struggled as it repeatedly slipped in the ice and snow. The last hundred yards proved to be the most challenging. Despite his efforts, the driver could not climb any further. He tried, but each attempt only sent him slipping backward instead of forward.

Bill was at his shop, so I called him on the intercom and asked that he help the driver before he tipped his truck over on the uneven slope. As I spoke I watched the truck try another futile ascent, only to gracefully slide back down the hill a few feet. Shortly I saw the bundled figure of my husband walking cautiously toward the truck waving his hands. He had to step carefully due to the ice. The driver rolled down his window and communicated with Bill. I could not hear them over the din of his engine, but the gesticulation led me to believe they had successfully communicated a plan. As the driver made three more failed attempts, Bill backed the tractor from its garage bay and continued backing it down to the truck. Next came the cold weather feat. Bill had to climb out of the warm cab and up onto the rear backhoe seat. He extended the backhoe legs to provide firm support on the ice. From here he began methodically chipping away at ice and snow with the bucket, trying to clear enough away to allow the vehicle to transit. It was a tedious process that required him to periodically climb back into the cab and relocate the tractor a few feet forward so he could attack a new section of ice and snow. It took him a half hour to clear a path. When he was done he signaled the driver to back up and try again. The truck's engine roared and the vehicle started its slow crawl back up the hill. It was over halfway through the slush when it slowed to a stop. The tires continued to spin as it slid backward again.

Bill walked down to speak with the driver once more. I had no idea what they were going to try next, so I just watched as the drama continue. Bill returned to the tractor and drove it back to the studio. He then retrieved the pickup truck, which had snow chains mounted on all four tires. He had little trouble backing it down to the box truck. After hooking several tow straps to both vehicles, he attempted to pull the truck up the hill. Penny had long since bored of this ordeal and returned to her bed, but the horses remained intrigued. The Ford F250 pulled on the tow cables, while the box truck belched huge plumes of diesel exhaust. Both vehicles were straining as hard as they could, and I feared the cables might snap at any moment, but slowly, inexorably, they started to move. It was a comical sight watching the smaller truck attempting to pull the much larger one the way a tug boat would maneuver a cargo ship. I started thinking of one of my favorite children's stories, *The Little Engine That Could.* Unconsciously I began reciting the familiar refrain from that book: *I think I can, I think I can, I think I can.* Pretty soon the two vehicles had cleared the ice patch and reached the top of our rise. Sonja and I cheered. *I knew I could, I knew I could, I knew I could.* Penny, aroused from her bed by our commotion, came to see what the excitement was all about. She too joined in the celebration. As we cheered, the vehicles stopped in front of my studio and I hurried over to assist with the unloading and installation. While Bill released his tow cables, I opened the door to the studio and welcomed the two delivery men with a friendly smile. "That was quite an ordeal; I'm glad you could make it."

The driver met my cheerful greeting with a sneer and an unpleasant remark about our rural location. I overlooked it and simply indicated where the oven should be placed. His assistant was much more pleasant, and the two of them moved the oven quickly into place and connected it. It took them less than ten minutes. All the while I listened politely as the driver complained furiously about having to bring such a big truck up our mountain. He was angry because a smaller van had not been available for this delivery. His complaints about the harrowing drive were only matched by his colorful description of his boss, whose parentage and lineage were both drawn into question. I reassured him that getting back down the mountain would be no trouble so long as he stayed in low gear. "If you get stuck, just call us. My husband will be glad to come assist."

He started to say something, but decided for once that discretion was the better course of action. He just grunted and left. His assistant remained polite and thanked me for the suggestion. We stood by the studio door and watched them crawl down the hill and disappear around the bend. We didn't receive any phone call of distress, so we assumed they traversed the road without further problems.

Penny tasted and sniffed the new oven multiple times; the horses called for their supper before departing to the stable; and I returned to the house to finish the meal. Another evening on the mountain was beginning at twilight. Everything was back to normal for a while.

Our foxy neighbor.

37

Age Before Beauty

I HEARD A SMALL sniff over the phone line and I knew Sandy was teary eyed. Her work at the local assisted living facility was taking a toll on her young spirit.

"It's so hard to believe he's gone," she quietly commented. "I'm used to seeing him every day. I didn't think he was that sick. I knew how he liked his coffee, and I always brought it to him before he had to ask. I even set aside his favorite dessert before they sold out."

It was the first time Sandy had dealt with the loss of a person she cared for and saw on a regular basis. I listened to her as she shared her shock and her grief. She was learning how to navigate life. It's a bitter lesson for all of us, and I tried to console her tender feelings.

"Sandy, I understand how it hurts you. You are in a place where people need help on a daily basis. Think about how much joy you gave your friend. He looked for you every day, and when you brought him his food, it was the bright spot in his day. You made a difference in the last months of his life. You talked to him and made him feel special. You helped him in ways you will never understand. He isn't suffering or alone anymore, and he is in a better place. It was his time. He lived a long life. I know it's difficult to cope with, but at some point we all have to face it."

"But he didn't have any family. He was forgotten. No one visited him."

"He wasn't forgotten completely. You were there for him, and he lived in a beautiful, clean environment, and your attention brightened his day. He received excellent care. Not everyone has those benefits."

"Mom, he was the one that kept telling me I was beautiful and he tried to hold my hand. Remember? I asked you if it was inappropriate, and you said it wasn't."

"I remember; he was trying to show his appreciation for your kindness to him. I thought it was a very sweet gesture. Sandy, did I ever tell you about what the Algonquian tribes believe?"

"I don't remember."

"They believe a man's story is never lost if it's shared by the campfire. The smoke will carry it up to the heavens. We may not be talking over a campfire, but the idea is the same. You are remembering him and honoring him by telling me about your experiences together. So now he will not be forgotten. The two of us will remember him."

"I suppose that's true."

"Sandy, while we were talking, steam was rising from my teacup. I think that counts as smoke under the circumstances. What do you think?"

"I guess you're right; I do feel a little better."

"As much as I hate to say it, you will most likely face a loss like this again. It's hard to be philosophical about it when you see the residents daily and help them with their needs. Just know you are having a positive effect on them."

"Even the grumpy ones?"

"Absolutely. Many of them are sick or confused and probably wouldn't act badly if they had control over themselves. Remember, dementia and other physical issues change their behavior. They probably were in a much more stable mindset earlier in their lives."

"I know; sometimes the things they do are sort of cute. The other day a few residents didn't want to wait to enter the dining room. Before I could remove the velvet ropes that blocks the entrance, people started crawling under them! I had to run over and take the ropes down before they got hurt. I do love talking to them and I have learned so much about history through their previous lives. It's like having lots of grandparents around."

"Sandy, just keep up your good work and it will get easier. Changing the subject, did I tell you about the new lemon bar recipe?"

"No."

"Your sister has been experimenting in the kitchen, and it turned out fabulous. You can have one tomorrow. It has a crust like a shortbread cookie, but with lemon in the base, then the filling is smooth with fresh lemon juice in it. It tastes like a lemon drop candy, only better and -"

"Don't tell me anymore; now I want one! I'll be dreaming about lemon cookies tonight."

I felt an inward sense of relief and was pleased the conversation had taken a more cheerful tone. I didn't want her fretting all night and feeling sad."Well, then all that's left to say is...sweet dreams."

38

The Wheeler Dealer

ALFRED WHEELER LOOKED DESPONDENT as he stirred his tea, gently tapping the spoon on the sides of his cup. He sat forlornly at our dining room table and I couldn't help but comment, "Alfred, you look like you lost your last friend in the world."

"I nearly have," he responded glumly. "My wife is moving in and I have to get rid of my pigs."

I looked at Bill in surprise. He was equally befuddled. I continued. "Alfred, I thought you were divorced."

"Well…not really…no…we've actually been separated these past few years. It's been so long that it seems like a divorce. But now the wife's decided she just can't live without me, poor soul, and so she told me she's moving to Montana to be reunited with me. She also said the pigs have to go."

"How do you feel about that, Alfred?" I cautiously responded.

"I'm upset about the impending separation. Pigs are such intelligent creatures you know."

"So I've been told, but it must present a dilemma for you. What'll become of your pigs?" I was trying to avoid another lecture on swineology and I immediately regretted asking my question.

"I don't know how I'm going to go about it. Who will take my pigs?" Alfred looked at me with pleading eyes and offered a weak smile. I felt a sudden alarm in the back of my head. *You've stepped in it now, Quinn.* "You and Bill could take my pigs, then I could visit them regularly! The separation wouldn't be nearly as painful if I knew they were being well cared for. Pigs are such emotionally sensitive creatures, you know."

I knew the sales pitch was coming, but I couldn't stop it. Alfred once more began extolling the virtues of his cloven hoofed friends. I felt a great urge to stop him, but fainting probably wouldn't work. He'd just try to convince Bill instead. "Alfred, I'm so sorry; we can't take your pigs."

"She's right, Alfred," Bill chimed in. "They would just become bacon bait here. We have enough trouble keeping the wolves, bears, and coyotes away."

"But Bill, you could protect them with your arms."

"My arms?"

"Of course the pigs would be safe with you! You're a military man; you must possess the means and skills to defend them."

"You're assuming I would be awake or at home when a predator comes calling."

Alfred was not deterred. "You're able to protect your horses and dogs."

"Not always," Bill replied sternly. "Penny lives inside, but the horses are often left entirely on their own. It's only their size and ability to run that protects them. But even poor Wilson was once chased by a cougar. He had to jump the corral panel, and crushed it in the process. He's lucky he didn't break a leg. I'm afraid your pigs, being hemmed in a pen, wouldn't last one night here on the mountain."

I had to support Bill's position. "It just isn't practical, Alfred. Why only yesterday I was teaching Wilson how to paint on canvas when a pack of wolves ran right past the corral. Two of them were viciously fighting. I don't know why—maybe the pack leader was being challenged. Whatever the reason, thankfully they were too engaged to notice us standing just thirty feet away in the round pen. One of the wolves was losing the fight and broke away to escape up the hill. If the rest of the pack hadn't pursued him, they might have turned their attention to us."

I paused to allow Alfred time to consider the possible consequences. He was silent and contemplative for a moment before replying, "Why were you teaching Wilson to paint?"

"It was for a video I'm planning, but that's not my point. Your pigs might not have been as lucky as we were if they had been there. Our home is right in the middle of a migratory path, which is why we don't want animals that would attract predators. It's the reason we don't have any chickens, goats, or sheep. For the safety and well-being of your pigs, we must regretfully decline your offer."

Alfred realized it was hopeless. We weren't about to budge. Forlornness returned to his face and he sat silently for a moment. I wanted to help him, but I couldn't think of anyone who would seriously consider keeping pigs as pets. Everyone I knew would want to raise them for slaughter. I told Alfred I would try to think of a way to help him, and that things had a way of working out. He didn't appear too convinced. He simply shook his head and remarked, "A wife without pigs, what is the world coming to? How will I carry on?"

"Did you say wife or life?" I asked.

"It's much the same in my case," Alfred sighed.

After his departure, Bill turned to me and said, "Did Alfred ever mention his wife's name?"

I shrugged my shoulders. "He never said. Why, are you looking forward to meeting her?"

"In a pig's eye," he winked.

"I'm not a Paint; I'm a painter!"

39

Of Mice and Women

SONJA RAN INTO THE house and slammed the door behind her with a loud smack. It shook the entire place. By the thumping sounds on the stairs I knew she had not removed her boots before her ascent.

"Mom! Eeww! I'm so glad you weren't in Dad's shop with me just now. Oh, it was so gross."

"Dad's shop is gross?"

"No, listen, I heard these weird squeaking noises coming out of Dad's old cash register.

"How odd." I pictured it in my mind. I always admired the big brass cash register. Bill had inherited it from his father, who had inherited it from an uncle. It must have been close to a century old and represented true art deco with its heavy scroll engraving and intricate floral patterns. It was a both a cash drawer and calculating machine. When the keys were pressed, numbers popped up in a glass display window. The same information was printed onto a roll of thin paper. Once the total sale was complete, it added that figure to the roll of paper, which was then torn off and handed to the customer. It was purely mechanical without a single electrical or electronic feature in it. It sat on a dark wood cabinet, really a sort of stacked dresser with lockable drawers. One of them still contained bottles of ink, rolls of paper used for receipts, candle wax for sealing letters, and hundreds of old keys. It weighed a ton (well, several hundred pounds) and my original intention had been to prominently display it in our front hallway. But we had to shrink the design of the house to fit the contour of the mountain. This left no suitable space for it, so it remained in the shop. My thoughts were interrupted by Sonja's story.

"Mom, I was helping Dad clean the shop and he asked me to check the register. When I opened the bottom drawer of the cabinet I saw five squirming mice. They had made a nest by shredding a roll of paper. And they had been—you know—using the drawer as a bathroom."

As much as I didn't want to think about it, I had a clear picture in my mind. For years I had tried to conquer my irrational fear of mice. Over time it became easier to tolerate them, but whenever I could avoid the squirmy vermin, I took the opportunity. I tried to imagine them as cute little Disney characters that would sew my clothes and help me with my housework. I looked at quaint photos of them sleeping in flowers and gently nibbling the petals. Friends sent me pictures of them dressed in fancy little costumes, and I tried to convince myself that most of them were no different than chipmunks or squirrels. But no, all I could see were nasty little vermin that were cousins to the rats who brought on the Black Plague or attacked their master's boss in the movie *Willard.* They had to go, and now, even if I had to kick them out with my pink cowgirl boots.

"Mom, did you hear me?"

"Yes, I'm sorry. That's awful, what did you do?"

"I slammed the drawer shut and told Dad. He sent me back to get traps."

I shook my head. "We must do more than that." I looked at her coyly. "Meaning you and Dad of course."

"What else can we do but set traps and try to catch 'em?"

"Well, we'll—you and Dad—have to get rid of the ones that are in there now, not just wait for them to step on a trap. And then you need to clean up their mess and sanitize the cabinet."

"Oh, gotcha."

"I don't want them to ruin that beautiful cabinet. I can't believe they're nesting in there. How did they get into the shop?"

Sonja shrugged.

"Perhaps you could pull the whole drawer out and then pitch the entire bunch of them, nest and all, into the woods. The side door is close to the cash register."

"I'll tell Dad what you said. I don't want them in there either."

Gratefully, I didn't have to face them. Sonja darted back down the stairs and slammed the rear door on her way back to the shop. I cringed and tried to return to my work. I was still upstairs ten minutes later when I heard the door slam again. *Doesn't anyone ever close a door properly anymore?*

I heard two voices climbing the stairs. Bill called up to me, "The mice have been relocated, but we had some escapees."

Sonja chimed in. "We really did try to catch them, but they jumped out of the drawer and ran all over the office!"

"Oh no!" It was all I could manage to say. I suppose it was somewhat comical, but if it had happened in the house I knew my reaction would have been quite different. I would have been forced to call a real estate agent and put the place up for sale.

"Dad had to clean out all the mess. The worst part was, we found one mouse almost mashed in half."

Bill flopped into the nearest chair and laughed. "Yes, when Sonja slammed the drawer shut she must have crushed it. That left four to deal with." Bill found it amusing, but it didn't have that effect on me.

"Bill, you need to clean it all out with Lysol disinfectant. Mice in the West carry diseases."

"You worry too much."

"Tell that to the neighbor who nearly died from Hantavirus. You should take this seriously, Bill. Your office must be cleaned too. Get some bleach and check the other drawers in the cabinet as well. This is serious and must be dealt with now."

"Yeah, Dad, we need to clean up that poop and pee now. It really smells."

Bill resigned himself to his fate. "Come on, Big Britches. You can help. I need you to go through all those keys and find the one that opens the back panel to the cabinet."

"Did you say keys?" Sonja's eyes lit up at the prospect. "I love old keys. They're much more interesting than modern keys. I tried some of them in the locks but they didn't work."

"Well now you can try them all."

"I'm on it." Down the stairs she flew, followed by the obligatory slamming of the door.

I stared at Bill, my arms crossed. "Well?"

"I'm on it," he sighed as he slowly rose from his chair and sauntered down the stairs. At least he didn't slam the back door. They spent the better part of an hour cleaning out all the drawers and sanitizing them. Sonja diligently tested each key in the back panel until she found the one that unlocked it. They were shocked by what they discovered when they opened it. They briefed me about their gruesome work once they returned to the house.

Bill shook his head in disgust. "They managed to build an estate in the cash register. It looked like they'd been at it for several years. The entire rear of the cabinet was compacted full with—you name it, a cornucopia of fuzz, paper, seeds, and droppings. It filled up two garage bags."

"I hope you wore a mask."

"Yes, Dear, and gloves. We vacuumed and sanitized everything with Lysol. I even sanitized the shop vac when we were done."

"Good," I sighed with relief.

"Good riddance."

"Bill, how did they get into it?"

"I found a small hole they'd chewed in the base of the cabinet. I glued a block of wood in it so they can't use it again."

"They aren't all gone yet?"

"They will be. Trust me. We set out six traps smeared with peanut butter. No mouse ever spawned can resist the seducing aroma of Peter Pan."

Bill was true to his word. His efforts were rewarded quickly, and he managed to catch two of them that evening. Over the next week he dispatched a dozen more. He was especially pleased by a two-for-one special that caught a pair of mice in the same trap. The rodent eradication plan was working, but our traps were starting to break from overuse. Bill bought more, then more still. Within a month over two dozen mice were sent to cheese heaven. We had learned the hard way that catching mice was a never ending process. We were living our own modest version of *Three Skeleton Key*. If you aren't familiar with that story, I suggest you read it or listen to an old time radio version. But I should warn you, it will give you the willies, or should I say, *Willards*?

"Oh, no...it's Nancy!"

40

Put a Sock in It

YES, IT WAS THE time of year when "the cows come home." Home, in this case, meant the heifers were released with bulls into the pastures that belong to Chase and his family. Their land bordered our own, which meant we often had bovine visitors. This is an annual event, and is as predictable as the sun rising in the morning.

When I have a few minutes I enjoy sitting in our loft and gazing out the large windows to the expanse of blue sky. I look for shapes in the clouds drifting by, and am often rewarded with some beautiful and comical sights, including racing horses, rabbits, puppies, deer, lions, Santa Clause, and even a mouse floating on a parachute. This time my musings were disrupted when I noticed Penny's ears perk up. She had been resting quietly at my side when she tilted her head, jumped up from her bed, and ran to the window. Her little tail began to spin wildly and a low growl emitted from deep in her chest.

"What is it, girl?"

I walked over to her and studied the outside surroundings. The horses were upset too. All three of them were standing still in the snow splattered pasture, facing north toward the Aspens. It is a thickly wooded section, so I could not spot any danger. Penny was insistent, and the horses were obviously quite concerned. Star began to stamp his feet, which was not a good sign. He backed up and snorted. I scanned intently for signs of bear, moose, or elk. At last I spotted movement in the tree line. Three different shadows, fairly large, were headed in the direction of the corral, but still shielded from view by the trees. A pang of fear gripped me. The shadows were low to the ground, like that of a mother bear and her cubs. I squinted to get a clearer view without my glasses, and was just about to call for Bill, when I nearly laughed instead. Emerging from the bushes into the meadow were three cows, two of them smaller than the first. They lumbered down the hill and through the pasture gate. *Of course, cows!*

Star did not share my relief. He began to buck and run in circles, expressing his desperation. He tried to galvanize Whiskey and Wilson into action. They were completely unimpressed, and slightly peeved that the cows had interrupted their lunch. Their heads returned to the ground and they continued eating the sparse grass.

Star continued to panic. He tried to convince his equine friends that danger was imminent, and they must run in circles, faster and faster! *We're about to be devoured by…by…something!* His wishes were ignored, so he became even more frantic. Now he was prancing in circles, throwing his head up and down, his tail flying high in the air, and he was squealing like a dinosaur.

I stepped onto the deck and called to Star. "Don't worry; it's just cows." He stopped dead in his tracks and turned his face upwards to me. "You're safe, believe me." Although he wasn't completely convinced, he stood still, confused and frustrated.

"Visitors?" Bill asked as he appeared on the deck.

"Cows. We better call Chase and have him collect them. Star is really upset. I don't think he's ever seen a cow before. He won't take his eyes off them."

The bovines began to walk closer to the horses. Now this was a whole different story. For some reason, Wilson felt that they were suddenly eating *his* grass. *This will not do, no, not at all.* Wilson began to stand his ground, and I saw him paw the grass, warning these interloping, grass-stealing, trespassing cows not to eat another bite of his grass. This was all Star needed to see. Convinced his assessment of danger was correct and that we were all wrong, he began racing repeatedly around the other two horses. I marveled at how swiftly and agilely he could move even with his damaged hip.

"I may have to go down there," I said.

"And do what? You don't want to tangle with cows, especially with so many icy snow patches still on the ground. Just let Chase deal with it. They're his problem."

Before I could reply, I was distracted by Sonja popping around the corner, holding up a red and white polka dot sock and asking, "Mom, I found this sock in the dryer. Is it yours?"

"Huh? Uh…no. That's odd; I emptied the dryer this morning. I don't recall seeing that sock. It's not Sandy's and clearly isn't Dad's." I was trying to keep one eye on the cows and horses and the other on Sonja and her lone sock.

"Maybe all the socks that disappear in other dryers are coming to us through the space-time continuum?" Sonja joked.

I replied, "Oh no, cows are appearing in the front yard and strange unfashionable socks are manifesting themselves in our dryer. We must be in some kind of vortex. I wonder who or what will show up next?

"Hopefully, Chase," Bill answered before departing.

That did not satisfy my curiosity about the enigma of the strange sock. I could never stand an unsolved mystery, but this one would have to wait. Then I heard Bill call me from the laundry room. I told him to come back; I could not leave my perch. He appeared a moment later with a black infant sock. "Is this yours?"

"No. Where did you find it?"

"I was helping Sonja look for the mate to your polka dot sock."

"It's not my sock," I injected. "I don't know where that polka dot sock came from and I don't know where that infant sock came from."

"Well, I found it behind the dryer. I don't know how it got there because we cleaned the entire floor when we installed the new dryer. It can't just have magically appeared, and I know how you hate any unsolved mysteries."

"It's the vortex," I replied.

"Right. Has Sandy been doing her laundry here?"

"Have you seen the size of Sandy's feet? She doesn't wear infant socks. I bet some poor mom is tearing her hair out looking for this sock right now. All joking aside, if it wasn't there when we installed the new dryer, then where did it come from?"

"You may be right about the vortex. These new computerized dryers are so complicated to operate. Tell me again how to make it work."

"Well, first you check inside for newly appearing socks."

It took a couple of hours, but Bill got his wish, not about the socks, but about Chase. When I opened the door, Chase was apologetic. "So glad you called about the cows, Nancy. I hate to lose any."

"I know. Can you herd them home?"

"I'll try. If I can't move 'em, I may have to bring my horse up here. Three are hard to move at once. They scatter faster than I can push them. They probably came through the fence somewhere."

"Are you going to look for a fence break?"

"No," he laughed. His answer didn't surprise me, and I kept my disappointment hidden. Ranchers figured it was their neighbor's duty to fence cows out, not theirs to fence them in, and state law supported them on this irritating point.

I soon heard the sound of his four wheeler and Chase shouting at the cows. The three cows burst onto the road and began running up the mountain, the exact opposite direction they needed to go. Chase swung the ATV around and came at the group from another direction. This time they scattered, so Chase picked the closest escapee and moved behind her as she grabbed one last mouthful of "Wilson's grass" and began munching. I watched this escapade continue for nearly half an hour. By now he had them grouped again, but they were headed east into our high pasture. He needed them to go north, down the road onto his grazing land. It was proving quite frustrating, particularly for Chase. He struggled with his four wheeler through muddy earth, snow, ice, and rocks. At last he jumped off his ATV and began chasing them on foot.

Surprisingly, he proved much more agile on his own two legs than he had on his vehicle. He ran through the field, waving his arms and shouting as if he was on horseback. I could tell Wilson was impressed because he had moved cows without a rider; Chase was moving cows without a horse. Within a few minutes Chase had pushed the cows down the road toward the north cattle guard entrance that separated our two properties. Meanwhile, Bill had removed the section of hog panel that flanked the cattle guard so Chase could take the cows through, much to the relief of Star, who could finally stop dancing to the calamity.

When I later saw Chase walking toward the house, I went out to meet him. "Nancy, the cows are back on our side. Now I have to get my ATV unstuck."

"Do you need any help?"

"Naw, I can get it."

"Do you want to come in for a cookie? You've earned one."

"I can't right now, got lots of work to do, but thanks."

As he walked away I shouted, "You don't happen to be missing a polka dot sock, do you?"

Chase looked back at me with a quizzical stare, shook his head, and walked on.

Bill turned to me and shrugged, "Eh, it was worth a shot."

41

A Good Omen

STAR LOOKED UP FROM his bowl and smacked his lips. His nose was full of white powder that clung lightly to his whiskers. To the uninitiated he might have looked like a coke addict, but it was simply his weight gain supplement. He seemed to be smiling, and his pink tongue efficiently enveloped his lips, retrieving every last speck of his nutritious snack. His facial expression and demeanor told me all I needed to know. He adored these special treats. Since he had come to live with us he was overflowing with happiness and shared this fact with us every day.

Six months had passed since the first snow, but it was one white powder that wouldn't completely disappear. It came and went at will, clinging to the ground and occasionally turning into slick ice sheets that threatened the most surefooted animal. According to the calendar, spring was just about over, but no one informed Montana. The temperatures were still below freezing most evenings.

"Nothing bothers you, does it boy?" I reached up to touch Star's ears. "You're as happy as a clam." Even as a child I wondered why my grandmother used that expression. *Are clams really happy? I suppose they are; they spend each day at the beach.*

I said my goodbyes to my three handsome fellows and headed back to the house. As I entered, Bill handed me the telephone. "It's your brother, Brian."

I fumbled to remove my coat while trying to put the phone to my ear. "Hello?"

Brian's voice was cheerful as always. "Hey, Nanc, how are you?"

"We haven't completely thawed out yet, but all is well here. I can't complain; I'm not knee deep in mud—yet."

"Oh, right, the dreaded mud and manure mix, I remember. I have a joke that should cheer you up, and it's a good one. I was telling a friend that my ninety-five-year-old grandfather was concerned about his health, so he started walking about five miles a day. It's been three months now and we have no idea where he is! HA!"

"Oh, cute. That is a good one. The girls will love it."

We continued conversing. It was nice to be able to talk to Brian on his day off. Usually we were a bit rushed when he called during the week, but it was a Saturday and he was resting at home. His only plan was to sit back and read a book he'd gotten from the library. There was nothing urgent or necessary about the call. It was just family staying in touch. For me this was a rare and cherished treat. When we finished talking I decided to take a page from his book, so to speak, and just relax for the afternoon. It was unusual for me. Relaxing does not come easily. My kind of personality is more like that of a doe, always alert to danger. Maybe it's a result of being petite and feeling vulnerable, or maybe it's due to having spent almost half my lifetime with no one but myself for backup. Whatever the reasons, snuggling into my glider with a blanket, a cup of tea, and the sounds of Penny snoring in her daybed beside me was very soothing. In no time I was asleep and dreaming. I don't recall exactly what those dreams were, some kaleidoscope of fleeting memories and pleasant sounds that melded into a vision of hands tapping a pair of drumsticks on a table. Brian played the drums, but he never played a table. *What is he doing? Why is my brother tapping his drumsticks over all my furniture? He's tap-dancing about the room in a tuxedo and tails, striking everything. Even his feet are making that sound. Of course, that's what tap shoes do, but where's the orchestra? There should be an orchestra, but all I hear is that tapping, tapping, tapping, like the sound of rain on a metal roof. Everything else is silent; only the gentle tapping sounds its rhythmic echo.*

I opened my eyes, but the tapping continued. I arose from my chair and looked out the window, still wrapped in my blanket. Small streams of water lightly clung to the glass and flowed down the panes to the sill, where they collected in tiny puddles. It was a light, gentle rain – not snow, but rain. My spirits lifted immediately. I glanced at the weather gauge on my side table. It registered fifty degrees. The raindrops hit the snow, leaving ever larger divots, melting the offending white substance. The sea of white was becoming a lake, a pond, a puddle. As the rain continued, it washed away the snow from my front garden, and I beheld a sight that made my heart sing. The first tiny green shoots were braving the cold soil and reaching for the sky. Purple Crocus, the first flowers of spring, had at last arrived to signify the change in seasons. Mother Nature finally had a change of heart. Better late than never.

42

Seeing Double

ONE OF THE JOYS of spring is an opportunity to see our surroundings come to life. The evergreens shed their snowy blankets and begin to produce pale green tips. The Aspen trees tiny buds are a promise of future shade from the summer sun.

I waited for the wildflowers to spring forth with their vibrant colors. I love the rebirth of nature after its dormancy. Spring is a time for the renewal of all living creatures, and today I watched in anticipation to see life moving again in the wilderness. It was poetry in motion. Fledgling eagles, baby chickadees, young foxes, and cute little cottontail rabbits were only a few of the offsprings that were now gracing our property, but my favorite sight, the fawns, remained hidden. Sometimes we found them tucked away in the tall grass under the Aspen trees near the horse corrals. They blended in so beautifully with the landscape that it was a small miracle the horses didn't step on them. On one occasion I nearly trod upon one. They look like dappled light among the iris plants or in the long grasses. When they close their eyes, they are nearly invisible.

Fawns are born with an instinct to remain perfectly still when they sense danger or see movement. Most animals run, but that would surely cause the demise of the little deer. They would not be able to outrun a predator, so they shut their eyes, slow their breathing and try to blend in with nature. At this age they do not have a scent, so a well camouflaged fawn can fool a coyote or cougar into walking right past them without being detected. Whenever we see them, we just continue on our way. We don't disturb them; they are frightened enough, and mom is usually nearby, watching over them.

As the years have passed, we have had generations of deer families bring their young into our gardens and front patio. I recognize some of them; they become tame very quickly and will listen to most any conversation you have to offer, provided you don't touch them and you allow them to munch on a bloom or two.

This particular morning I was sitting on the back porch listening to the water spill from our three-tiered cast iron fountain. I often wondered if the sound attracted the wildlife. I know Star had a keen interest in it. He drank from my fountains and bird baths at every opportunity—that is when he thought I wasn't looking. It was such a comical sight, but Star found it more convenient than going back to the stable for water. Sometime I had to pick bits of chewed grass out of the pristine water.

Today Star chose to hang out at a different water cooler. I was sitting quietly alone on the patio as a doe silently stepped out from the trees and gingerly moved toward me. She was quite delicate, and her eyes were wide and trusting. Behind her, four little feet followed in her footsteps and stood close to her mother. I spoke softly to her. "You brought your baby today. She is a beauty. Look at those pretty white spots."

The doe's ears perked, but she did not run.

"You two have your lunch? It's a pretty day to eat alfresco—as long as it doesn't involve my garden."

The young mother sniffed the ground and began to nibble at a small weed. As she turned her head, the nearest tree moved, and another fawn popped out with exuberance!

"You had two fawns this year! Good for you; they are both very *dear.*"

The second fawn stepped forward awkwardly, and almost took a bow, enjoying the attention. *There's one in every family.*

I watched them browse for some time. It was a calming experience until I had to lecture them once again which greens were acceptable to eat. They clearly felt safe in my presence, but I refused to feed or handle them. I wanted them to stay wary of humans. I was surrounded by hunters, and I didn't want my "deer" friends to be turned into sausage and jerky. I'm not against hunting, but it's not an activity I particularly enjoy. Anyway, they would be safe here.

As they munched I thought about the generations of deer that came before them, before us, before the first white settlers. For how many millennia had this ritual gone on in this same spot with only the native Indian to threaten them? Deer were highly prized as a source of meat and leather. Certainly they had hunted these grounds. I had proof. I remembered finding an arrowhead on our property a decade earlier when the construction crew was improving our driveway. I marveled at how the Indians could shape obsidian with primitive tools to form both a sharp edge and a recess for securing the head to a shaft using tallow. Holding an ancient relic of history in my hand connected me to the past.

The Blackfoot tribe had roamed our property for centuries. Blackfoot is the English translation of the work *Siksika*, a reference to the dark colored bottoms of the moccasins they wore on their feet. They were a nomadic people who made *tipis* (teepees) from lodge poles covered with buffalo skins. The four poles that served as the foundation for the structure were elegantly fashioned and decorated. The entrance always faced the east and the fireplace was in the center of the tipi. The place of honor was in the rear, where they also kept their important ceremonial objects.

A warrior usually had several wives due to the shortage of men. In summer the tribe hunted, fished the rivers, and gathering wild fruit. However, winter must have been perilous. They rubbed bear grease on their skin to help keep their bodies warm. The thought of it made my overly sensitive nose wrinkle.

Lifestyles have changed dramatically since the coming of white men, but knowing I walked in the same places, looked upon the same mountains, and planted in the same soil was a comforting thought. Time would continue to march on, and perhaps in the distant future someone would think of my family, our lifestyle, and our contribution to the land in what was once considered a modern culture.

During my musings the clouds had gathered and it began to drizzle. I said goodbye to the deer, entered my house, and closed the door, effectively shielding myself from the weather outside. I was grateful to escape the dampness and enjoy the comforts of my own *tipi.*

My gardening companions.

43

Horsing Around

I SPRANG UP INSTANTLY from my chair when I heard the familiar cry of a horse. Sonja came running from her room. "Did you hear that, Mom?"

"Yes," I replied as we both rushed to the windows. Whiskey was calmly standing in the front meadow, but Star was running and stamping his feet. He darted in and out of the trees at the meadow's edge. He threw his head back again and called to his herd members in a panic.

"Sonja, do you see Wilson?"

"No, Mom."

"Star must be calling him. I bet Wilson went down to the creek bottom. Star knows how dangerous that is and he won't follow."

"C'mon Mom, we better find Wilson."

We were out the door and headed down to the barn in two minutes. Star seemed relieved at our presence, but still danced about with nervous energy. He continued to whinny and snort, his way of demanding that we find Wilson. Sonja was irritable as we neared the corral. "Wilson!" she shouted, "You're upsetting your brother. Come home!"

Normally this would work, but Wilson was nowhere to be seen. We paused near the south end of the corral and waited. Star stomped his feet and snorted, throwing his head about wildly so that his mane kept flying in the air. Wilson didn't appear. We walked around the bend and I searched the narrow trail leading down the hill to the back of our property. It was like a canyon, with high cliffs on both sides and a stream running through the bottom, a very vulnerable place for anyone to be trapped. Except for the logging trail, the land was as undisturbed as it had been for millennia. It was a perfect spot for predators to catch their prey whenever they came for water. I dared not go down there unarmed, but all I had was my walking staff. Normally Wilson would come poking up the road in his typically carefree gait as though nothing was wrong, but not this time. Perhaps he did not hear me. Perhaps the sight of fresh green buds of grass was too irresistible. Perhaps he was injured.

Now I had to make a choice. Go back to the house and arm myself, take the risk and walk further down the trail, or continue to remain where I was. I decided to wait a bit longer, but Sonja was growing impatient. We shouted again. Always before, our horses responded when we called them home. Like faithful dogs, they would emerge from the trees and come to the sound of our voices.

I looked into Sonja's worried face. "Let's go back and get the car; we can't look for him unarmed, and frankly, Honey, I don't feel like hiking the mountain right now. We can cover more ground on four wheels."

We trudged back up the hill and found Bill waiting for us at the door. "I heard your yelling. Is Wilson on a walkabout?"

"I think he went into the back forty," I puffed, out of breath. "I came back for the car."

"Sonja and I can drive down for you."

"In that case I'm going back to get Star. We can walk down partway. Maybe he can help me locate Wilson."

Bill and Sonja backed the car out of the garage and met me at the corral. I waited for them to pass before letting Star out the front gate. "We'll find your buddy," I reassured him. "Just come with me."

I feared Star might try to follow the vehicle instead, but he stayed with me. His eyes grew large and round, and he pranced to relieve nervous energy when we reached the beginning of the ravine. I touched his neck and said, "Easy, boy, we'll find Wilson; don't worry."

This seemed to momentarily calm Star. We both stood and waited, looking down the road with anticipation. It proved to be a short wait. I heard a distant sound of hooves striking the ground. It grew louder and more pronounced until Wilson ran past us without even a sideways glance. He continued on to the gate and darted quickly through it into the corral. He then stopped and meekly stood by the corral panels with a nonchalant air of innocence. *What's the problem? What are you talking about? I've been here the whole time.* He really knew he was in trouble.

Bill drove up beside me and rolled down the window. "Wilson was at the bottom of the gorge by the creek, lollygagging, but as soon he saw us he made a beeline for home. I've never seen him run so fast."

"I know, he shot by us like a streak of lightning. Now look at him, as innocent as a lamb. The only thing missing is the halo. He knows better. Now I have to go lecture Wilson on our barn safety rules again. I'm glad Star didn't follow him, and decided to call us for help instead."

"Yep, Star's a bit of a wuss and a tattletale."

"Hey, he did the right thing. You should be proud of him. You're just mad because you had to get off the couch."

"I love that couch, and what's more, it loves me. We're simpatico." Bill grinned as he rolled up the window and roared off, leaving me and Star to breathe dust. He paused momentarily by the gate to drop off Sonja before scurrying back to his beloved sofa.

Sonja and I approached Wilson. Star was close behind us muttering, "Boy are you gonna get it now." During this entire affair our senior horse, Whiskey, stood by the feeder, looking completely bored and content to chew the same mouthful of straw he'd been chewing for the past twenty minutes. He was such a dignified fellow who would never consider breaking the rules. He just tolerated the antics of his two goofball friends.

Star had appointed himself as mother hen/hall monitor and watched over the herd. If anything was amiss he would always run home and call to us. Now he stood by eagerly awaiting our judgement and punishment of his delinquent older brother.

Wilson remained silent and accepted his lecture. I spoke in the scolding tone of any parent who has just caught her child performing a dangerous stunt. "You know this is for your own good. The cougars and wolves have just emerged from a very lean winter and are eagerly scouting for food to fill not just their aching bellies, but those of their young. Even the bears are hungry enough to attack anyone in their path, especially those with young cubs. This is a very dangerous time for you to go gallivanting off on your own. And the ravine is the worst place to be. They can trap you down there between the fence and the road. And you can't jump across the back gate. Who would even know you were in trouble if it wasn't for Star sounding the alarm. I thought you had better sense than this, Wilson. Shame on you. What do you have to say for yourself?"

The whole time I was scolding him, Wilson was eyeing Sonja beside me. She was busy trying to balance herself on one leg while removing a boot full of sand and pebbles. She had to sit down to complete the task. As soon as she did, she set the boot aside and concentrated on brushing off her sock. In that moment, when I had just finished my lecture, Wilson lowered his head, snatched the boot, and walked away!

"Wilson!" Sonja called, "Bring back my boot!"

Wilson had no intention of returning his prize. I couldn't ascertain whether it was a playful attempt at forgiveness or a protest for having interrupted his grazing in the ravine. Either way, he was not about to return the boot.

I turned to Sonja, "I'll get it; wait here."

"Wilson, give me that boot," I demanded. He turned from me, the boot flapping in his mouth like some prize, then strutted away with pride.

"Wilson, give me Sonja's boot."

Nope!

"Very funny, return it now."

No way! I like it!

"Don't make me get your halter." I cut to the left and stood in front of him. "Give me that boot!"

He looked me in the eye and shook it vigorously while neighing, "I'll give you the boot."

"Enough of your sassiness." I was trying not to laugh, for it was hard to take his play seriously. I stretched my hand out. Wilson dropped the boot to the ground. I bent down to retrieve it, noting the drool marks where he had held it in his mouth. With disgust I added, "You could at least have set it in my hand."

I carried it to the tack room to clean it with a rag while Sonja hobbled after me on one foot. "Sonja," I sighed while looking at the holes in the leather, "I think we need to get you some new boots."

Wilson thrust his head in the doorway and grunted, "Do I get a treat now?"

"No treats for a boot thief," Sonja insisted as she slid her foot back into her boot.

Wilson was not going to apologize. He simply stood expectantly by the door. *What about me? I want a treat!*

"Back up! Back up!" Sonja shooed him away. We followed him toward the round pen. "Do you want me to get his halter, Mom?"

"Yes, I think he needs some training."

Sonja turned around and called out, "Mom, Star's in the tack room!"

All we saw was a white hind quarter protruding from the tack room. "We need to get him out of there before he panics." No sooner had I said it and the hind quarter disappeared into the cramped confines of the tack room. "Oh great! Now what do we do?"

There wasn't enough room to squeeze in and back him out, plus it would have been far too dangerous to attempt. If he panicked and started kicking, he could well injure himself and kill one of us. All we could do was talk softly to him and try to coax him into backing out.

"Back up, Star!" I commanded.

"Star, come here!" Sonja called.

Star looked about unconcerned, sniffed at the saddle pads, and quietly backed out of the room. *No treats here. I wonder why Wilson stuck his head in.*

Sonja was at Star's side, rubbing him gently. "Good boy, Star, good boy." She turned to me scornfully and said, "Mom, Wilson is teaching Star bad habits."

"I agree. The next thing you know he'll be stealing your boots."

"Whiskey would never behave this way."

"Whiskey is a well behaved gentleman. He is too dignified to indulge in juvenile pranks." I heard a snort from the hay feeder where Whiskey stood, followed by a loud and long display of flatulence.

"So much for higher standards," smirked Sonja.

Star learning proper manners.

44

My Ring of Fire

I GAZED OUT THE picture windows from our second floor loft. It was always a comfort for me to see such an expansive view through the plate glass. I checked on our horses every time I passed these windows or walked down the stairs. Even on days when I was rushed, my head automatically turned to take a quick glance outside, satisfying myself that all was well. On this new spring day circumstances were far from satisfactory. Our three boys were very upset and I immediately saw the source of their discomfort. One of Chase's bulls had managed to find his way into the horse corral. He was a big brute of a fellow, a huge Black Angus, and he was pushing at the sides of the panels, eyeing the hay storage area. These were lightweight panels not intended for cattle, and I did not want him damaging them. When he couldn't move them, he became agitated and paced the perimeter looking for access. The horses stayed clear of him, but the bull was becoming more frustrated and angry by the second. I called Chase, but had to leave a voice message. I hoped he would get it and come immediately. An angry bull can cause quite a bit of harm, and I knew they were a big investment for a rancher.

Bill and I stood on the front deck so the horses could see us. I was hoping it would calm them and give them a little comfort. Bill shook his head and said, "I can't wait here all day for Chase. I don't think the bull will cause much trouble, so I'm going back to my shop. Call me if you need anything."

"He may not get the message for a while."

"Honey, there's really nothing I can do unless he becomes violent."

"Well he is angry."

"Angry isn't violent." With that last remark he left. I kept my vigil and called to the boys occasionally to reassure them I was there. After an hour the bull left the corral and wandered down the road toward the creek until I lost sight of him. The horses calmed down, so I sent Bill to close the gate. I had my usual household duties of cleaning, laundry, and paperwork to attend to, and most of the afternoon passed without further incident. In time I heard the hum of a four-wheeler and knew Chase was entering our driveway. When he arrived at the door I explained the situation and told him I had no idea where the bull had wandered. Chase looked very concerned. "I just got your message and came right over. I have to find him. Bulls can be quite dangerous and this is one I know is mean. He must have gotten through your fence somewhere. I'll find him."

Chase jumped onto his ATV, waved his hand, and sped off down the road. After a half hour had passed I didn't see or hear a bull or cowboy in our fields. I decided to step out and have a look around. My timing was impeccable. I walked outside and partway down the road, keeping my eyes on the horses. Much to my surprise the bull had a similar idea. We saw each other at the same moment. Chase was nowhere to be seen, but I heard his voice shouting to me loud and clear, "Nancy, don't move; don't run. He's looking right at you!"

I immediately froze. *I'm a statue, I'm a statue, not moving, hardly breathing.* I remembered the stories Gail and Chase used to tell me of cowboys being "taken" by a bull. Some of the men were seriously wounded and permanently injured. Even Gail had suffered bruising, gouging, and a broken bone or two in the past, although she always told me she "put on her man pants" and continued to work through the pain. *But I'm a tiny little thing. A bull will make short work of me and just leave a spot in the road where I used to be.*

Time hung in the air and I was vaguely aware of the dull monotone sound of Chase's four-wheeler as he slowly moved in my direction. Following his instructions, I didn't move a muscle, but my mind continued racing a mile a minute. *I might be able to sprint to the front door if he starts to move. I can run about twenty miles per hour in a short sprint; a bull runs about thirty-five miles per hour. He's faster; I probably wouldn't make it. Chase might be able to intervene with the bike. There are no trees I can climb, no vehicle or rock to hide behind, and I don't have a weapon, not even my staff. Boy, it sucks to be me right now.*

There was no more time to think; the bull chose me as the target and moved toward me like a freight train. I remained still. Chase hit the gas and I heard the engine wind up. He cut in front of the bull and spun around, placing himself and the bike in front of the irritable creature. The beast turned away and Chase continued to push him down the hill and toward the road alongside the horse corral. With the bull's attention diverted from me, I shook off my fear and ran to the safety of the house. I didn't stop running until I was on the second floor bedroom balcony where I could get a better view of our front acreage. Chase slowly approached the bull and gently nudged him with the four-wheeler. I was surprised the animal didn't move, and instead stood his ground stubbornly. This clumsy ballet continued for well over an hour as Chase slowly maneuvered the bull toward the front of our property. I lost sight of them, but decided not to go investigate his progress. It was much later in the evening when I heard the doorbell ring. I invited Chase in for a visit. He sat on his usual bar stool by the kitchen counter and began talking.

"I finally got that bull back with his cows. When he saw them he went right to 'em. I'm so glad you did what I said, Nancy. He was looking at you and I knew if you ran, he would chase you down. I was afraid he would hurt you 'cause he's my meanest bull. I have trouble with him too."

I smiled and replied, "I'm just glad you came to the rescue. I wasn't up to a game of 'ring of fire.'"

"No, no, don't want that!" Chase laughed. "Too many people get hurt in that game. Standing in a circle with a bull is more than a bit dicey; it can be deadly if you don't know how to read the signs."

"I can't believe you entered that competition at the rodeo and won."

"I promised Mom and Dad I won't do that again. The money was great, but not really worth the risk."

"Then stop accepting the 'triple dog dare', it's unhealthy."

"No kidding!"

"At least you aren't dealing with Red Kangaroos in your paddocks like my friend in Australia. They're about five feet tall and weigh over a hundred pounds. She has them come into her corrals and cause all kinds of trouble. A kick from one of them could kill a man."

"I'll take my bulls any day; I know how to handle them."

As we laughed and chatted, I spied Bill walking across the patio from his shop. He came through the doors and quickly inquired, "Chase, did you ever find your bull?"

Chase and I just looked at each other and burst out laughing. Bill was puzzled and earnestly asked, "Did I miss something?"

"If I had a red cape I could have had a new career as a bull fighter."

"Yeah, the world's shortest career as a bull fighter," Chase added.

45

Putting on My Woman Boots

SOME DAYS YOU JUST have to put on your pretty boots and step out in the rain. I peered down at the toes of my brand-new rubber mud boots with their delicate floral patterns of leaves and flowers in pink, green, and yellow. I didn't want to ruin my pink leather cowgirl boots, since they were not waterproof. I had purchased the mud boots at a Ross Discount Department Store. They weren't as rugged as the ones you would get from a ranch supplier, but they suited me for light duty in wet weather. Every time I slipped on these cheerful boots I could picture my old friend Gail rolling her eyes. I knew any rancher would laugh me out of the corral if I showed up wearing them. Even Sonja eyed them with suspicion and disdain. I consoled myself with the idea that if I could stand ankle deep in a slurry of mud and manure and still keep a smile on my face, then the flowered mud boots had served two purposes. My feet would be dry and I'd still be stylish.

This spring my little boots were getting a workout. It was surprising how much rain we had so far. It had become a daily affair. The snow and ice were gone, for which I was eternally thankful, but mud now consumed us. Even the fields, with all their lush green grass, were soggy to the point that I dared not let the horses spend much time in them, lest they foundered.

It was unusual to hear the almost constant tapping of rain on the roof. When it was light it was soothing, but when it poured it was so noisy that I could not relax or sleep. I watched the beads of water roll off the toes of my boots and kept telling myself that it made the grass grow and would produce an abundance of hay. Hay benefited the ranchers because it fed the cattle and the horses. But did they have to benefit so much?

Bill and I were trying to plant flowers in the back patio garden. The rain was light enough that it only slightly inconvenienced us. It did soften the soil, making planting easier, if also messier. A few bright rays broke through the clouds and I cheered with delight and shouted, "Come on, Ray, you can shine through those wimpy clouds. Let's have some sunbeams down here."

"Does begging the sun to come out work?"

"I don't know, but it makes me feel better."

I was anticipating a few minutes of fresh air and sunshine, so I drew in a deep breath, when my olfactory sense was assaulted. I covered my hand over my nose and gagged. "Do you smell that horrible odor?"

I was surprised when Bill answered, "Yes, I do, and I can only imagine how offensive it must be to your super sniffer. I noticed it earlier this morning too."

A light breeze kicked up and within a minute the foul smell was gone. We puzzled what it could be. I wrinkled my nose again and grimaced, "It's not horse or cow."

"It doesn't smell like skunk or a dead animal. What are you using for fertilizer, Quinn?"

"Nothing. Could it be some kind of weed killer? It smells like bleach. Oh no, there it is again. I have to go inside."

"I'm coming with you."

I hurriedly shut the door. "I suppose I should laugh, our first chance for sunshine and we can't even be outside. I'm going to research that weird smell."

I spent several hours scanning the internet for an explanation of this particular odor. I scratched many possible sources off my list, including various animal urines. What could possibly be out there that was causing an intermittent smell that was carried by the wind? My only feasible conclusion was that it was produced by the Mycenoid species of mushrooms. They are small, with fragile stems and bell-shaped caps, and usually grow in clusters. They are known to have a strong chemical or bleach-like odor. I surmised these mushrooms were a product of the seemingly continuous rain we had been experiencing. I assumed once it dried out, the odor would dissipate. I decided to think about it as another gift from nature, but I secretly wished it was the kind of gift that could be boxed up and returned.

I glanced down at my boots sitting by the back door. "Well, maybe I can't enjoy gardening in the sunshine, but at least I look good in the rain."

46

Keep the Faith

IT WAS MY FAVORITE time of year, the time when my cousin Faith made her annual sojourn to Cimarron. We had a lot of fun activities planned, including a trip to the Museum of the Rockies to tour the Genghis Kahn exhibit, visit a working 19th century farmhouse, and take in their planetarium show. I was particularly looking forward to the Mongol exhibit. It is always a treat for me to go back in time and view artifacts from daily life long ago. It surprised me that the women of the Mongol empire had such beautifully crafted toiletries. I was intrigued by their metal work. Their cosmetic compacts were intricately carved and their hair pins were similarly detailed works of art. The Mongols were skilled craftsmen who made suits of armor out of small metal strips fastened together. Even some of their passports were carved from metal (the fact that they used passports impressed me). They didn't mince their words either. One of the passports contained a single statement which read "Let me pass or die." Now that's being a minimalist.

I especially enjoyed viewing their musical instruments such as the two-stringed *morin khuur* (horsehead fiddle). Its name was derived from the use of multiple strands of horse hair taken from the tails of both a stallion and a mare to form the larger (male) and smaller (female) strings. The musical displays and descriptions of its importance in

Mongol culture provided me an interesting respite from constantly reading about the weapons and brutality of the time period. Bill, on the other hand, was fascinated by a giant crossbow that was mounted on two wheels and towed like artillery.

I understood that the opulence displayed in the glass cabinets represented people of a particularly high place in their society. Not everyone lived with such beauty and splendor. I remember one informative plaque in the exhibit that explained how the average peasant wore the same clothes until they had almost completely disintegrated off of the body. Their dining habits were even worse. It was not uncommon to eat your own body lice in order to stave off starvation. It was obvious that various members within their empire lived as polar opposites.

We jumped forward to the 19th century with our tour of the working farmhouse. It was an eclectic affair that included a house with women in costume baking in the kitchen (no, we weren't allowed to eat the pastries, though Bill was tempted), several barns and stables filled with over a century old collection of farm implements, small fields and gardens around and near the farm house where popular edible plants of the period were growing, and my least favorite spot – the root cellar. Bill and Sonja went down into the dark earth while I remained topside. When they returned I asked what it was like and the reply was "Dark, cool, and smelling of dirt". The very thought made me cringe. Little wonder I enjoy the wide open spaces of Big Sky country.

Our visit to the planetarium held a special significance for me. The program commemorated the 50th anniversary of the United States moon walk on July 20th, 1969. It was a life changing day for America, but even more so for me. That morning my father took my brother out for breakfast and never returned. The two events would be forever linked in my mind.

For once I put aside these memories and focused on the planetarium program. I learned some new information that truly surprised me. I was unaware how a slight miscalculation in the lunar module's speed caused them to overshoot their intended landing site by over three miles, or that the onboard landing computer was overheating, or that they were using fuel at an alarming rate. Neil Armstrong searched desperately for a suitable landing spot and placed the Eagle down with only 30 seconds of fuel left. Even though I already knew the outcome, the presentation at the planetarium was heart pounding. I felt like I was floating in space and landing on the moon with the astronauts. I have always loved my country, but a renewed surge of pride coursed through my veins to think that our nation produced such men and such a craft as this a half century before now. It reminded me again how far one can go in life with the right attitude, faith, and preparation, not to mention the will to succeed.

We had to cut the day a little short and return home because Penny would need to be let out and the horses required their evening feed. As our vehicle rounded the corner to Cimarron, I saw the boys look up from grazing and begin to run alongside the car. Faith exclaimed, "Look at Star run; it's amazing!"

I felt great joy at the sight and proclaimed, "He isn't the same horse he was when he first arrived." It was true. His long silver hair waved in the wind, and even though his gait was unsteady and a little gawky, he was fast on his feet, and looked like he reveled in the feel of the wind he generated. Being of mostly Arabian breeding, his emotions were always visible. I could tell how Star was feeling every time I glanced in his direction.

All the horses filed into the corral and hung their heads over the fence, watching with anticipation. Dinnertime! As we approached the garage Penny's head popped into view from the second story window just like a Jack-in-the-box. Her face was sternly disapproving as though saying, "It's about time!"

"Oh, Nancy, she doesn't look happy at all," Faith remarked.

"She always looks that way. We call it the disapproving Penny head in the window. But wait until we get inside, then she'll be an ecstatic pup."

True to my prediction we were met with a wiggling little mass of gelatin with a spinning tail. Penny's eyes were bright and joyful at our return. I sat on the staircase and she popped onto the first tread to begin her chorus of happy grunts and sneezes at our reunion. Over the din I could hear the horses calling to us, and I suggested we quickly change our clothes and head down to the barn to feed our impatient fellows. Once we got to the tack room, Faith helped me with the feed buckets. We placed Whiskey in the round pen and set his rubber bucket on the ground. Within moments, The Three Stooges and their kin positioned themselves outside the corral. They paused until everyone was assembled, then suddenly raced full force toward us. "They're attacking us!" Faith cried out. "I don't want to get bitten."

"They won't bite. They aren't afraid of you though, and will run right over your feet to get to the bowl."

"Not mine!" Faith started stomping her feet at them and chasing them around the pen.

"Faith, it's a trick! Check your left flank! They're coming up your way."

Faith spun around and threw a rock at her closest foe. "Look at him run now!" Despite her initial fear, Faith seemed to take on the task of defending Whiskey's food with zeal.

I had an idea. "Let's stand side to side. You take the gophers to the left; I'll take the ones on the right."

I extended my right arm and placed the tip of my walking stick on the ground.

Faith laughed. "You look like a gladiator ready for battle."

"I feel like one. Where's your walking stick?" I barely finished my sentence when about eight rodents rushed me. I swung my stick close to the ground, but they were not deterred. They tried to run between my feet, though a couple of them hesitated and stopped in front of me. I gently popped them on their bottoms and they moved a few inches away, looking up in surprise. *Hey man, you hit me. That's not fair, dude.*

"Faith, look out behind you!"

Faith spun around to see another half dozen furry rodents heading in her direction. I tossed her the other walking stick that had been leaning against the corral panel and she went to work on them. She bopped a couple of them on the head, and it made me realize we were playing a live version of Whack-a-Mole.

By now Faith was getting slightly out of breath. "Nancy, I'm getting tired."

"I'll keep them at bay. You check on Star and see if they're bothering his bowl." By this time I had counted over twenty of the little scudders in all shapes and sizes. Some were plumper than last time, and one reminded me of the pup Rolly from the movie *101 Dalmatians* because he was dragging his belly in the dirt and leaving a trail. Nearly overrun with vermin, we continued to fight the good fight and kept them from jumping inside the food bowls. As I glanced up the hill I saw Bill making his way down in our direction. I called up to him, "We have a target rich environment here."

"I'm ready for them," he yelled back. Bill came through the gates and surveyed the fray. "I can't shoot any of them this close to the horses." He positioned himself away from us and the horses before firing a couple of shots into the mass of wiggling, jumping, chewing ground squirrels. The crack of a bullet was all it took to send the whole gaggle running for home. They dispersed into different holes or darted down the hill. No sooner had their rumps disappeared into these holes than their heads reemerged and the barking and scolding began. *How dare you interrupt our dinner hour. I shall complain to the authorities.* POW! They darted underground, only to emerge elsewhere and continue their rants. This act was unsuccessfully repeated several times until Bill exclaimed, "My blasted sights are way off."

King of the misses I thought, but I said nothing. He adjusted his point of aim to compensate, and after nearly sending several of them to Valhalla, they decided discretion was the better part of valor and departed into their subterranean world. For the present all was quiet on the western front.

"Wow, I'm glad that's over," Faith remarked. "I've never seen anything like it."

"Most unsanitary," I replied as I attempted to clean out poor Whisky's fouled supper dish.

"Nancy, why weren't you afraid of them?"

"Because they aren't mice."

"But they are rodents."

"So are squirrels, but they don't bother me either. These are just cute, fat, irritating, disgusting ground squirrels, not mice or rats."

"Oh, yes, that explains it. I have an idea. It's something we do at our barn in Michigan. I'll tell you about it on the way home. I'm hungry; can we get something to eat?"

"Everyone else has eaten; I guess it's our turn."

Bill grumbled as he headed back to his shop to clean his .22 and check his sights. Faith and I released the horses and talked all the way up the hill toward home. I had to admit, it was a cunning plan she had.

We found ourselves at Higgin's the next day. Faith showed me a bucket style feeder that hung over the corral panels where the gophers couldn't reach it. We purchased three sizes in different colors, one for each horse.

"I can't wait for you to try these; nothing can crawl into them while the horses are eating, and if they drop any food from their mouths, it usually falls back into the container. I think this will solve your problem."

Upon arriving home we got to work. The now cautious critters gathered near us, but refused to step into the round pen. Apparently they were having flashbacks from the previous day. Faith and I filled the buckets with feed and hung them on the second rung from the top of each panel. Star and Wilson began to munch happily, but Whiskey refused to eat.

"Oh, no, Whiskey won't eat." I felt deflated.

Faith said, "Give him a little time; he'll get used to it."

I wondered how long it would take Whiskey to become acclimated to his new dinner pail. He was a particular fellow. I could only hope his hunger would force him to get over his fear of change. By the next morning Whiskey was standing at his new feeding place, staring at the corral panel and willing his food to appear.

Seeing this from the house, Faith and I went to the barn and fed the horses early. If Whiskey was showing any willingness to eat, I wanted to accommodate him. We were soon rewarded by the site of our three horses with their muzzles buried in their respective feed troughs. Success! I felt a sense of peace and turned to Faith to share my thoughts. "Now this is more like what they promised us in the brochure."

47

The Tea Cattle

I WAS IN THE kitchen attempting to brew tea the English way. I poured the boiling water over my silver tea ball and into a charming hand painted burgundy and gold porcelain teacup, which itself came from England. It was signed and numbered, and a treasure of my small teacup collection. I placed it on its matching saucer and allowed the tea to steep. This is the point where the British have an advantage over their American cousins. We are an inherently impatient lot, and I found myself very much wanting to hurry the process along by stirring the tea with an engraved silver spoon that I acquired for these occasions. I had read that doing so might increase its bitterness, so I resisted the urge. Instead, I glanced into the water and watched the color darken as tea began to seep from the ball in cloudlike billows. Instinctively, I picked up the ball and gently dunked it again. *I'm such a typical American; my friends in England would admonish me, I'm sure.*

I waited for another few minutes, resisting the urge to further dunk, swirl, or stir my tea. Satisfied it had steeped long enough, I sprinkled a little sugar in the still steaming vessel and gently stirred it. The silver spoon ringed against the side of the cup. *Oh dear, another ghastly mistake, one never hits the cup with the spoon.* I consoled myself with the idea that had I been in polite company I would have behaved with greater dignity and poise.

As I sipped the flavorful brew, I was reminded of a story about the history of English tea. Robert Fortune was a Scottish botanist and a tea spy! In the 1840s he disguised himself as a Chinese Mandarin and smuggled tea plants and leaves to India. The Chinese had been very keen to keep tea a secret, and it was forbidden to sell the plants to other countries. I could only imagine the intrigue and adventures of a tea smuggler.

I carried my cup and saucer upstairs, pausing to gaze out the window. The bucolic setting was marred only by the presence of one of Chase's free ranging cows in our driveway. I wanted to call Chase and have him come get her, but Bill said it would be easier to shoo her off our land with the pickup truck. Sonja was game for the idea, so they rolled out the truck and drove after her. She dutifully trotted ahead of them, occasionally peering back to see if the big bad pickup truck was still following. She complained the whole way, but when they reached the cattle guard, she did something quite unexpected. She gingerly stepped through the guard and leaped to other side. This should have been impossible because the cattle guard is formed of a series of narrow metal slats laid parallel to each other, with wide gaps between them. Underneath is a ditch, so any animal attempting to cross it would find its legs falling into the gaps and likely being broken. Upon close examination, Bill discovered the ditch under the slats had disappeared. He concluded that runoff from the melting snow had deposited a good deal of silt under the cattle guard, forming a solid barrier of dirt just beneath the slats. The entrance no longer served as a deterrent to inquisitive cows. Within a few minutes she returned. More drastic action would be called for.

Bill returned to the house for the necessary hand tools. I called Chase to help. Together they spent the next two hours tediously removing dirt from between the guards. The space between the slats was too narrow for anything other than a hand pick or claw hammer to loosen the soil and a plastic cup to retrieve it. Once the job was completed, Chase reclaimed his stray cow and left. I congratulated Bill on a job well done.

The next morning I opened my eyes to the sounds of mooing. I let out the sigh that Bill claims comes too often from me. Without looking, I knew the cow was in my front yard again. Bill entered the bedroom and told me what I already knew. "The cow is back and this time she brought her calf."

"The two for one special?" I arose from the bed and donned my robe. I peered out the window and noted that the Black Angus cow and her baby were munching the plants in my front garden near the fountain. "Star will not like her drinking out of his birdbath."

Bill appeared surprised. "Star drinks out of the bird bath? I knew he drank out of the fountain and the waterfall, but the birdbath?"

"He does; I often pick grass out of it. He's too lazy to walk back to the barn, so he finds the nearest watering hole. I think he's puzzled why the bird bath doesn't refill itself."

Another long moo erupted from outside. Bill shook his head and said, "I'd better chase them off and find out how they got in this time."

"Do you think it's a hole in the fence line?"

"I hope not. I don't relish the thought of having to climb up and down those hills trying to find a break. I kinda think she feels the same way too. Maybe the break's close by. We'll see."

I went downstairs to make my breakfast and that all important first cup of tea of the day. I cannot handle coffee or caffeine, so decaffeinated tea suffices. Bill and Sonja had already eaten and were now getting out the truck to herd the cows back to the cattle guard entrance. This time mama cow exited our property by walking along the ditch between the fence and cattle guard. There was just enough room for her to squeeze through. Baby took a detour and ended up on our hillside where she cried for mama. Bill had the foresight to bring tools along, including extra fence wire. He began tying wire from the fence down to the cattle guard, creating pockets of tripwires to close the gap. When he was done, he stood there admiring his handiwork. Mama cow gingerly stepped between the newly laid wires and came back inside to fetch her young one. However, once inside, the miscreant decided to lounge a while and enjoy our sumptuous grass.

Bill returned to the house for more wire and to provide me a progress report. It infuriated me to think how she was happily stuffing her cow pie hole at our expense. I didn't have enough grass for my own three horses now that Star was part of the family. The pastures were eaten down very quickly by him because Star did really eat like a horse. I offered to assist, but Bill declined. He and Sonja had the situation in hand, or more precisely, he was a man on a mission and didn't want to be bothered by well-intentioned interlopers (meaning me). All I could do at this point was sit down and try to enjoy another cup of tea while waiting for Chase to arrive again. It gave me something to do.

Bill managed to contain the cows in the high meadow until Chase showed up, not that they had any intention of going elsewhere. After Chase retrieved them, Bill dug the side drainage ditch deeper and erected a more elaborate system of trip wires that were interlaced with dead logs. This time the cows refrained from entering.

When I congratulated Bill on his success, he laconically replied, "The cows are utterly disappointed." This is what passes for humor in our household.

48

A Stitch in Time

NOW THAT I WAS convinced our pastures were secure from bovine interlopers, I retired to my glider and picked up the newspaper. A front page article caught my eye. The upcoming Tri-County fair was advertising all of its contest categories. It's no secret that I have always enjoyed home décor, interior designing, architecture, baking, furniture restoration, and sewing, so I was pleased to find a category for stuffed toys. Only a year earlier, Sonja had expressed a desire to learn how to sew. I was thrilled at the prospect of teaching her. I have been sewing since I was a teenager. I had acquired a very high-end machine while in my early twenties, and I still use it to make clothes, curtains, and for reupholstering chairs. I started Sonja on simple pattern designs, and I soon found she had a natural talent for sewing and pattern making. She even mastered its embroidery feature. Within a year she was creating a wide variety of complex plush animal toys shaped like birds, wolves, horses, trucks, and jeeps. The contest sounded like the perfect venue for her to display her art, so I broached the idea with her. We read the rules and entry requirements, and began making our plans. Sonja had three weeks to sew her entry for the competition—a wolf cub of her own design.

Throughout the afternoon I listened to the sewing machine running nonstop. Sonja was very enthusiastic about her creation. By dinnertime she had produced a nearly completed plush wolf. It was made with faux fur purchased from a fabric store. We had selected the most realistic looking fur we could find, and the grey and silver tones suited the project perfectly. She designed this one in a sitting position, and it was about seventeen inches high, with a large tail positioned forward, next to the body.

"This is a blue ribbon effort," I told her, as I patted the soft head of the wolf.

"I'm a little nervous about entering."

"Everyone is. When I show a new artwork, or the publisher says my book is ready, I wonder how it will be received. Don't compare yourself to other people; run your own race. This is easier said than done, but it's an important lesson to remember. Personally, I think you have a prize winner."

"That's because you love me."

"That's true, but it's not the reason I said it. I think your wolf plush is really well done. I wouldn't give you false flattery, Sonja. If I see something about it I think is wrong or can be improved, I'll tell you. Even if you don't win this contest, it doesn't mean your work is inferior. It just means, in the judge's subjective opinion, somebody else did better. It's never a mistake to try, and you may learn something from the experience."

"I understand, Mom, thanks."

We didn't have any time to waste. We only had a window of a few hours to deliver Sonja's entry to the fair. When we arrived at the fairgrounds, Sonja's wolf was tagged and accepted, then placed in a glass display case with the other entries. After the judging was over, it would remain on display for a week, then we could pick it up once the fair closed. There was some amazing homespun talent on display throughout the fair—sewing, baking, weaving, woodworking, painting, pencil drawing, canning, and more. It made me feel good knowing these kinds of hands-on activities were still popular, and the fair was a wonderful venue for displaying them. My only regret was that we were on a tight schedule, as usual, and we could not linger to examine each entry in greater detail.

For the next week Sonja often mentioned the fair, and I knew she was excited to see if she had won a prize. We had planned to take her to the fair, but we were unable to attend due to other commitments. I suppose it was for the best because the day we were supposed to go had turned into a tragedy. One of the cars in the live derby event spun out of control and crashed into the bleachers, causing several injuries and killing a volunteer first responder. It was a terrible way to end an otherwise grand festival.

The day arrived to pick up Sonja's wolf from the fair. When we entered the building they were taking down all the displays, and Sonja's entry had been moved to a higher shelf. As I reached up for it I heard Sonja say, "I don't see any ribbon." She paused and then added, "It's okay; I still love my wolf and I'm glad I entered the competition."

As I fumbled to retrieve it, I replied, "I'm sorry, Honey Girl; we can try again next year. I must say, I'm very proud of your attitude." When I picked up the plush toy, I saw a flash of blue flutter behind it. I turned the wolf over and proudly displayed the blue ribbon to her. "You did win! The ribbon was attached to the back with a pin."

"That's great! Let me see him! I can't wait to tell Dad!"

Sonja was beaming; she hugged her wolf and felt the bright blue satin ribbon with her fingers. It had the gold embossed words "First Place" and the name and date of the fair. As we left the building, we stopped to admire the other entries in various categories. When we approached the car, I gave Bill a thumbs up sign and he smiled back at us. Upon our return home I asked Sonja what she wanted to do to celebrate. She replied, "I want ice cream and a trip to the dump!"

Sonja accompanied Bill to our local trash dump at every opportunity. She thought it was fun to see what had been discarded and could be salvaged. One day she found several hard bound history books in good condition, including a biography of Abraham Lincoln, which they saved and used in class. Today her good luck continued. At the dumpsite she found a metal bobbin on the ground that was a perfect fit for my old sewing machine! Perhaps you do reap what you sew.

49

Fantasy Foster Family

ALFRED WHEELER SAT AT our dining room table eyeing the plate of pumpkin chocolate chip cookies suspiciously. "These are one of your recipes?"

"Yes, a family favorite, would you like to try one?"

"Perhaps…the wife doesn't bake much—chronic dieting you know, and the fear of diabetes…although it doesn't run in her family."

"How does she like living in Montana?" I politely inquired.

"Well, she loves the summer weather and the scenery, but that's about it, I'm afraid. She has not really taken to the culture here. I understand completely because I share her feelings. She is a scholarly woman, not as knowledgeable as I, but she continues to grow. She tries, bless her, sort of like you with your baking. Never give up I say."

I turned the subject to another matter. "Alfred, you never mentioned your wife's name, we would like to meet her."

"You should bring her over for a visit," I heard Bill call as he came down the stairs. He approached the dining room and sat down at the table. "Pumpkin chocolate chip! These are really good, Alfred; try one."

Alfred reached for the serving tray, "Husbands can be so supportive, don't you think, Nancy?"

"Oh, yes." I bit my lip.

Alfred continued chatting, but it didn't escape my notice that he had yet to reveal to us his wife's name. He continued to talk about the constraints of having his wife in the house and how much he missed his pigs. He had found them a temporary home in the college's agriculture program, but was still looking for the perfect place for his beloved swine.

"I suppose I should find a more suitable pet for the wife. Your Penny is very sweet. I suppose you wouldn't part with her?"

Bill and I were aghast. Before I could even speak, Bill quickly responded, "No, Alfred, Penny is part of the family. We wouldn't consider giving her to anyone."

"How about for your vacations? She would need someone to care for her and that would free you up to do as you please? We could watch her for you. She's not a pig, of course, but a very nice little dog I must say."

"That is a kind offer, Alfred, but we take Penny with us on our trips." I actually found the idea of leaving Penny in his care so upsetting that I picked up the cookie plate from the table, announced I was refilling it, and excused myself to the kitchen. While I placed a new batch onto the tray, I heard Alfred trying to convince Bill to let him have Penny for a while to improve her training.

"She'll be a better mannered dog after I've trained her."

I breezed into the dining room. "Another cookie, Alfred?"

"No thank you," he replied as he absentmindedly took two off the tray.

I rejoined the conversation. "Penny doesn't need a foster family. She is very happy with us. I think she would find it upsetting to be away from her loved ones."

"I know you mean well, but don't you want what is best for her?"

"Alfred, we are what is best for her. Have you thought of going to the animal shelter and adopting a dog of your own?"

"I don't know how the wife would feel about it, but it may give her someone else to focus on. She is so devoted to me, you know. She even tolerates the new mountain life just to be by my side." He paused for a moment, then wistfully added, "I miss my pigs though. Still, I suppose it's a small price to pay for saving a woman's sanity. The weaker sex must be handled so carefully."

Bill saw an opportunity and posed a question. "Alfred, I understand you never return the affections or the advances of your female admirers, but I must ask—what is your secret? They do seem to flock to you."

"No secret, Bill. I treat them like pigs."

"Pigs?"

Swine I thought to myself.

"Of course, I treat them all like queens. My pigs have the best of everything. I treat the ladies the same way. I listen to them and compliment them. All females desire that. Human or animal, it's a feminine need to feel important. They want to be understood, that they have a purpose, no matter how trivial it may be."

Alfred seemed to be talking to himself, and I noticed a look of nobility as he raised his chin to the air. At that moment I saw him not as a man, but as a prize winning razorback. He finished the last few sips from his teacup and announced his departure. As I closed the front door behind him, I playfully fell against it.

"Don't worry, Penny Pup; you are here to stay."

Penny looked up at me, her tail constantly wagging. There was no fear in her brown eyes. She knew she was always safe with us.

Bill chuckled, "Poor Alfred, a legend in his own mind." He squatted down and patted Penny on the head. "He must be dreaming if he thinks we'd ever leave you with him. Now who's your Daddy?" Penny squirmed with delight as he rubbed her velvety ears and continued. "There's just one thing I'm puzzled about."

"What's that?"

"We still don't know his wife's name."

50

The Winds of Change

IT FELT UNUSUALLY COLD. I sat up in the bed and shivered slightly. My first thought was how much comfort I would get from my morning tea. I noticed the sun was absent from the rear window. Normally it overlooked the tree covered mountain in back of the house. Although it was the last days of summer, this felt very much like a winter day. Over the past two months I had grown used to the sun cheerfully greeting me with its glorious beams shining through the window, urging me to start my day. I liked to watch it dance across the floor, warming the carpet as it traveled along its predestined path.

Penny was still snoozing in her bed, but I could hear her slight nasal snores as she slept. She looked so cozy in her big pillow, with her blanket tucked around her tummy. It was a bed meant for a much larger dog, but when I saw it in the store I knew it was perfect for our "Precious Petunia." It was about three feet in diameter and eight inches high. Being brown, it didn't match my décor at all, but it had a soft furry texture, and I wanted to buy it the moment I set my eyes on it. When we brought it home and put it near our bed, Penny was ecstatic about her new accommodations and promptly plopped into the center, sinking into its depths.

I looked back on the memory fondly. Our original plan had been for Penny to sleep in her "Penny House." It was a collapsible mesh carrier which she slept in when she was first adopted. It was located near the heater in the laundry room, making it the warmest place in the house. Penny loved it, but all that changed the first night my cousin Faith stayed with us in the adjoining guest room. Penny would have none of it, and she flatly refused to enter the Penny House again, preferring to sleep upstairs with the rest of her pack. It's still a running joke in the family, and we "blame" Faith for our having to acquire a new "Penny bed". I couldn't let her sleep on the floor (she sheds too much).

I later had to admit to myself that our acquiescence came with a larger price tag than just a new bed. Sometimes it was hard to sleep with Penny in the bedroom. She and Bill would fall asleep almost instantly and have snoring competitions. They each made their own unusual sounds, but Penny would always be first, beginning with not always muted barks, followed by unconscious baying. I was really surprised one night when she belted out a wail that sounded just like Snoopy in a Charlie Brown cartoon. Her noises never seemed to awaken her, and my greatest fear has remained that someday she will unwittingly teach Bill to join with her in her nightly repertoire.

Somehow aware that I was thinking about her and staring at her, she peeled open one eye, let out a grunt, and squirmed out of her bed. She began the morning Penny stretch, flapped herself until small hairs flew in every direction, then trotted over to my side of the bed where she popped her face up to my pillow. We exchanged good morning greetings while she thumped her tail wildly. Bill was already up and out, and I knew closing my eyes would not deceive her.

"Why don't you go find Daddy?"

The tail thumping continued, only now her eyes were pleading with me. *I really have to go, Mommy.*

"Can your sister take you out?"

No, it has to be you this time. We need to bond.

I sighed. "Let me get my robe on." I retrieved my robe from the closet and descended the stairs. I could hear the jingle of Penny's tags clinking together on her collar as her little feet paddled alongside me. I was always happy to have my little shadow accompany me throughout the house.

Bill was in the kitchen preparing breakfast. "Good morning, Nancy. You look sparking as always, my love."

I smirked and returned my affection with a kiss. I knew how I really looked, but he never seemed to notice. "What's the temperature today?"

"A little chilly," he replied. "It's one below zero."

The shock registered on my face. "What! That wasn't in the forecast, or the brochure, I might add."

Bill took no notice. He had grown accustomed to my constant reference to an imaginary sales brochure when we originally bought the land.

"I wasn't expecting it either."

"Is winter here already? We haven't even started fall?"

"Yes, it does have a winter-like feel to it, but I'm sure it will pass quickly."

"Bill, the horses don't have their winter coats yet, and—oh, no—my vegetables!"

I didn't feel like braving the cold to visit the green house, so instead I ran to the upstairs window to check on our equine companions. *Where are my boys? This is miserably cold and they're unprepared for it. I suppose they're tough enough, but my little gentleman, Whiskey, and our new boy, Star, aren't as strong as Wilson. Perhaps I should blanket them? But I only have one blanket. Now where have they gone? They must be in the stable. I sure hope so. Montana is so capricious!*

I continued my search of the corral and fields, but saw no sign of them. *Have they gone down in the tree line to get out of the wind? Are they in the stable? I can't see the stalls; that big fir tree is in the way. Maybe if I use the binoculars I can see them.* I pulled the field glasses from the case I kept on the windowsill. Within a few moments relief flooded over me as I saw the three amigos in the main stall. I was uplifted by the picture of Wilson and Star, with Whiskey pressed in between them for warmth. It was a wonderful sight. We now had a truly functioning herd. Knowing they were helping each other eased my mind.

"Your tea is ready," Bill called up the stairs.

"The horses are just fine, and they just invented a Whiskey sandwich."

"Eh? I think somebody needs her breakfast."

I recounted the picturesque scene at the barn as I returned to the kitchen. I held the mug of steaming brew in my hands. It was not the kind of weather suited for a fine bone china teacup, which made this mug a perfect choice. I wrapped my hands around the smooth ceramic vessel. I felt the warmth move through my palms and fingers, and with each sip the chill began to leave my body.

"This is just a weird cold snap. It won't last," Bill reassured me. "In a few days the summer weather will return."

"Tell that to my vegetables. Oh, I need to call Sandy and make sure she's turned on the heat in the condo and is warmly dressed for work."

Bill didn't argue as I reached for the phone. Penny had flopped down on the floor in front of the fireplace and was once again slumbering. By the time I finished my conversation with Sandy, Penny was panting. Her little tummy was glowing red from the heat of the fire. "Penny, come away from the fire; it's too hot." Instead of obeying, Penny just rolled onto her back and banged her tail on the floor, asking for rubs on her luminous belly.

Bill's prediction was correct. The cold only lasted for a couple of days and we were soon experiencing more typical weather for the season. The sun returned with warmer days, giving us a feeling of renewal and reprieve. I wish I could say the same for my garden. When I entered the green house, I was disheartened. Nearly all of my vegetables had frozen. Their leaves and vines hung shriveled, limp, and broken. The vibrant green was now a mix of brown with a sickly pale cast of greenish-white. I checked to see if any of the immature vegetables could perhaps be salvaged, but many of them were mushy and misshapen. It wasn't worth the risk of a food borne illness to harvest the damaged ones.

I thought about how the early pioneers must have felt when they lost their crops to weather, insects, fungus, or vermin. Whatever the reason, the unexpected end to months of hard work was difficult to accept. At least I could go to the grocery store and purchase our food. All I was really facing was disappointment. I consoled myself with the knowledge that we had already harvested many of the vegetables, but some of these plants never got a chance to mature, including Sonja's favorite vegetable, cauliflower.

It was an omen. I now knew summer was over and fall would be short. Soon the landscape would change drastically and more permanently. We were once again about to face the harshest season of the year.

51

The Best Laid Plans

THE SUNSHINE ONLY LASTED a few days, to be replaced by heavy rains and colder than normal temperatures. Autumn had arrived prematurely, but there was a bright spot. Bill and I were scheduled to attend a writer's conference in the Great Falls area. We were meeting another author and his wife there, and I was pleased by our budding friendship. I was also looking forward to learning new techniques for film writing and the opportunity to hear a lecture from a New York Times Bestselling author. It was set for the end of September.

I was telling Sonja more about our plans as we brushed the horses. I pulled a curry comb out of the bucket and began to work it into Whiskey's hair. "Sonja, come here. Do you notice something?"

"I see it, Mom. Whiskey's putting on his winter coat early. Why?"

"He knows we're going to have an early winter, and a harsh one to boot."

"That would explain all the rain and wind we've been having, but September has barely started."

"I know; let's just enjoy what we have for now. It will only get worse." I continued brushing, but a sense of foreboding was already forming in the back regions of my mind.

It was obvious my horses were right. The days continued to be cold and wet. Whiskey's coat was even thicker now, and although Arabians don't develop shaggy coats, Star's hair was thickening quickly. Wilson was the lone holdout, but he usually waited until the last minute and then, poof, his winter coat seemed to appear almost overnight.

I looked into the two stalls that served as our hay storage area. They were stuffed full. I always felt better when the winter hay was snugly under shelter. I knew the gates that Bill had hung the previous year would keep the elk and deer at bay. We had purchased an extra ton of hay this season, so I felt comfortable we had enough food for a long winter.

As I walked home, a cold wind bit into my neck and the clouds gathered for more rain. "You can't rain on my parade," I called out loudly as I climbed the hill. I knew that soon I would be leaving on my trip, come rain or shine. I hung up my jacket and placed my boots neatly on the tray by the closet door.

I heard Bill's voice calling me from upstairs. "Is that you, Hon?"

"Yes, I just came in from the barn."

"Come up here; we need to talk."

Oh no, not the dreaded "we need to talk." I climbed the stairs with trepidation.

"I don't want to worry you, but it looks like a snow storm is coming in this weekend. It's a big one and covering several states in the West. They're expecting about two feet of snow in Great Falls."

"It's September! But it's also Montana. I guess we have to cancel our trip."

"Honey, don't get too upset. Let's watch it for a day or so, then make a decision."

I agreed, but an uneasiness was settling into my gut, and that feeling was rarely wrong. It was my inherent early warning system. Bill called it my "Spidey senses."

As the days passed, we watched the weather reports. The West was bracing for the storm. Travelers were told to cancel their plans and only drive in an emergency. Because the trees still had their foliage, the likelihood of falling branches and downed power lines was high. Heavy snowfall, blowing snow, and icing conditions would make driving dangerous, if not impossible. The last straw came when my new friend called to let us know he and his wife had decided not to risk the long drive. I understood completely, and decided we should cancel as well. I emailed the director of the organization hosting the conference and inquired if they had plans to reschedule the event. The reply I received was a bit flippant. She stated they had no plans to cancel, and added if I was worried about the snow, just bring a coat. It was a bitter disappointment in more ways than one. Once again the weather had ruined my plans, but I hadn't time to despair.We had to winterize Cimarron now. We brought in all the outside furniture and ceramic planters. Bill disconnected the water fountains and brought in the pump motors, underwater lights, and hoses. He put the plow blade on the tractor and chained up its tires.

Sonja and I salvaged what we could from the greenhouse and sealed it shut. I wasn't holding out much hope for my few surviving tomatoes, Brussel sprouts, or any other vegetables. Sonja pulled out the carrots with their lovely long green stems, only to find tiny orange roots. "Look Mom, it's sort of a carrot."

"It looks like a candy corn, but it's better than nothing."

Sonja just laughed. "I wish it had more time to grow."

"I know, but it will be good on a salad, if you can find it!"

We filled the bins with firewood and prepped the fireplace. We also closed the vents under the house and cleaned out the tack room. This meant bringing all the saddles and bridle gear into Bill's shop. I turned on the heat in my art studio and checked to make sure all the windows were tightly closed. We were now ready for the storm.

And what a storm it was. The Governor declared a state of emergency for the Great Falls area. We had snow too, but it was not as severe as the pounding they received north of us. After the weekend passed, the snow began to melt, and we returned to our normal daily chores. At least all the winter preparations could be crossed off our checklist.

As I was sitting at my desk, Bill inquired, "In all the storm prep, I forgot to ask, how would you like to celebrate your birthday this Saturday? I can take you out to dinner."

"That might be fun. I've had a craving for crab cakes lately. I do miss having the fresh seafood we enjoyed in Florida."

"I'll do whatever makes you happy."

"Perfect!"

I was looking forward to it. After the disappointment of the previous week, I wanted to have an enjoyable day. I put my work away and told Sonja it was time to feed the horses. Whiskey once again was eating less than he should, and we were having to entice him to finish his meals. Some days he ate well, while other days he ate less than half of his food. He wasn't in any danger yet, but I wanted to keep a close eye on him so I could stay ahead of any problems.

As we came back from the barn, I heard Bill's voice call from the stairway.

"Come on up; I have something to tell you."

Oh, please not again. I met Bill at the top of the stairs.

"Nancy, we have another snowstorm on the way."

"When?"

"Saturday."

"Oh, no—happy birthday to me. Am I allowed to sigh now? It will be a big one."

"Go ahead."

I shook my head instead. "I know we have to make a supply run in Helena. Let's pick up some food I like, and celebrate at home. It'll be fine. Sandy will be here this weekend too, so we can all celebrate together."

"That sounds like a plan."

I smiled and put on a good face, but Bill could see through my façade. He knew how disappointed I was, but said nothing.

The weather held for our day in town. The girls had promised to stay home and clean the house while their Dad and I shopped in Helena. I found everything on our list except for the one thing I most wanted, crab cakes. We were told they were seasonal, and there was not a fresh or frozen one to be found in any of the local stores. On the way home Bill told me we had a couple more errands to accomplish. He took me to a bakery and picked out a carrot cake and had my name and a birthday wish placed on it. He also took me to Higgin's Ranch Supply and steered me toward their Montana Silversmith jewelry case. I tried on earrings and bracelets, and thought about each stunning design. I removed my compact from my purse to use the mirror. As I opened it and held it up to my face, the round mirror fell from it and shattered at my feet.

Bill shook his head and I waited for him to say the inevitable "Tsk, tsk. Seven years of bad luck, Quinn," but he remained mute. I apologized to the salesgirl while she swept up the shards. She was very polite, but I was thoroughly embarrassed.

Bill pointed to the display case and said, "I'm sorry about your compact, but take another few minutes to pick something out for your birthday. Go look at those earrings in the big mirror in the dressing room."

"I'll take you there," the salesgirl offered. "I don't know why we don't have a mirror at this display."

The feather earrings I tried on were a bit heavy for my ears, and of course, I liked the most expensive bracelet in the collection. I didn't know it until I turned the box over and spied the price tag. It was pretty, a delicate cuff style bracelet with cutouts in the design of mountains, and above those shapes, a round piece of turquoise that resembled a blue moon.

Even in the dressing room I could hear the wind buffeting the building. *Please, can't I escape bad weather for just a few minutes so I can enjoy a little shopping?* The wind howled back a definitive no! Now I was feeling rushed. I shrugged and left the dressing room just in time to see snow beginning to fall outside. Bill noticed it too.

"We should get home; the storm is starting early."

"I know; I'm glad Sandy is already at Cimarron."

"We'll come back another day when we have more time."

I thanked the young lady that helped us and rushed out the door without purchasing anything. So much for my birthday present. The drive wasn't too bad. We had navigated worse conditions, but clearly the storm was building. As soon as we got home we began unloading the groceries. Sandy and Sonja cheerfully helped out, which was a bit unusual. Clearly they were excited about something. When everything was unloaded, I sat down on the bottom of the staircase and hugged my little Penny.

"Tired, Quinny?" Bill asked.

"A little."

Before I could say another word, the girls burst around the corner calling out, "Surprise! We couldn't wait until tomorrow!" In their hands, on a pedestal plate, sat a two layer carrot cake.

"I am surprised! Bill are you surprised? This is beautiful, girls; I love it!"

"It's carrot cake!" Sonja proudly announced. "We worked on it all afternoon. We even ran out of eggs, and Sandy drove me to the Mullen Store to get some more."

"Yes," Sandy agreed. "I brought the carrots from town, but I didn't know we needed eggs."

Sonja added, "I've never baked a whole cake before, and I was afraid you might miss the cream cheese that I used for the frosting."

They both said, "Are you surprised?"

"Absolutely, and I have a surprise for you too. Bill, will you show them?"

Bill came into the kitchen with our store bought carrot cake in hand. At first the girls looked disappointed, until they realized it meant more cake for us all. The rest of the evening was uneventful, and I had a lovely birthday the next day. The snow fell, but I was snug and cozy with my family. Sonja's first attempt at cake baking proved to be a great success. It tasted wonderful, though I had to pick out the oversized chunks of carrot that somehow missed the chopper blade during dicing. I found them in the piece that was cut for me, but I considered them a reminder of all her effort on my behalf.

My last, but not least, surprise of the day was the gift Bill had hidden from me. When I opened the box, it revealed the silver bracelet with the landscape design and the little blue moon rising above them. Somehow Bill had managed to purchase it behind my back. I was worried about the price, but he simply said, "It's your birthday. Besides, I got it on sale."

It turned into a wonderful birthday, even without a crab cake. Sometimes the best laid plans can fail, yet everything still turns out alright. What more could you hope for?

52

Till the Cows Come Home—to the Wrong Home

THE CLOUDS GATHERED TOGETHER until they were woven into a single heavy cloak, so that the sun was unable to penetrate the dense murk.

"This wasn't in the forecast," Bill remarked as he stood closer to the fire blazing in the living room. "It was supposed to be clear. Hey, Nancy, did you ever get your lunch?"

"No, I wasn't hungry until now. I'll just make a sandwich."

We heard Sonja shriek from the top of the stairs, "Cows! They're in the corral and surrounding my Wilson!"

"What?"

I ran to the window and saw about thirty cows milling in and around the horse corral. My boys were upset, especially Star. "She's right, Bill. It's an invasion. We need some cow catchers."

Bill peered over my shoulder, seemingly unperturbed. "I see them. Great. I hope there isn't a breech in the fence. Hold on, look, here comes your cow catcher now." One lone horseman was attempting to gather the cattle. I assumed it was Chase, but the cowboy was so bundled up I could not identify him. Bill continued, "I better go down there and see what's going on. Maybe I can help."

Sonja was recovering from a head cold, and I wanted her to stay inside. She'd already gone out earlier to feed the horses against my wishes. She was not happy about my decision and grumbled the entire way back to her room. Bill donned his coat and boots and hurried down to the paddock. Black Angus were milling about and making a lot of racket. The mooing was loud enough to be heard in the next county. I watched as the two men conversed, then Bill and the rider tried to separate our horses from the encroaching cattle by moving our boys toward the round pen. They would not follow them, even after the cowboy dismounted and walked his horse into the pen. Bill knew our boys well, so he decided to bribe them with treats. We kept senior feed in a large storage bin in the tack room. As soon as Bill walked into it, our horses marched through the cows and stood at the door, waiting with anticipation. Not even a herd of Black Angus were going to keep the boys from a snack. Bill returned with three treat pans and the horses dutifully followed him into the round pen. With the boys safely separated from the cows, the rancher began moving his herd out of the corral. Bill pointed in the direction to take the cows, then began his trek home. As soon as he entered the house, I popped down the stairs to quiz him for details.

"What's going on?"

"Well, it's not Chase. It's another rancher I've never met named Josh Appleton. He's been grazing on land further west of us, but some of his cows got lost in the recent snowstorm and wandered onto Chase's land. Appleton rounded them up and is trying to herd them down to the bottom. He wasn't sure where he was, so when he saw our road he started pushing the cows down it, thinking it would link up with his lease. If I had known he was coming I would have closed the corral gate. He's getting them out of there now and will be heading them back down the road. I told him the only place to cross over to his parcel was at the bottom of the hill, so I still have to open the panel at our cattle guard to let them out. I just came back to get the truck 'cause I don't want to walk in front of that herd. "And there's one more thing. Where's Sonja?"

"Upstairs. Do you want me to get her?"

Bill nodded without speaking.

When Sonja came down, Bill began to lecture her. "When I got down there the corral gate was open. That's how the cattle got into it. You were the last person down there and you failed to secure the gate. When I went into the tack room to get some senior feed I found the bin was completely empty. I had to scrape the bottom of the bin for a small handful of feed to split between all three horses. You know it's your responsibility to let me know when the bin is low so we can refill it. It can hold ten bags of feed, so there's no excuse for neglecting it. And this was the worst possible time for it to be empty."

"I'm sorry. I was going to tell you later."

"That doesn't cut it. I've told you before to keep it full. What if one of those cows had gored Wilson while I was wasting time trying to scrape together some feed? What if we'd had a blizzard and couldn't get the truck down there to resupply the bin? You know all this, Sonja."

By now my little angel was welling up with tears.

"Well, Sonja, I'm waiting for an answer," Bill demanded.

The dam broke and Sonja rushed up the stairs crying. Bill shook his head.

"What did you expect?" I asked.

"I expect her to do her job."

"You can take off the colonel's eagles, Bill. This isn't the Air Force, and she's your daughter. I'll bet you never spoke to your men this way?"

"I didn't have to. They did their jobs."

"Well she's still a child who looks up to you."

"She's a teenager with responsibilities. It's not the first time she's ignored them and I've told her as much."

"You're just irritated because everything didn't go the way you planned. Let me talk to her. You need to open the front entrance for the cows."

Bill left and I went upstairs to Sonja's room. I could hear her sobbing in there. I tapped gently on the door. "Honey, can I speak with you?"

Through the sobbing she replied, "What for?"

I entered the room and sat down beside her on the bed. Her face was buried in the pillow. "I understand you're upset, but so is your father. It will pass."

"I screwed up. I didn't mean to."

"I know." I wasn't sure what else to say. "Your father can be a bit demanding sometimes, but he loves you."

"I know that, but I made a mistake and it could have cost one of my horses his life."

"Honey, I think that's unlikely. It was a chain of events that caused the problem. The rancher's cattle wandering, his getting lost, the gate being left open—"

Sonja bolted upright and replied, "Mom, I didn't leave the gate open; I swear it. I'm always careful to close it. Wilson knows how to open the gate."

"And what about the feed bin being empty?"

She lowered her head. "That was my fault."

"I know it can be hard, but mistakes are part of growing up. When you have animals to care for, you take on an important responsibility. You're pretty good at it."

"Not this time."

"Maybe, but have you learned anything from it?"

"Yes, I'll keep the feed bin filled and I'll double-check the gate latch, but I know it was closed."

"No one got hurt, Honey, so learn from it, keep calm, and carry on, as the English say. That reminds me, would you care to have some tea with me?"

"No, Mom. I need to get some feed down to the barn."

"No, you have a cold to recover from first."

"I'm over it."

"You don't sound like you're over it."

"You worry too much. I feel fine. I just have to blow my nose once in a while. I can handle the feed bags."

"We'll discuss it after the cattle are gone and your father returns. If he says it's alright, you can help him load the truck and take the feed down, okay?"

"Okay."

I gave her a big hug and left. I returned to the window to watch the progress. Josh Appleton had mounted his horse and began to circle the bovines, forcing them out of the corral. From the window I could clearly see how well-trained his cow horse was. In a quick trot, Josh's horse obeyed the cues and instinctively moved the cattle into a group. A few cows wanted to stay or eat in the next field, but they were dissuaded and forced back into the line. Once he had them all out of the corral, he closed the gate, but then he started herding them around behind the barn. *What are you doing? You're supposed to take them down the road. There's no way to get to the exit through the back pasture fencing. Once they're in there, they'll scatter into the field and wood line.* I started to go down and warn him, but I saw Bill arrive at the corral in the truck. After a short discussion and much nodding of heads, Josh began to redirect the cows back onto the road. Bill drove ahead of them. I'd have to await his return for a report. I watched the parade begin to march down the road and around the corner, heading away from our mountain. *At least they didn't get to lick my windows this time, but I'm going to have to watch my step at the barn.* It seemed one of the cows was reading my thoughts, for at that moment she stopped, lifted her tail, and relieved herself on the road in front of the corral gate. *That pudding pile is nearly impossible to clean up, you—you old cow!*

A half hour later Bill returned to the house. He flopped down into the chair next to mine.

"You got back just in time; it's starting to snow again."

Bill nodded, "I went down and opened the side panel. The cows were scared to use the exit, but Josh managed to move them through. After we got them to the other side, he asked for my name. When I told him, his face lit up and he said, "I know you. Your dog, Kobi, used to visit us sometimes.'"

"That's right! I remember when his wife called us one day to pick him up after he escaped from his kennel. Remember? I sent her a thank you note in the mail. It was one of the cards I designed; I even signed it in case she wanted to frame it."

"Yeah, I recall something about it." Bill seemed preoccupied with other thoughts.

"I hope this is the end of our bovine convention. We've had a lot of visiting cattle this year. My nose knows it."

"Did you speak to Sonja?"

"Yes, she's feeling better now."

"Then I need to see her."

"Bill—"

"It's alright, Nancy."

He called to her and she came out to the loft, still a bit apprehensive.

"Sonja, why was the feed bin empty. We refilled it only a couple of weeks ago."

"I've been giving feed and supplement to all the horses because of the snow."

"Honey, it costs less to feed them hay, and right now they can still eat grass a while longer. Only Whiskey needs senior feed. The others can have a small amount, but they don't need a steady diet of it and we can't afford such an expenditure. As for the supplements, just give them to Whiskey. I'll try to buy the next batch on sale."

"Dad, I called Higgin's while you were gone. There's a sale on today, but it ends this evening."

I looked at Bill; it was his turn to sigh. "Then I guess you and I had better go get a load. Want to back the truck out?"

Sonja's eyes lit up at the prospect.

"I'll take that as a yes," he added as he tossed her the keys.

I asked, "Can I make you some supper first?"

Bill checked his watch. "No thanks, we have just enough time to get to town. I'll call the store and reserve a half pallet." As he got up to leave I gave him a parting kiss.

"What was that for, lady?"

"Oh, just because I love you and because you're a good father."

"Sometimes I wonder," he responded.

"I don't."

I watched them drive away in the blowing snow. It was a passing squall line, just a light downfall and nothing to be concerned about. The house was quiet now with only Penny and me present. Only the light snowfall and an occasional gust of wind disrupted the silence. I settled into my glider and read a book on house design. Oh, I had so many new ideas I wanted to run past Bill—when he was in the right frame of mind, of course.

53

Brian's Song

I SAW SONJA DASH off as the phone rang. I rarely answered the phone anymore. It was usually for Sonja. She and her friend talked for endless hours. I didn't mind. I was happy she had such a great friendship.

"Mom," I heard her voice over the intercom, "it's for you."

I picked up the receiver and heard the familiar voice of my brother singing off-key. "Happy belated birthday to you, happy belated birthday to you, I should have called sooner, but I for-got to. Hello, Nanc!"

"Hi, Brian, what's going on in the sunny South?"

"Oh, the usual. Just enjoying life. Anything happening up your way?"

"Not too much." I paused before continuing, debating whether or not to burden him with a report on Whiskey's health. It wasn't his concern, but then again, he knew Whiskey and might want to know if anything was wrong rather than be surprised if the worst happened. "I guess I should tell you that Whiskey hasn't been eating regularly again. I talked to the vet, but she still thinks it might be old age catching up with him. Right now it's just wait and see."

"Sorry to hear that, Sis. I know that waiting is the worst part. Please let me know how he does."

"I will, thanks. I'm sorry to sound like a wet blanket."

"No, no problem. Hey, I have a story that might cheer you up a bit."

Brian's stories were always amusing and did distract me, even if only for a few minutes. "You ready for this? A lady came into the dealership today, marched into my office, and told me in no uncertain terms I had to fix her car right away. I asked her what was wrong, and she said every time she touched her brakes she felt like someone was 'bumping me in the rear.' That's exactly what she said, 'bumping me in the rear.' I wasn't quite sure what she meant, but you can imagine the image I was forming in my mind. I tried real hard to keep a poker face, but I think maybe she saw through it because she got pretty angry. I assured her we'd get to the bottom of it."

"That was a poor choice of words."

"Yeah, I realized that a split second after I said it."

"Were you able to calm her down?"

"It took some doing. I told her we'd check the car out immediately while she waited in my office."

"You were being mighty accommodating."

"You didn't see the look on her face. I was afraid not to. Well, I got one of my techs to test-drive it, but he couldn't find anything wrong. She was watching us through my office window, and I have to tell you, Nanc, I could feel those eyes boring right through me. I'm not saying she was crazy, but she was one of those women 'who will not be ignored,' if you catch my drift."

"I know the kind. What did you do?"

"I told the tech to take out the seat and examine it carefully, and I said to do this in plain sight of her so she'd think we were serious about tracking down the problem."

"Did it work?"

Brian started to chuckle. "With a little bit of guile on my part, yes. I went back in the office and gave her a serious look. I said we'd checked the seat and found a loose nut which the tech was tightening up. Her whole demeanor changed, and now she was all smiles. I sweetened the deal by assuring her there would be no charge, and I said just bring it back if it happens again."

"Probably a wise choice. Did you really find a loose nut?"

"Yes, I just didn't tell her it was in her head." Brian got me, and I burst out laughing.

"See, I told you I'd make you laugh. Hey, my lunch break is almost up. I only had a minute to talk today, but a little voice inside told me I should call."

"I'm glad you did."

"Let me leave you with a joke. This ham sandwich walks into a bar and sits down. He orders a beer, and the bartender says, 'Hey, you have to leave. We don't serve food here.' HA! Good clean humor never hurt anyone."

"I completely agree; that was a cute one. I'll tell it to the girls."

"Gotta keep you laughing. Talk to you later, bye."

54

Penny Candy

WE HAD DESCENDED THE mountain pass on our tri-weekly sojourn to Helena. I say tri-weekly, though our goal had always been to "try weekly". Regrettably, the latter case was becoming increasingly problematic. As we entered the outskirts of town I retrieved our schedule from my purse and read the top line. "Orthodontics is our first stop after we pick up Sandy."

Sonja moaned, "When am I going to get my braces off?"

"Only when the orthodontist and dentist both agree they should come off," I responded. "We don't want a repeat of what happened to Sandy." I was referring to the extended time Sandy had to wear her braces. The orthodontist removed them prematurely. We only discovered this fact when Sandy went for her next cleaning. Our dentist informed us the teeth were not yet in an ideal position, so the braces had to go back on. I was not going to allow this mistake to happen again. Before Sonja's braces came off, I wanted confirmation from both doctors that the time was right.

"I'm tired of them. I wish I'd never gotten them. I don't care how my teeth look."

"You say that now, but you aren't considering that they'd continue to shift and cause you greater problems in the future if left untreated. One day this will all be over and you'll have a beautiful smile and healthy teeth."

"That doesn't make me happy," Sonja responded.

Bill jumped into the conversation. "Spending money on braces doesn't make me happy either, so we're even."

"And when it's finally over I'm going to miss watching the home improvement shows in the waiting room." I was only partly joking. I actually did look forward to the decorating and remodeling programs. Where we lived it was impossible to get television reception except by satellite. There was little we wanted to watch and the cost was so high that we eschewed it and never looked back. We still had the internet and mail order DVDs, the advantage of which was that we could pick and choose what we wanted to see and when we wanted to see it. This extended to music and old time radio programs from the 1930s to 1950s. Of course, each of us also read a great deal, and our home was practically a library of books, records, CDs, VHS tapes, and DVDs.

We picked up Sandy and went directly to the orthodontist. Bill no sooner parked the car than both girls jumped out and ran into the building. "What's their hurry?" I asked.

"Maybe they want to watch the Disney channel."

Bill and I went over our list and snuggled Penny into her bed. "You be a good girl. We won't be here too long." Penny looked up at me from under her blanket, her big brown eyes pleading with me not to leave her alone. "Oh, Penny, you'll be fine. When we get back I'll give you a treat." The sound of her favorite word perked her up and I saw her tail fanning back and forth under the blanket.

We went into the building and I settled down to watch the Home Network. The two appointments lasted less than an hour, enough time for me to find out if the homeowners were going to love it or list it. "Oh, they decided to keep it. That's a mistake. They should have bought the place with the big back yard next to the creek."

"I guess they aren't country folk," Bill added with a wink.

As we headed back to the car I discussed our next destination with Bill. "We have Wal-Mart, Lowe's, and COSTCO."

"The usual suspects," Bill replied as he opened the door and got in.

"Hello? What's this?" His voice was agitated. "Look at this. Penny tore into the snack bag."

"She's never done that before. What was in it?"

"Just granola and protein bars."

"Let me see the wrappers."

Bill searched about until he located the remains of a shredded protein bar wrapper and handed it to me. I read the ingredient list with alarm. "It has chocolate in it. That's deadly for dogs."

"Don't sound the alarm just yet, Quinn, there's hardly any chocolate in them. A little won't hurt her."

"Any chocolate is harmful, Bill. How much did she eat?"

I watched him gather all the wrappers. The expression on his face turned somber when he said, "She ate four of them. This could be a problem."

"I'll call the vet." I fumbled for my cell phone as Bill started the car and pulled out of the parking lot.

"I'm going to head straight to the vets. Find out if they're open. If they aren't, I'll try one of the other clinics."

Sandy and Sonja were busy scolding Penny while taking turns holding her in their arms. She was befuddled by all the sudden attention, so I told the girls to watch her reactions. I didn't want her slipping into a comma unnoticed. As I dialed the phone I wondered if we were making a mistake driving all the way across town when there were closer vets. On the other hand, none of them had ever treated Penny before and knew nothing of her history. It was a calculated risk, and I prayed we were not making a mistake. I made contact with the office. Thank heavens they had not closed for lunch. The assistant looked up the brand of protein bar and informed me that it did indeed contain a good deal of cocoa. She quizzed me about how long it had been since ingestion and told us to get there as quickly as possible. They would be ready for us.

Bill drove like Mario Andretti, darting though traffic. All the time I watched the clock on the dashboard and ran the mental calculations. We had been inside the orthodontist's office for about forty-five minutes, so nearly an hour had now passed. *When did she eat the chocolate? Was it right after we left her alone?* If we could get Penny to the vet within an hour, her chances for survival were much greater. Penny was quite chipper and happy and not showing any ill effects—yet. Of course we hit every red light in the city, causing a delay in our mission. The minutes ticked by and I felt the tension mount. *My Penny Person, she has to be alright.*

We waited for another traffic light to change. No one was speaking; we were all lost in our own thoughts. I could see the strain on everyone's faces as each person dealt with their fear privately. At last we pulled into the vet's parking lot, scooped up Penny, and raced through the front door. We made it with less than five minutes to spare. I gave the chewed wrappers to the receptionist, while an assistant took Penny into a back room. She tried to comfort us by saying, "I believe you got her here in time. You're sure it's been about an hour? If it's longer, we may not be able to help her."

"I'm sure of it," but my voice was shaky. *Am I certain or is it wishful thinking?* All of us nodded in agreement. *I hope I'm right.*

"We'll give her something to bring it all up. We have to induce vomiting. The chocolate is probably still in her stomach and hasn't gotten further into her digestive track. She's going to be sick for a long time. Can you leave her with us for a few hours? We don't close until five."

Bill agreed it was a reasonable solution, but I wanted to stay with Penny. I offered to sit with her or in the reception room.

"That won't be necessary. If there's any complications, we'll call you straight away." The receptionist was right, but I felt like I was abandoning my little baby. I reluctantly agreed. The young lady rested her hand on my arm. "I believe you got her here in time. It would be a different story if most of the day had passed. That happens sometimes. I think Penny will be okay. You can pick her up soon."

We left the vet's office to continue our errands. I tried focusing on our shopping, but found myself constantly glancing at my watch. It was hard for me to concentrate. I knew Penny was in good hands. I had read about giving hydrogen peroxide to animals who had ingested poisons, so I was familiar with the procedure for emptying their stomachs. The cell phone did not ring, so I presumed all was well. It was approaching 5:00 p.m. and we were headed to the clinic to see how Precious Pup was doing.

"How is Penny?" I asked with some trepidation while standing at the reception desk.

My fears were immediately dispersed when I heard a resounding, "She was awesome! We couldn't believe how much she had consumed, but it's gone now. None of it got down in her digestive tract."

All of us were elated.

"We'll bring Penny out. She recovered very quickly. She's quite a remarkable dog."

I heard the familiar scuffling sound of tiny toenails tapping across the tile floor and knew Penny was scrambling down the hall to her family. She burst around the corner with her tail spinning full throttle. One would never have known what she had just endured. She jumped into our waiting arms and greeted each one of us with a happy lick. Now we had to settle a hefty bill, but it was worth the money. Our Penny was safe and healthy. Even Bill did not complain as he paid the fee. As for Penny, she was still looking for that promised treat.

55

The Body Electric

I STOOD ALONE ON our covered balcony and stared at the fleeting orange sky. It was quickly consumed by clouds composed of various shades of deep blue and gray. They moved swiftly eastward, blown by a strong wind through the wide expanse of the heavens. Yet the illusion they projected was one of such closeness to the Earth that it appeared all I had to do was reach out to touch them and they would halt. But I could not reach them, nor hold them in my grasp. They continued their journey over the Divide, unimpeded by my actions or my thoughts. Here and there jagged streaks of light slashed through the cracks like massive search lights. Their soft glow warmed the flowers and grass for a moment before moving on to greener pastures. I could feel the electricity in the air and smell the rain that had yet to fall. The beams of light grew dimmer until the inky clouds were all that enshrouded us. Rain began to fall and the wind grew stronger.

I had been watching this drama unfold for the past half hour, powerless to stop it, mesmerized by its strength, swallowed up by its grandeur, suffocated by its intoxicating beauty. Splashes of water pelted my face and broke the enchantment. I called to my family for a video camera. I wanted to record the event and share it with others before it reached its zenith. Sonja heard me from the adjoining loft and quickly produced both camera and tripod. The thunder began to roll with the wind, and the house shuddered. I fumbled momentarily with the controls before filming the light show. The visual aura was matched by the sounds of wind through the leaves, the drumroll of rain on a metal roof, and the boom of nature's artillery. The thunder was different from any I'd heard before. It roared with ferocity through the trees and echoed off the rocky cliffs. The rain pounded harder and harder until it reached hurricane force. I could no longer hear myself think. It was overpowering and more than a little unnerving, yet strangely exhilarating, as the vibrations pierced my body. Mother Nature was now displaying her full fury as the rain turned to hail. The sound became deafening and I was forced to go inside and shut the sliding glass door.

I had never before experienced this much lightning and gale on the mountain. Every few seconds a brilliant flash would sting my eyes, but I could not turn away from the amazing beauty of each cracking white line. Its zigzag stripes fanned out like branches on a tree, and the almost instantaneous booms rattled the house, reminding me just how close these strikes were. One should be wary of lightning storms, but I am not, despite having lived in two homes that were struck by lightning, including one which caught fire. Yet to this day I'm still unafraid of storms; I just have a healthy respect of them.

The tempest was now ebbing and moving on toward the Pass where it would soon frighten livestock and small children before crossing the Divide. I returned to my perch on the balcony where the camera was still faithfully recording the fading fury. The sun had not completely set and the clouds continued to drift away. Now a fog was settling in between the rolling hills and valleys of the mountain peaks. The eerie yellow-orange glow returned to the skyline, competing with the mist that arose from the Earth like primordial steam. It had a soft ethereal quality, making the panorama appear slightly out of focus. The lightning had waned and the atmosphere began to calm. That strange feeling of electric currents in the air was rapidly fading. This wasn't a typical storm that one watches passively; it had been an all-consuming physical experience. As quickly as it had arrived, it was gone. I could still hear the distant bands of thunder and a gentle tapping of soft rain on the metal roof above my head. The drama was over and the storm took its last bow before disappearing over the mountains to the east.

In its aftermath the creek below the house filled quickly and the water overflowed its banks along the journey to the river beyond. It was one more reminder to me that the West was still very wild.

56

Picture Perfect

THE CLOUDS GATHERING IN the sky raced easterly, high above my head, blown by an incessant western wind. I sat on a large boulder above the front meadow and thought about the fickle nature of Montana weather. I knew at any moment I could experience rain, hail, snow, or any combination of the three, as atmospheric conditions changed while the clouds passed over our mountain on their way to the Continental Divide. With so much intense beauty surrounding us, my interest in photography had rapidly grown. I looked at the digital camera in my lap and realized my skills as a photographer had come a long way. I recalled the Kodak Instamatic camera I used in my youth which required film cartridges that snapped into the back of the unit. It then had to be wound until a click indicated the film was taut and aligned with the lens and aperture. There were few controls or adjustments I could make aside from mounting a flash cube for low light photos. Luck was the primary factor in photo quality. Then it was off to the processing center for a week or two before I knew whether or not I had any worthwhile prints. Normally there were only a few photos from the role that were worth keeping. The rest tended to be blurry, muddied, or so distant as to be useless. One had to pay for all viewable prints, or as the photo center manager, Mr. Kruger, always liked to say, "They're commercially acceptable." I think this meant they weren't completely black.

When I later acquired my first 35mm camera I learned about F-stop (lens speed), focus, lighting, perspective, and zoom. I even learned how to develop film with the help of a friend who was a professional photographer. The digital world may not be as glamorous as developing film in a dark room, but it certainly is far easier and faster, making for a much more enjoyable experience. I get a devilish satisfaction each time I review and delete the photos that in earlier times would be labeled commercially acceptable. Take that, Mr Kruger!

Once again I gazed at the expansive breathtaking view before me and wondered what early settlers and American Indians thought of it. The image before me could easily have been one of those captured in shades of black, grey, and white by noted Western photographer, Evelyn Cameron. She was a pioneer who came from Britain to eastern Montana in 1894 with her husband Ewen to begin a new life as horse ranchers. They established the Eve Ranch near the town of Fallon. It was a long and arduous journey, fraught with the same difficulties we faced, but without the aid of any modern conveniences or even a decent road. They were entering an environment unlike anything in their previous experience. I can only imagine how they felt when they reached the prairie badlands of eastern Montana with its surreal, mushroom-like sandstone rock formations and gumbo clay. Lacking any notable humidity, it is a dry and windy climate, punctuated by the occasional petrified tree to match the ghostly landscape. The forces of nature have created buttes of various heights that sternly overlook the harsh and sparsely populated environment. The passing of time has worn away portions of the weaker sediment, creating bizarre formations that point upwards toward the unending sky.

There were only a few ranches in the area, each surviving on the limited sources of water and the ability for their cattle, horses, and sheep to graze on the open range. It would seem unlikely that people could survive without much vegetation, but nature provided some vital compensations. Bands of coal abounded in the nearby hills, and the pioneers dug through the soft sediment to retrieve enough for fuel. Wildlife was abundant, so meat was available for the skilled hunter.

The stark silence was only broken by the call of a wild animal or the whispering winds, which could change into a howl without warning. The terrain was desolate, but it held an unusual kind of beauty. The red and orange colored streaks of clay and rock decorated the buttes like ribbons on a precious gift. It must have been a welcome sight against the seemingly limitless expanse of blue sky.

As with most homesteaders, life was a constant struggle. Whether sleeping on the frozen ground, hunting for food, building their first living quarters, or facing wild animals, weather, and disease, nothing in their aristocratic upbringing could have prepared these two members of the English gentry for their new life. Yet they did not shy away from such hardships, not the Camerons. Evelyn actually seemed to thrive on the new challenges.

Try as they did, the elements proved to be too much and the ranch failed, but the Camerons remained. Evelyn turned to photography as a way to provide an income. She was an educated and intellectual woman whose diaries are sprinkled with phrases in German, French, and Italian. She initially shunned her new social circle, but, perhaps serendipitously, photography provided her a unique opportunity to record local social events without fear of rejection. Over time Evelyn was accepted by the women in the nearby communities, and they often looked to her for help and advice. Her story reminded me of how circumstances can change for the benefit of everyone involved. While reading her biography, I could not help but notice some of the parallels between our lives. I don't dare to say that my struggle to learn and adapt equals hers; it does not, but I did discover we shared many of the same ideas and concerns. Her experiences offered the reward of a new way of living. It was a test of her grit and determination that eventually led to a life of satisfaction and happiness. I hope my story ends as well as Evelyn's did.

57

Doe–Hay–Me

IT WAS A WELCOME relief from winter's daily chores to sit in my rocking chair for a few minutes and read a book about architecture and decorating. Each glossy page contained photos describing the different styles of structures, indulging my fascination with the subject. The thick pages felt good between my fingers. As I gently turned each one I caught a faint scent of printer's ink. All was quiet. I sipped my tea and dreamed of the homes presented in the large hardback book.

"Feeding time!" Sonja announced as she strode by my chair. "I'll take care of it, Mom. I love seeing the boys." She passed by with hardly a glance in my direction and continued down the stairs.

"Okay, thanks," I called after her as she hurried away. A gust of wind hit the house and I was suddenly more grateful for Sonja's independent spirit and love of our horses. However, after a few minutes my mothering instincts prodded me out of my chair. I set my book aside and walked over to the big front windows to check on Sonja. I noted with satisfaction that she was performing her duties undisturbed and the horses were quite content. However, I realized they weren't alone. A petite doe was gently stepping away from the horses' water fountain. She stood in the stall only ten feet from our friendly equines as if a shy member of the herd. I glanced around the corrals and front meadow, expecting to see her companions, but she was completely alone. I felt bad for this little gal; the cold weather was so hard on the deer, and I didn't like the idea that she was friendless. As Sonja emerged from the tack room, the doe scampered under the corral panel and disappeared into the tree line. When Sonja returned home I asked her if she had seen the doe in the paddock.

"No, I didn't. How could I miss that?"

"So you didn't see any deer at all?"

"No Mom, just the boys." Sonja shrugged her shoulders and continued to her room to resume her studies. I returned to reading my book, but my inquisitive nature never liked an unsolved mystery. I repeatedly returned to pondering the question of why this dainty doe was without a companion.

A cold snap was predicted for our area and it soon came to pass. The temperatures dropped below zero, so we checked on the horses every time one of us passed by the windows. I stood by the dining room fireplace warming my backside while watching the horses huddled together, insulating each other from the wind and cold. They stood in their shelter as the wind whipped by them. I could feel the house shudder with each gust. *At least they're out of the wind; that must help them, but it all looks so miserable.* I knew the horses were bred to withstand the cold. All the wildlife had their own innate ways of surviving the climate, but these thoughts were providing me little solace. It was simply a harsh time of year for all creatures.

I continued to gaze out the windows when I noticed some movement at the tree line. There she was again, the little doe. She walked to the paddock and crawled under the pipe panels, then proceeded to the feeder and hay storage area. Because of the large fir tree in the corral, I lost sight of her, but watched with anticipation for her next move. After a few moments I spotted her at the edge of the feeder, nibbling hay from the ground. She looked quite at home, and after a few more bites she walked over to the horses and stood beside them. Wilson, Star, and Whiskey graciously shared their food and water with her, and I suppose they understood her need for some company. Perhaps she had found a surrogate family after all. This made me feel better about her solitary life. She was so young, it was clear she needed some help and a respite from her lack of companionship.

When the wind subsided she wandered around with the horses for some time, then I saw her walk through the open gate and into the front yard with our three horses in tow! This further lifted my spirits, watching as she pushed the snow around with her nose, searching for bits of grass. She looked like the smallest horse of them all. *This little gal thinks she's a horse! We have a new herd member. I guess I'm not the only one who collects strays. My horses take them in too.*

Our smallest herd member.

58

White Lightning

"WHAT WOULD YOU LIKE for supper, Sonja?"

"Pizza."

"What else?"

"Mac and cheese."

"How about a salad?"

"Mom, I need real food."

"Salad is real food."

"So's hamburger, only more so."

"Okay, you can have a hamburger, but no bun, and I want you to eat some green beans."

"It's a deal."

I was becoming concerned about Sonja's diet. She was eating more and more like a Montana rancher, but without the caloric workload to match it. My not so subtle hints failed to have the desired effect. At least I had convinced her not to wear her hat inside. I turned and called upstairs to ask Bill what he wanted for supper.

"I'm having air tonight."

"What?"

"I'm not eating, Honey."

"If you're not eating honey, what are you eating?"

"Ha-ha-ha."

"See, you don't think I'm funny, but I am."

"Don't give up your day job, Babe."

"So I guess it's just Sonja and me."

"I," spoke the voice from above.

"What?"

"It's Sonja and I."

"I thought you weren't eating."

"Oh, you are a witty one. Yo-har, yo-har, yo-har."

"I told you so."

Supper was over by 6:15, and I reminded Sonja it was time to let Whiskey out of the round pen. "He should be through with supper by now."

"Right, Mom. I want to finish cleaning the kitchen first."

"That can wait. I think it's starting to snow." I turned on the outside lights and witnessed a torrent of heavy snow mixed with sleet. The wind began to gust and rattle the house. "You'd better hurry."

Sonja put on her coat and muck boots. The voice from above spoke again. "Take the flashlight from the kitchen drawer. I just put fresh batteries in it today."

"Okay, Dad."

Sonja quickly departed for the barn. I called up to Bill, "What's the weather report?"

"They're predicting a flash snowstorm, over a half inch of downfall for the next hour, then it ends for the night. Right now the winds are gusting to twenty-six miles per hour." Bill was interrupted by a flash of lightning and a loud boom. "Did you see that?"

"A thunder snowstorm? I've never heard of such a thing. Is Sonja alright?"

I heard Bill get up from his computer and walk to the picture windows. "The barn lights are on. I can see her getting Whiskey out of the round pen. She's okay."

"I wish she'd hurry back before it happens again." There was another flash of lightning, but the boom was delayed for ten seconds."

"That one was a good two miles away, Nancy. No need to worry."

That was easier said than done. "My girl is in a thunder snowstorm with lightning. How is that even possible?"

"Check the outside temperature."

"It's registering thirty-eight degrees."

"That's what I thought. It's just warm enough to be a thunderstorm. We've had them before, at least once that I can recall. It's pretty rare."

"Well I don't remember it. Is she on her way back yet?"

"I can't tell." Bill came down the stairs and went to the front door. "Hold Penny. I don't want her going out in this."

"How? She had a bath earlier and her collar's still off."

"Hold her by the ears."

I rolled my eyes at the thought, then held Penny next to me with my hands placed firmly around her shoulders. Bill stepped out onto the front porch. "It's like a blizzard, near whiteout conditions."

"I'm glad we're not driving in it. What a freakish storm."

Bill stepped back inside just as Penny broke loose from my hold. He closed the door before she could investigate further. Bill turned on the front deck lights and said to me, "She'll be back any minute. It's not cold outside."

Sure enough, Sonja came stomping in a minute later. The entire brim of her hat was filled with snow and hail. "Well that was exciting. Poor Star jumped up at the first flash of lightning. I think the thunder's what actually scared him."

"What about Whiskey and Wilson?"

"Wilson never stopped eating at the feeder. He hardly noticed it."

"Did Whiskey eat his supper?"

"All of it."

"That's good. Where are they now?"

"They're all hanging out by the hay bin. They're okay, Mom."

Just then the snowing stopped and turned to light rain, which passed within a minute. It was over. Bill looked at Sonja and shook his head. "You have great timing, kid. You just barely got to enjoy the brunt of the storm. Now you can finish cleaning the kitchen."

59

Saving My Whiskey

IT WAS SUPPERTIME FOR the horses, so I joined Sonja on her twice daily trek to the barn. She distracted Wilson and Star with two pans of treats while I placed Whiskey's feed dish in the center of the round pen and encouraged him to come get it. I was concerned by Sonja's morning report that Whiskey was having difficulty walking. I kept a careful watch on him, but instead of traveling the ten yards from the corral to the round pen, Whiskey simply stood his ground and trembled. I could plainly see the pain on his face and knew something was seriously wrong. Despite my coaxing, our little Morgan refused to budge. His age was catching up with him. He was now thirty-three years old and had exceeded the life span of the average horse by three to eight years. If his legs or feet were failing him now, there was nothing anyone could do about it. Fear gripped me at the thought of what might have to be done. His sudden decline in health was hard to watch and I desperately wanted to help him. I picked up the dish and carried it to the tree where he stood. I placed the bowl at his feet and murmured some words of encouragement while I rubbed his ears. It was all I could do to keep from crying. I didn't want Whiskey or Sonja to know what I was thinking.

"We'll have to watch him for the next few days and see if his condition improves any," I told Sonja. She just nodded without replying.

She may have had the same thoughts about him, but she kept them to herself.

Over the next three days we watched his appetite wane. He moved with difficulty, making one short painful step after another to get water. Instead of remaining in the corral, he found solace fifty yards away among the leafless Quaking Aspen trees. He was isolating himself from Wilson and Star. Winter had fully set in and the winds were wicked. They whipped the trees where Whiskey had sought refuge. He was in a shallow depression, out of sight, which worried me, but it offered him some protection from the frigid blasts of air. Twice a day Sonja took him food and water, but each time she returned to report that he was consuming less and less of each. He was down to three pounds of meal a day, an insufficient amount to sustain him. It was time to seek the vet's advice. This I truly dreaded.

Our regular vet, Jeannie, was unavailable. I had to deal with a new partner in their practice, Robert Jackson. After I explained Whiskey's symptoms and expressed my concern about his emotional state, his first thought was it might be colic. Even he agreed it seemed an unlikely diagnosis, and so he offered to come out that afternoon for a more complete examination.

The road to the stable was still passable, and we met him down at the corral. Robert was older than the other vets in the practice, and had the demeanor and confidence that comes with age and experience. He began with a cursory examination which started at Whiskey's head, continued to his stomach, then down his legs to his feet. He held the foot and probed it while he spoke. "His right foot feels warm, like a laminitis condition. Has he ever foundered?"

"No, his health has been wonderful. The farrier says he has excellent feet. We've never known him to have any inflammatory problems."

Robert released the foot and stood up. "His heart and lungs sound fine and his temperature is normal, but I wish I heard more gut sounds. However, you're right; this isn't colic."

"He hasn't been eating as much as he normally does, but he's still producing manure."

Robert removed the stethoscope from his ears and looked me in the eye. "He's very old you know."

I just nodded my head in agreement. My knees felt weak and a wave of anxiety passed through me. I gripped the side of the corral panel with my right hand and found myself being surprisingly candid as I suddenly blurted out, "Is he dying?"

There was a long silence, at least it seemed long – interminably long to me, before Robert replied, "I think he's showing his age and may be shutting down. I don't really think I can do anything for him. I could give him a little pain medication and see if that makes him more comfortable, unless you want me to…do something else."

I felt a little sick. "I don't think he is suffering that much. Do you?"

"No, probably not, but understand he is very old."

"Then I want to try to help him. Let's give him the medicine and see if it works. I won't let him suffer and linger, but I won't give up on him this quickly. He wants to live. He's trying; I can feel it. Let's give him that chance."

"I think that's reasonable. I'll give him an injection of an anti-inflammatory and leave you some Butte pain medication. Give him one gram a day. I'll be on call this weekend, so let me know if you need us or have any questions."

Whiskey received his injection with dignity. I felt my heart go out to my elderly gentleman. I rubbed his shoulders and silently sent a prayer to heaven for his recovery.

The next day Whiskey showed some improvement. He was still unable to walk much, but he had managed to eat a few extra pounds of food. While I found this encouraging, it was not what I was hoping for. He was still hurting. What was worse is he was rejecting his medicine. We decided to disguise it in an apple. Bill cut a plug from the apple, spread in the paste, and replaced the plug. "That should do it," he said with satisfaction. "He won't be able to taste or smell it. Take this to him, Sonja." He handed the treat to her and she was out the door in a flash.

Sonja returned from the barn looking forlorn and speaking with frustration. "He spit it out! He smelled it immediately and refused to eat it. Star and Wilson wanted it, but not Whiskey."

"So let's try plan B," Bill replied. He pulled out a small packet of instant flavored oatmeal from the cabinet. "This tastes like apples. Let's see if he'll eat an oatmeal ball." He added some water to make a paste, mixed in the medicine, and rolled it in his hands.

"It's a masterpiece," I declared. "Sonja, take this to Whiskey and set it in his bowl. Act like you don't really want him to eat it. If you force it on him, he'll get suspicious and turn away."

Sonja was somber. "I'll let you know if he eats it, but he's being difficult. I don't know if he will."

I watched her from the loft windows and saw Whiskey take a bite and begin to spit it out.

When she came through the door, I was waiting. "Did he ingest any?"

"I think so; he got most of it. I looked on the ground to make sure."

"Good, but we'll have to come up with a new idea for tomorrow."

I went to my glider, snuggled under a blanket, and began to rock and think. I let the rhythmic motion calm my mind. *What is Whiskey's favorite treat other than apples? What would make him eat without suspicion?* My thoughts were scattered and seemed to jump back and forth as I rocked in the chair. Then suddenly it came to me. *Peppermint, the answer is peppermint.* I knew Whiskey could no longer chew a hard mint, however, if I dosed his oatmeal ball with peppermint extract, he wouldn't be able to smell the medication, so he might be more inclined to eat it.

My idea proved successful. The following day Whiskey ate his medicine with relish and we began to see him improve once again. For five days in a row he was walking and eating more food than he had in weeks. I was thrilled we had turned a corner. Whiskey was on the mend. I could finally relax and get back to the more mundane everyday chores. Then the next morning brought news that buckled my confidence.

"Mom," Sonja said quietly, "Whiskey couldn't walk this morning."

I hurried to the window to see for myself. He was trying to take a step, but he threw his head up in pain. He gingerly put his foot back down and pushed his front feet forward, resting his weight on his back heels. He stood like a rocking horse, but did not move. For reasons I didn't understand, the medicine had stopped working. His stance concerned me enough to call the vet, but nobody answered. I decided not to leave a message. I wanted to speak to someone in person. A phone recording is so easily ignored or lost in the daily shuffle.

"I'll keep calling, Sonja; don't worry."

"I'll be in my room," Sonja replied, dejected.

I too was discouraged, but my coping mechanism required that I do something. I started to research the problem on my computer. I read through page after page of possible medications and side-effects. I reviewed natural remedies. I studied skeletal diagrams, hoping to pinpoint the source of his pain and why it had suddenly occurred. I was quite bleary-eyed a few hours later and decided to check my messages. It was a pleasure to see a text from a new friend in Australia. Bonnie enjoyed reading my books and had contacted me through one of my social media accounts. Over time we had developed a lively correspondence that led to friendship. When I told her about Whiskey's decline, she was very supportive and sympathetic. I continued to read through her comments and felt encouraged when she mentioned a specific medication that had helped her horse with arthritis. I immediately replied and we began messaging each other. My fingers were typing so fast, they were starting to ache. I glanced at the clock and realized I needed to try calling the vet again. I asked Bonnie to stand by. This time I was able to reach Robert and I quickly explained the situation. "I'm concerned about Whiskey. The Butte you prescribed as an anti-inflammatory isn't working anymore. He had relief for about five days, but now he is barely walking again. He clearly has pain in his feet. A friend suggested a medication called Previcox. I would like to discuss the possibility of prescribing it for Whiskey."

"I've heard of it. It's been used successfully on dogs, however there's recently been a formula made for horses."

"Is it effective"?

"It's not as harsh on the digestive track, but it won't cure Whiskey."

"Will it bring his pain level down? If we can get his pain under control I think he will eat more and walk better."

"It might work, but there is a risk involved with any medicine. It could lead to organ failure or other problems. I don't like to write prescriptions unless it's absolutely necessary."

"I can't let him go on like this; I have to do something. I would like to give this medication a try."

"I suppose I can prescribe it. You do understand that I'm only doing it to make him comfortable."

"That's what I want too. He may or may not respond to it, but I think he deserves this chance. Right now he's uncomfortable rather than suffering great pain. I'm willing to come and pick up the Previcox today if you'll leave it at the desk for me. I can be there in about 30 minutes."

"It'll be there. Give him a half tablet each day. I'll give you eight pills; that's about two weeks' worth of treatment."

"Thank you, I'm very grateful for your help." I hung up the phone feeling hopeful again. I quickly sent an email to Bonnie. "The vet agreed to the prescription; we are leaving now to pick it up. Our rescue mission is underway! Many thanks and a big hug for your suggestion."

Three days later my dismay was rising again. I watched Whiskey from the loft windows. It was obvious he was feeling miserable as he stood still in the middle of the corral, rarely moving, and only with great difficulty. The miracle drug was not working and time was running out.

"What are you looking at, Quinny?"

It was the wrong question for that moment in time. I couldn't hold myself together another minute. I burst into tears. In between my sobs I managed to voice my thoughts as I clung to Bill. "The miracle drug isn't working. I don't think I can save him this time," I cried. "I know he's old, but he should fall asleep on a warm sunny day and not wake up. I don't him want to die like this in the middle of winter. I don't want to have to decide for him when his life is over. I may have to end his suffering, but mine is just beginning."

Bill comforted me in his arms while I moistened his shirt with my tears. "I'm sorry, Nancy; I've been thinking about it too." He lifted my chin with his hand and looked directly into my eyes. "You won't be making this decision alone; I'll be there to help. I am concerned about the frozen ground. Before we do anything else, I need to test it with the backhoe. I know you want him buried on the property, but if the ground is too hard, I'm not sure what to do."

Bill was right and being practical. This same idea had crossed my mind as well. While I cleaned my face and dried my eyes, a new thought occurred to me. *I can call the vet to ask about a different medication, but maybe I'm looking at this all wrong. If the pain is in his feet, I should call the farrier. Wilson has shoes for sore feet. Maybe Whiskey is having a laminitic episode. Perhaps some orthopedic shoes will help.*

My mood immediately brightened. I had to leave a message for my farrier, Brant, on his cell phone. I described the problem and asked him to return my call as soon as possible. I left a message on the vet's phone as well. For the next few hours I felt like I was on hold. Hillary returned my call. She had worked with Whiskey in the past and remembered him. I quickly gave her an update and asked for an alternative medication.

"Nancy, Whiskey is an old horse. We can't do anything more for him. I won't authorize another medication."

"I've been reading about other options. Perhaps if we tried -"

"We won't write another prescription for him."

I was silent for a moment. "What do you think of the possibility of some kind of corrective shoes? I've been investigating the idea and I called my farrier."

"I understand you want to exhaust every possibility for him, but I wouldn't use the farrier just yet. You can try a boot on him. They're sold at Higgin's Ranch Supply, but they're spendy."

I thanked her and was hanging up the phone when another call came through. It was Brant. I described the situation and the vet's recommendation. Brant had reservations of his own.

"Nancy, I doubt those boots will work. It's a moot point anyway.

Higgin's stopped carrying them, so you'd have to special order them. It may be possible he needs corrective shoes. If so, I can fit him with a pair. I can make it out tomorrow if you like."

I was ecstatic, but tried to remain calm. Perhaps all was not lost. I shared the news with Bill. "This will work," I told him. "I'm going to save our Whiskey. I'm tired of everyone giving up on him because he's old. He can still have some quality of life, even if it's only a year or two. I have a plan!"

"That's my girl. I'm glad you didn't give up; I like seeing you back in the fight. It must be the Irish in you."

My hope was rising again. Tomorrow was another day and another opportunity to save my Whiskey.

60

Lucky Horseshoes

PRIOR TO BRANT'S ARRIVAL I had Bill pull our truck out of the garage bay so Whiskey could be examined inside, away from the wind and snow. It was a more comfortable setting, but despite my heavy coat, I remained cold. I kept my hands in my pockets, trying to warm them while our farrier studied Whiskey. Brant appeared to be unfazed by the weather. For him this was a pleasant improvement. Bill and Sonja appeared equally immune. Was everyone but I a penguin?

Brant examined Whiskey's posture, his painful movements, his legs, and then his hooves. Sonja and I stood by silently and awaited his assessment. Brant was quiet and methodical as he handled Whiskey's feet. At last he spoke. "Nancy, I found the pain source. It's not the bottom of his feet. It's higher up in the toe. I'm not making any promises, but I think he's having a laminitic episode. It's not real serious yet. In fact it's rather mild, like a pebble in your boot. I think corrective shoes will get him walking again. Keep him on the medicine for a few more days. Sometimes Previcox takes a week to work. Meanwhile, let's see how he does with these new shoes."

"Do you think he can get better? Do horses recover from this problem?"

"Yes, they can. I can't make any promises. We don't know what flared this up in the first place, but the bones in his feet have not moved or collapsed. I believe we caught it in time."

I could have kissed him. "Brant, thank you for helping us. I didn't know where else to turn."

"I know how you feel. The vets often give up on old horses way too soon. Their first thought is to euthanize them. Look at him; he's at a good weight, his ribs aren't showing, but most importantly, look at his eyes. He's bright and alert. He's in there and he hasn't given up." Brant patted Whiskey on the neck as he turned to me and sincerely added, "I'm glad you didn't either. Anytime you have a foot issue, call me."

With the tension now broken, Bill excused himself and returned to the house to calm Penny. She was in the loft window staring down at us with envy. Oh, how she wanted to be part of the action. Sonja and I remained to assist Brant. We watched and listened with fascination as he described the shoe he was going to custom fit to both of Whiskey's front feet. "This pad is made out of a thick heavy duty plastic-resin material. I can shape it to relieve the pressure on the front feet when Whiskey is standing. It will help him walk too, and provide comfort when he has to pivot or make a turn. I'll put screws in the bottom to give him some traction on the ice."

"Like snow tires," I beamed.

"Exactly."

Brant went to work grinding the shoes to his own specifications. His trailer had everything he needed to perform his duties, including a forge, sander, and all kinds of hand tools, along with salves and a myriad of horse shoes.

My mood was improving by the minute. "Wow, Whiskey, you're a lucky boy. I would like a pair of custom made boots too."

Brant overheard me and grinned, but remained focused on his work. I was surprised to see that Whiskey's orthopedic shoes were being screwed into his front hooves, rather than the more typical nailing.

"This will provide him some stability," Brant shouted over the whirring of the screw gun. During the entire process Whiskey was gentle and patient. When he finished, Brant patted his ears. "Such a good boy, you're always so easy to work with. Now, let's see if you can walk."

As Sonja led Whiskey out to the parking pad, I saw Bill in the upstairs windows waving at us with little Penny in his arms. I gave him a thumbs up sign and he soon joined us again outside. Whiskey was a little stiff, but clearly responded immediately to the comfort of his new shoes. He cautiously walked up and down the driveway.

Brant appeared pleased. "He's walking better already. This is great."

It was a pleasure and a relief to finally see some progress. Brant made a few small adjustments on the shoes and announced his work was completed. "Call me in a few days and let me know how he's doing. I'll be away for a week, so if there's a problem, I'll attend to it when I get back. By the way, it's a good thing you called yesterday. I've been out of town for a while. This is the only day I'm back home. I leave again in the morning for Ohio."

This came as a surprise to me. "We were fortunate to catch you in between your travels. I'll get my check book from the house, and I have a surprise for you. It isn't much."

I returned with Brant's payment and a batch of peach oatmeal bars. "I made them this morning to say thank you for coming out so quickly. If this was the medieval period, you would be the knight in shining armor. Thanks again for helping us."

Brant happily accepted the treats. "It's all good, and I know these peach bars will be too. I love cookies, and the apple cake you gave me a few weeks ago was great."

Brant drove away while I watched Whiskey march across the meadow back to the corrals where Wilson and Star anxiously waited. It was old home week again for the herd. They were literally welcoming his return to the stable and to the good life.

A week later I was positively gleeful as I watched Whiskey behave as a normal horse once more. He stood at the feeder and tried to chew hay with his friends. Even though he couldn't eat it because of his lack of teeth, it was wonderful to see him socializing. He returned to his normal feed consumption even as we weaned him off his pain medication. He now walked without hesitation and confidently strode onto the ice, calling Wilson and Star to follow him. I watched him lead his herd with authority into the meadow toward the Aspen trees. After he led them back to the corral for supper, Whiskey waited in his private dining room, complaining to Sonja that his supper was eleven minutes late. Things were back to normal.

I knew from past experience how quickly it could all change, but I was comforted by the knowledge that we would have more time with our Whiskey. Someday he would behold a pale horse, but not this day or the next. Time would have to wait until that soft summer day I wished for him, that perfect day when the spirit is willing and the flesh is naught.

Whiskey enjoys his new pedicure and custom shoes.

61

The Fruits of My Labor

I WAS GRATEFUL FOR the hot mug of tea because it warmed my hands when I wrapped them around the cup. The heat permeated my fingers and began to remove the chill from my bones. Like Penny, I was sitting on the floor by the back window where the sunbeams lighted the carpet. The warmth it produced was very comforting, so I had joined my little gal, who now thumped her tail in delight at the company. We sat silently together, I enjoying the view from the window and she enjoying my caressing strokes on her ears.

I stared through the glass, now covered by delicate etchings of ice that formed a gentle laced pattern. It did not obscure my view of the leafless Aspen trees encased in hoar frost. This effect was created by partially melted snow that refreezes the water vapors into a single seamless crystalline form, thus turning every tree into ersatz ice sculptures. The result was stunning, like thousands of diamonds had spontaneously erupted onto the surface of each tree. They glinted and glittered in the light, creating the illusion that the ice was dancing. It was a beautiful gift of winter that I welcomed in these bitter cold days that seemed unending. I snuggled Penny closer to my side. She responded with soft grunts of satisfaction. I wiggled my toes in the sun and felt relief at having a moment to relax with my thoughts.

Bing-bong came the sound of the door chime. I was surprised by the interruption. Penny scrambled up quickly, thumping her feet and tail off my stomach as she lurched toward the front windows. I rubbed my belly to relieve the pain of her sudden blows, and slowly got up to investigate. I presumed it was our UPS man, Jim. No matter how severe the conditions, I could always count on him to brave the elements to deliver any package. *Who else would come out in such bitter weather?*

I couldn't see the vehicle, so I turned to Precious Pup and said, "Let's find out who's at the door, Penny." Down the stairs she trotted, trying to keep pace with my much slower gait. I, in turn, tried not to trip over her. It was a complicated dance, but somehow we always managed to avoid collision. I opened the front door and beheld the Michelin Tire Man, at least that was my first impression. It took me a moment to recognize the heavily bundled figure was actually Alfred Wheeler. I was a bit startled that he had attempted the drive up, given the current road conditions and the extremely cold weather. But true to Montana tradition, he had not bothered calling first.

"Alfred, come in. You shouldn't be out in such weather." I stepped aside to let him pass, took his fur bomber cap and mittens, and waited as he sat down on the closet bench and unstrapped his snow boots. Penny sniffed him intently.

"Hello, Penny. How are you doing, my little friend?" He rubbed her head briskly with one hand while fumbling a boot buckle with the other. "Nancy, I just had to get out of the house for a while, go for a ride, and enjoy the fresh air."

I couldn't help but wonder if Alfred was being completely forthright. I also suddenly realized my own dishevelment. I was not presentable for company. I felt unpolished wearing no make-up and dressed in frumpy sweats and fuzzy pink socks. "I wasn't expecting company."

"Obviously," he replied as he eyed me carefully. "Don't worry about your appearance or a messy house. I like to see how people really live. Considering you didn't know I was coming, the place looks pretty good. But I knew I would get what I would get."

Oh, I'd like you to get, alright. I just smiled and said, "Well, Alfred, now you know. Have a seat at the dining room table and I'll tell Bill you're here. Can I offer you some tea? It's no problem."

"That would be most welcomed."

I placed the kettle on to boil and hurried up the stairs to the bedroom to alert Bill over the intercom that we had company. I considered sprucing myself up, but decided against it. A quick comb of my hair and some lip balm would have to suffice. I had tea to finish preparing. When I returned a few minutes later, Bill and Alfred were settled down at the dining room table near the fireplace.

"Honey, your kettle's been whistling a while."

I gave Bill "the look" and dashed into the kitchen. Earlier in the day I had created a new fruit crisp. It sat on the counter next to the stove. Did I dare offer it to Alfred? *In for a penny, in for a pound.*

"Care to try a slice of fruit crisp, Alfred?" I brought the treat in on a white feather patterned plate, along with his mug of tea.

Alfred poked at the dessert with his fork and closely surveyed the fruit slice, eyeing it sideways with his head placed level to table. "What kind is this? Are you sure you used the right ingredients? I know you're still working on your baking skills."

Without sighing I replied, "It's a plumcot. Do you like it? We enjoy them."

"You mean a kumquat. I believe that is the correct pronunciation."

"No, I mean a plumcot. It's a hybrid mix of a plumb and an apricot."

As Alfred continued examining the treat suspiciously, Bill backed me up. "She's right, we found them in town. They're really quite tasty."

Reassured, Alfred took a bite. "It's very interesting. While I prefer blueberry crisp, this is quite edible."

"I'm glad you like it."

I was about to cut another piece for Bill and myself when Sonja appeared.

"Did someone say fruit crisp?"

"Yes, would you like some?"

"Oh, yes, please," Sonja responded as she joined us at the table.

Alfred changed the conservation to focus on our recent arctic front and the effect it might have on his poor pigs. "I do worry about my pigs in such extreme cold, even though I'm sure the students are taking good care of them. We've had nothing but subzero weather for over a week. I trust they aren't suffering or homesick for my companionship."

"Do you ever think you'll get them back?" Bill inquired.

"Perhaps, perhaps not, it depends upon the wife."

Bill sensed his opportunity and glanced at me. "Alfred, you never did mention your wife's name."

"Didn't I, oh, I thought for sure I had. You know that's probably part of the reason I'm here today."

"I thought you needed a drive and some fresh air," I remarked.

"Well, yes, of course, that's true too."

"Too?"

Alfred looked mildly uncomfortable and said, "I guess we needed some time apart."

An image flashed into my mind of Alfred staying in our guest room, and me still trying to guess the name of his wife. I quickly banned the thought. "What do you mean?"

"She is a bit upset with me. I know her love for me will prevail, but for now I decided an afternoon apart was the best course of action. You see, she found out I named two of my pigs after her. Instead of being complimented, she was quite angry."

"I'm sorry to hear that." As I spoke, I kept trying to remember the names of his pigs. Hermione—that was his ghost buster pig. Were there any others?

Bill chimed in. "Well tell us about it."

"Yes, you see my two favorite pigs are Peggy and Sue."

Bill laughed, "Do you mean like Piggy and Sue-ee?"

To my relief, Alfred laughed too. "No, Bill, that wasn't my intention. I just don't understand why she isn't honored by my effort. Nancy, you're female."

"Yes, my whole life."

"All the other ladies I named my pigs after felt honored. Wouldn't you feel the same way?"

Oh dear, why is he asking me this question? Think fast, Nancy. "You mentioned other ladies; perhaps she is upset because she is not the first woman who received such a gracious gesture."

That idea seemed to surprise Alfred. "You may have a point. I should have considered that." Alfred looked at his watch. "I'd like to stay longer, but I think I should be going home now and talk to Peggy Sue. No point in making her distraught by a prolonged absence."

I vigorously nodded in agreement. "It will be dark soon and it's more dangerous to drive at night. I'm sure everything will work out."

We walked Alfred to the door and helped him with his winter gear. He continued his pondering. "No doubt she's worried about me and wants me home soon. I won't disappoint her. You know, she's a fetching woman…in her own way."

We waved goodbye as Alfred drove off. When he was out of sight, Bill gave me a hug and asked, "How about another piece of that kumquat crisp?"

"Very funny, it's Plumcot crisp."

"Whatever. Oh yeah, and don't forget the vanilla ice cream this time."

"Don't you want to wait until after dinner?"

"This is my dinner."

"Hmm, don't let Sonja find out."

Bill trailed me into the kitchen, quite pleased with himself.

"What are smiling about, your ice cream and crisp supper?"

"No, I'm relieved Alfred didn't christen one of his pigs 'Nancy'."

62

Anniversary Blues

"WHAT ARE YOU LISTENING to, Bill?"

"*Ode to Spring* by Joachim Raff."

"I've never heard of it."

"Neither had I; but I ran across the title and thought it appropriate, given the change in weather."

"But spring is still a few weeks away."

"Officially, yes, but for once it arrived early, so why not celebrate it in song?"

"Because you might jinx it."

Bill laughed and shook his head. "I don't believe in spooks or jinxes—knock on wood." He wrapped the edge of the table several times for emphasis. "Quinny, what would you like to do for our anniversary?"

The question caught me off-guard. "I don't know; I hadn't given it any thought."

"Well give it some thought now; it'll be here soon enough. I was thinking maybe you'd like to have a quiet romantic dinner in some swank bistro, this time without the kids. Sandy is on her own and Sonja is old enough to stay home and guard the fortress with Penny and the boys."

"Do you know of any swank bistros in Montana?"

"I'm sure we can find one. There's that new restaurant—the remodeled period home, remember?"

"The place where everything is covered in goat cheese and fennel?"

"That's the one—Hasenpfeffer House, or something like that."

"I looked at their menu online. It's pretty pricey."

"It's our anniversary. I don't care."

"It's a bit avant-garde and, honestly, I didn't find anything that appealed to me."

"Okay, pick another place. How about the Greek restaurant or the Italian bistro?"

"You really have a thing for bistros."

"No, I just like saying *bistro.* It sounds sophisticated."

I could see this conversation was not going anywhere and therefore I asked if I could sleep on it. Bill agreed, but he wanted to know soon so he could book reservations. He added, "Pick something swanky so you can wear one of your evening gowns."

I was excited by the prospect of choosing just the right evening attire for this special occasion, but which outfit should I pick? I knew of no dining establishment in Montana where an evening gown would be appropriate, however there were several where I could get away with wearing a cocktail dress. I opted for the Italian restaurant, thus I was able to narrow my selection to two choices, the first being a black velvet dress with rhinestone trim along the wrists and V-neck, and the second being a navy blue number with a jeweled pin at the waist. I realized I would be somewhat overdressed with either one, but since it was our anniversary, I wanted to indulge myself. While I pondered my final decision, Bill stepped into the doorway.

"Honey…we need to talk."

I didn't have to look at him to know the meaning of those four words which I had grown to dread. "What's wrong?"

"A snowstorm is hitting Friday night and Saturday. We're expecting over six inches."

"Six inches! I thought you said winter ended early."

"I guess Mother Nature didn't get the memo. I know you were looking forward to Saturday because it's our actual anniversary, but we can celebrate it at home and still have the dinner next week. Think of it as a two-for."

I put on a good face as I returned the two dresses to the closet. Then I chided myself for feeling a bit blue. *This isn't your first rodeo, Quinn.*

I was looking forward to our belated anniversary dinner. The skies were clear, the days were mild, the latest snow had melted, and I had decided to wear the black dress. Sonja and I were enjoying an early lunch of baked chicken. I didn't want to eat too much and spoil the evening's fun, so I settled on one small piece of white meat.

"Mom, don't worry; I can handle things here tonight while you and Dad go out."

"I know you can, Honey Girl, but I want you to call me when you finish feeding the horses, okay?"

"No problem."

"And be sure to—OUCH!" There was a loud crack which even Sonja heard.

"Mom, are you alright? What was that noise?"

"Oh no, I think I may have cracked a tooth—on this!" I held out the boneless piece of meat. I felt a sharp stabbing pain in the back of my mouth. It arced across the top and bottom molars. As I rubbed my jaw, the pain began to throb. I knew something was wrong. I turned to Sonja. "Please, get your father."

I was fortunate in a way. The dentist was able to seem me that afternoon, however, the prognosis wasn't good. He couldn't simply repair the tooth; I would need a crown. Bill tried to cheer me up.

"We still have time to go home and change for our dinner engagement."

I shook my head. "I'm sorry, Honey, I really don't feel like it now. I'm in too much pain and would make a poor dinner companion."

"Okay, Quinny; I'll take a raincheck, but you still owe me one anniversary supper. Okay?"

"Okay," I replied, but my smile masked my disappointment. I should have picked the blue dress because that's how I now felt.

63

Macy's Day Had No Parade

THE DENTIST COULD NOT repair my tooth for two weeks, which meant our anniversary celebration had to be postponed indefinitely. Bill wanted to make up for the fiasco by taking me to Macy's for a shopping spree. I was ambivalent at the prospect because the store was closing. This fact saddened me, but on the other hand, each week their closeout discounts increased, and they had such a beautiful selection of clothing and footwear that I accepted his offer.

As we pulled into the parking lot, Bill glanced my direction. "What's bugging you, Babe? You look like you've lost your best friend."

"Oh, I was thinking how much I'll miss Macy's. It saddens me to realize how many stores have closed in the last few years. Three of them are in this same shopping center. It doesn't bode well for Helena."

"The town will recover; it always does because it's the state capitol."

"I guess you're right, but it's a bit depressing to see another business shuttered."

"Well just think about all the money you're going to save on clothing during their liquidation sale."

"I may not find anything I like."

"Yeah, right, like that's going to happen."

Actually, I did find some very nice boots which I bought. I eyed a few shirts and dresses I really wanted, but I was content to wait until prices dropped further. Bill promised we would return next week, and each succeeding week, as the sale discounts continued to increase. I reminded him we still had a new crown to pay for, but he waived it off, assuring me we could afford both. "If I'm buying you a crown for your anniversary, it better come studded with jewels."

There was no sense in arguing with him; once Bill got an idea into his head, he was like a dog with a bone. I relented, but my feeling of guilt at splurging on unnecessary clothing came back to haunt me. The temporary crown on my tooth did not ease my pain, and after a week of it the dentist sent me to the oral surgeon. I knew what this meant, a root canal. Now I was really feeling guilty, but Bill didn't seem to mind. When I told him the bad news, he insisted we go to Macy's and shop for the latest bargains. The fun was going out of it for me, but I reluctantly agreed. Even as Bill sat in a chair outside the dressing room while I tried on clothes he had picked out for me, he scoffed at my concerns. "Nancy, you're paying twenty-five cents on the dollar, so get them now."

"I really don't need anything."

"That's not the point. You didn't get your swanky anniversary dinner or any anniversary gift, so think of this as an offset."

"You just bought me several nice watches and a purse. They're more than enough."

"All on sale and heavily marked down. It makes me seem cheap, so you can compensate for that with volume. If it really bothers you, then think of these gifts as early birthday and Christmas presents."

I could tell he was sincere, and saying no would disappoint him. "Okay, but that red coat I saw is too expensive. Promise me you won't buy it for me."

"I promise—unless they mark it down 75%. Now, are you ready to purchase that blouse?"

I nodded and headed toward the checkout counter. Bill followed me, carrying the chair he had been sitting in. "What are you doing with that chair?"

"While you were changing, I bought it."

"What on earth for?"

"It's a good chair and I talked them down to five bucks."

"But what do you need a chair for?"

"For five bucks, who needs a reason?"

64

Finding Whiskey's Sweet Spot

MY ELDERLY GENTLEMAN WAS beginning to wane again. It wasn't as bad as before, but I could see discomfort in the way he walked, gently and cautiously, as if he had to calculate each step in advance. I decided more research was in order. There was no point in contacting the vet's office; I already knew what they would say. I began my information quest on the internet and found a possible cause for his symptoms – insulin resistance. This condition results in pain and swelling in the legs when an animal has difficulty processing sugar. Since Whiskey was on a steady diet of manufactured feed, the idea appeared to have merit. The only way to confirm it would be through bloodwork. I was prepared to argue my case with the vet, but when I contacted the office, they were surprisingly receptive to the idea. When Robert Jackson arrived to draw Whiskey's blood, he was surprised and impressed at how well our Morgan was doing.

"Nancy, Whiskey is doing much better than I expected. Those custom shoes are really helping him." Robert inspected Whiskey's legs before drawing blood. "I don't feel any heat. That's good."

"Yes, but you should have seen him last week. He was walking normally and in full spirit. Now he's beginning to slow down again."

"There could be several causes for that. When I run the blood test, I'll check for insulin resistance and Cushing's Disease."

"I don't think it's Cushing's. He's always been able to shed his winter coat."

"That's a good sign it's not Cushing's, but the test will eliminate it as a possible candidate. I'll call you when I have the results. If it turns out to be insulin resistance, you'll need to switch to a low sugar, high protein feed."

While awaiting the test results, I researched alternative feeds and found what might be a suitable substitute at Higgin's. Availability was limited, but I could always order more. When Robert called us, he had good news. "The test results indicate insulin resistance. There's no cure for it, but it can be controlled by proper feed. Have you found anything locally?"

Bill read off the ingredients of a low sugar brand. Robert agreed we should get some right away and begin a transition period. Bill and Sonja went to town that afternoon and swapped out part of our existing feed for the low sugar product. Knowing Whiskey's reluctance to accept any change in diet, we began by mixing in a pound of the new feed with his old feed at each meal. Every couple of days we increased the amount of new feed by one more pound. If he showed any reluctance to eat it, we backed off for a while. It took a week, but by the end of that time he was enjoying his new feed even more than his old feed. But most importantly, the spring returned to his step and he was once again our frisky Whiskey.

Bill and I watched him finish off a bowl of food in relatively short order. Bill scratched his ears and commented, "I think he's in a pickle."

I replied with a bit of alarm, "Why do you say that?"

"Because he's eating his meal with relish."

"Ha-ha, very funny. It really is working well, isn't it?"

"Too bad it costs more than the old feed."

"That's to be expected. Magic potions are never cheap."

"Yeah, well, just be glad we got it when we did, but it's not going to be enough to get him through the spring."

"Can we get more?"

"Sonja's been checking. A small supply came in today. We'll run in and get what we can."

"Will it be enough?"

"I think so; but Sonja and I had better go now before somebody else snags it."

I watched them depart, then spent much of the intervening time with my elderly gentleman, telling him how wonderful he looked as I combed and brushed his hair. He snorted and mumbled, not sounds of pain or distress, but relaxing noises that showed his contentment. When the truck returned, I eagerly asked how much feed they bought.

"Not as much as I'd like, but more than we'll need to get us through the next two months."

I saw concern on Bill's face. "Is something wrong?"

"Not really. I'm just a little disappointed by what I saw in town. Things are changing in Helena."

"In what way?"

"Well, I stopped by Macy's to see if they still had that red coat you liked. I wanted to surprise you with it, but the store has been closed permanently."

"So soon? I thought they'd be open a few more weeks."

"The governor just issued an order to shutter all nonessential businesses. I guess between that and the general fear of uncertainty about the future, they decided to cut their losses and leave early."

I knew what he meant. The fear wasn't just in town; it was spreading over the nation and the world. I worried we might not be ready for it. Unlike Whiskey, there was no magic potion to overcome the threat of the growing pandemic.

65

Going Viral

"BLOW, WINDS! BLOW UNTIL your cheeks crack! Rage on, blow! Let tornadoes spew water until the steeples of our churches and the weathervanes are all drowned."

Sonja watched her father in dismay as he stood before the loft picture windows, shouting to the spring blizzard outside that had turned our world opaque overnight. "What are you doing, Dad, besides murdering Shakespeare?"

"All the world's a stage…and everyone's a critic," Bill responded.

"Sonja, can't you tell your father's feeling contemplative?" I felt a need to offer some defense. It was the beginning of the second week of the nation's self-imposed quarantine to slow the spread of the coronavirus. Despite keeping busy, the tedium occasionally crept in and reminded us of those things we could not or should not do. It wasn't so much that we wanted to go anywhere; it was the idea that we seemed to lack the flexibility to do so. It was an alien concept and a constant presence in the back of everyone's mind.

Bill continued his poetic allusions, unperturbed by our comments. "Is this the way the world will end, not with a bang, but with a whimper?"

Penny rose from her bed and sauntered over to Bill, performed the Penny stretch, and hopped up, placing her front paws on the window sill so she could see what all the hubbub was about. *Nothing but snow... nothing to see...nothing to chase...it's time to wee.* She turned to Bill and glommed onto his leg, clawing his trousers with her paws.

Bill looked down and said, "Do you need to go outside?" The magic word "outside" made her jump and sneeze. "Sonja, would you take Penny out to piddle?"

"Come along, Spaz."

"Don't forget your jacket and hat."

"Mom, I'm not a kid anymore. I know what to do."

She hurried down the stairs with Penny before I could respond. Bill turned to me from his perch, "How sharper than a serpent's tooth it is to have a thankless child."

"It's not Sonja I'm worried about. She's behaving like a teenager. It's this weather. I thought we were in spring."

"How many years have you lived here, Quinn?"

"I know, I know. I keep telling myself to expect the unexpected, but good grief. We've had eight inches of snow in two days. We hardly got that amount all winter. Are you planning to plow?"

"Why, is there any place we need to go during the quarantine?"

"Not for a couple of days."

"Are we not fully stocked to ride out the next two months?"

"No—I mean yes— I mean we are stocked up—mostly."

"Then I see no need to plow. This too shall pass." Bill waved his arm at the white blanket outside. "Give it a day or two."

"And then what?"

"With any luck this snow will melt quickly before your root canal appointment. I must say though, this is the most boring pandemic I've ever been through. Strange times—" The windows began to rattle loudly. "Wind, Quinn?"

"No, earthquake." Is Sonja back inside?"

"I don't know." The noise ceased. Bill continued. "That wasn't too bad, hardly a jostle. I wonder what it measured."

I heard the door open and the stomping of feet. Sonja soon joined us upstairs. "Spaz piddled."

"Did you feel the earthquake, Honey Bear?"

"What earthquake?"

"Strange times indeed," Bill repeated.

"You'd better check on Sandy."

"She's still at work, Nancy."

"Do you think Helena got hit hard?"

"No, they should have felt it no more than we did. I wonder where the epicenter is. There should be a report posted by now." Bill pulled up an alert on the internet. "Six-point-five! It didn't feel like it to me. Oh, here's why. It originated 400 miles away in Idaho. No reports of serious damage. That's good." Bill stood up and started to walk to his recliner, but he bumped into a nearby cardboard box that had shifted during the quake. "OW!"

"Are you alright?"

"I think I cracked a toe." He pulled off his left sock and found his third toe canted far to the left. "Oh, trouble's afoot."

"Should we go to the doctor?"

"No, I'd have to plow first, and all he'd do is wrap it. It doesn't hurt— yet. I think it's dislocated. I should be able to move it back myself." I heard five distinct clicks as Bill repositioned his toe."

"You'd better put some ice on that."

"I will, but first I want to tape it up."

Soon we were both sitting in our respective chairs, Bill nursing his foot with an ice pack and I trying not to think about my upcoming root canal amidst the pandemic. When evening approached, I called Sandy to make sure she was alright and to receive an update from her. "How are the residents at the retirement center holding up?"

"Well, we had to close the central dining room. Now everyone is having their meals brought to their apartments. I was told to drive around to the independent cottages and hand out meals."

"That must have been quite a change in your routine."

"It was, and I was worried at first. I didn't know any of these people and I had to knock on their doors and introduce myself. I also had to take their temperatures and pulse rates. I've never done that before."

"How did you handle it?"

"At first I was intimidated, but then I felt really good about the added responsibility, like I was a nurse in training. And they really seemed to appreciate it. You know I ended up spending a little time with everyone, chatting and trying to lift their spirits."

"That's great, Sandy. You really make us proud. Just remember you're on the front lines of this war. You and the rest of the staff are protecting the most vulnerable members of our society."

"I know, Mom. We spend most of our time constantly sanitizing everything. Since family members can no longer come in and visit, we're trying to create new ways to entertain everyone. And the management decided the staff has to eat here from now on. We're not allowed to go out for meals."

"How's the food?"

'Oh, it's great. We had Shrimp Scampi tonight, and last night we ate Steak Diane, and before that it was Chicken Kiev."

"Wow, you're eating a whole lot better than we are. Maybe your Dad and I should move there."

"We feel the same way. Management said if it gets bad enough we may have to stay here."

"Hopefully it won't come to that, but just to be on the safe side, your Dad and I won't drop by the condo when we're in town unless you need us to buy you some supplies."

"No, I'm pretty well set. I have plenty of Clorox wipes and a large pack of bathroom paper thanks to COSTCO."

"What about food?"

"I get to take home leftovers, and they give us gloves and masks."

"That's good to know. We'll be in town for my root canal on Friday, but we won't stop by. Take care, Sandy. I love you."

"I love you too, Mom, and I miss you guys."

That was the sweetest music to my ears. It only took a pandemic to hear them.

Because it was considered emergency surgery, the root canal went as planned, but the permanent crown would have to wait. Bill used the time to hobble about town, picking up several dozen essential items we determined would make any extended stay at Cimarron more bearable. On the drive back home he told me about the changes he'd seen in the stores.

"Many of the stores are closed, but the ones I visited are taking serious measures. At Lowe's and COSTCO they've placed tape on the floor every six feet so customers don't crowd each other at checkout."

"That's sounds sensible. What else?"

"Well, they also put up giant Plexiglas sneeze guards. After each customer passes, they have to spray them and the countertops with antiseptic. One clerk at Lowe's told me if they failed to do it each time, they would be instantly fired."

"Wow. Were there very many people in the stores?"

"No, I think much of the panic buying has passed. Just to make sure, COSTCO brought in a warehouse full of TP. They had it stacked everywhere. It's a good thing you didn't need to go in and use the facilities because the women's restroom was closed."

"What about the men's?"

"It was open except for the stalls." Bill glanced at my expression and continued. "Hey, I don't make the rules, I just benefit from them."

I rolled my eyes. "Was anyone wearing a mask?"

"I saw some, but most folks were just giving everyone else a wide berth. I think masks are in short supply right now, but I suspect they'll become more commonly seen over time."

"Did you manage to find everything on the list?"

"Everything but Panda Express Orange Sauce."

"I think we can survive without it."

"Ha, then you tell Sonja."

66

Music of the Night

ONE OF THE GREATEST advantages of living in a rural setting is the feeling I am always connected to the wildlife in their natural environment. This connection is never greater than during the summer months. The morning sun brings to the world the blessing of a new day when all the creatures, big and small, begin their daily tasks. It is a joy to see and hear, but there is something special about the evenings that is difficult to put into words. As the darkness sets in, the mountains seem wilder. I often see the bats in flight catching mosquitoes and hear the owls calling to each other with their solemn hoots. It is a haunting sound, especially when it echoes through the hills. Bill and I sometimes sit for hours in the darkness and listen to the sounds of the night.

We were now ready to enjoy a little night music. Bill opened the rear window in our bedroom and settled in with me on our blue loveseat. A cool breeze brushed our faces through the screen mesh as we watched the moon rise above the forest peaks. A familiar sound danced through the air, something we hadn't heard in years. It had a clicking repetitive rhythm to it.

"Do you recognize that?" Bill asked in a hushed voice.

"Crickets. We haven't heard them since we left Florida."

I listened more intently. Far off in the forest I heard the high pitched squeal of an elk bugling. It rose above the dim sound of the crickets, a lonely soliloquy or perhaps a cry for a mate. It was accompanied by the rush of the wind, which gently rustled the leaves of the nearby Aspen trees like chimes. Next came the even lonelier howl of a coyote, followed by the sound of laughter, which was really the yapping reply of younger pack members. I wondered how the other animals felt about the night. Some had settled in quietly and were hiding from the predators. Others were spreading their wings or crouching in the tree lines, ready to pounce silently on their supper.

This was our summer evening symphony, performed by an ensemble of wind instruments and a featured soloist. I closed my eyes and listened to the music of the night. Each concert evoked a different feeling, and I looked forward to every single one, but tonight was special. We sat without speaking and watched the moon, full and bright, arcing above the fast moving clouds as they formed eerie ghostly aberrations.

I broke the silence. "It reminds me of something you would see on Halloween."

"Nancy, it's summer."

"But it is spooky," I replied.

"I'll tell you what's spooky. Listen."

"It's quiet. I don't even hear the creek."

Bill whispered, "The wind's died down for the moment and so have the night people."

"Night people? What night people?"

"The predators and the crickets, of course."

I shook my head. *He's trying to frighten me. What nonsense. We usually hear something, the wind, the animals, anything. I hear nothing. I wonder if something is out there frightening them.* "Don't they usually kick up a fuss if a predator is nearby?"

"Sometimes, but not always. They might call attention to themselves."

"Maybe everyone is asleep."

"It sure seems that way. Why do you ask? Are you ready to go to bed?"

"No," I replied, "I just find it a bit odd, but comforting too." It was simply the sound of silence. There was no sound inside or outside the house. "I can't remember the last time it's been this quiet."

"So just enjoy it, Nancy."

"Oh I am," I replied as I burrowed into his chest. *Now I am getting sleepy. Why can't every night be like this one?* We sat in the silence and I thought to myself that it must have sounded like this a hundred years ago. No background noise from electric lines, passing cars, or any other distractions. It lasted for nearly an hour, just the clouds moving stealthily one direction as the moon passed silently the other. The world itself seemed to have stopped. Bill put his arm around me and hugged me close. Like our mountain, I was soon deep in slumber. The silence was the sweetest music of all.

67

Out of the West

BILL AND I SAT in our favorite love seat facing the rear window of our bedroom. It was another glorious summer evening that offered a clear stunning view of the night sky. We were enjoying a relaxed, almost whimsical conversation in the semidarkness.

"What would you do if you had a lot of money?" I suddenly inquired.

"How much money, Honey?"

"I don't know, millions, maybe billions?"

"Did I earn it or win it?"

"What difference does it make?'

"It makes a lot of difference, Nancy. If I earned it, it means most of it is probably tied up in my business."

"Fine, you won the lottery."

"How much?"

"I don't know—800 million dollars."

"Is that before or after taxes?"

"It's just for fun."

"I still need to know."

"It's just a game. What would you want to do if your money was unlimited?"

"I don't know; I have everything I need."

"Well suppose you could have more?"

"I haven't given it much thought. Aside from the usual stuff like buying a few homes or land around the country or maybe around the world, I might buy a few man toys like some airplanes. I'm not sure what I'd do with the rest of it. I suppose I'd donate some of it to my favorite charities and causes. Why, what would you do with it?"

"I would like to design and construct all new buildings for the animal rescue and adoption centers around the country. They would have a reception area, private offices, a clinic, a room to get acquainted with the dogs and cats, a kitchen, and all the animals would have an indoor kennel that connects to a private run so they can be outdoors at will."

"Wow, you've been planning this a while."

"Yes, I also would like to create a company to produce all my art on dishes, kitchenware, and home décor items like pillows and blankets. Of course, I'd set aside some money for the girls to inherit, and then give the rest to my favorite children's charity without blinking an eye. I wouldn't miss it at all!"

"What about that Spanish style villa you always dreamed of?"

"Okay, I'd save a few million for that and to take care of the horses."

The conversation ended as quickly as it had begun, creating a long period of silence. It was only broken when Bill asked the obvious question. "What are you thinking about now?

"What do you mean?"

"What do I mean? Nancy, anytime you go this long without saying something, I know you're either asleep or deep in thought. Well, you're not asleep, so what is it? What's bothering you?"

After so many years together, I could not mask my concerns. An element of foreboding was pervading me, and Bill could sense it.

"What is it, Quinny? What's bothering you?"

"What makes you think anything is bothering me?

"You're pensive. I can see it in your body language."

"In the dark?"

"Yes, even in shadows I can tell you're not relaxed."

I turned to him and replied, "What about our future, Bill?"

"What do you mean?"

"Sandy's left. When Sonja's ready for her next step in life it will change everything. It's not like either one of them will ever take over this place and start a second generation here."

"That's to be expected. What of it?"

"What will we do next, once it's just the two of us? What do you want to do in the next chapters of our lives?"

"Well, I hadn't really thought about it, hmm—do you see that! Look!

Bill was pointing to a meteor streaking across the sky. I had never seen one so bright and dramatic. It seemed to leave a trail of glitter in its wake.

Bill gripped my hand tightly. "Quick, make a wish!"

I closed my eyes and searched my thoughts.

"Did you make one?"

"Yes, of course, but I can't tell you. Did you make a wish too?"

"Yes, but if I can't tell you either," he smiled. "Don't worry, you were part of it. I can't say anymore." He pursed his lips and turned an imaginary key which he then threw away.

"I get it, James Bond; keep your secret safe. I'm not worried." I leaned back and looked out at the stars. "Isn't it amazing? I don't ever get tired of it. How many stars do see up there?"

Bill leaned forward, trying to get a better view. "Oh, I don't know, a few hundred, maybe a thousand we can see from here. If we stepped outside for a better view we could count them, but we'd be at it all night."

"It's been an incredible thirteen years. Hard to believe Sonja was only three when we moved here. It all seems rather bittersweet to me now."

"Why's that?"

"I suppose it's part of being a mother, that mix of happiness and melancholy. Now I don't know what to do?"

"Sounds like me when I retired. After thirty years of doing what you love most, what do you do next?"

"You did what you always dreamed of doing. You retired to a small ranch in Montana."

"Yeah, Cripple Horse Ranch, where the lame and the lost go to live."

"Is that so bad?"

"Not for them, but what about for you? Are you happy?" I didn't want to say anything, but he persisted. "Are you, happy, Nancy?"

"For the most part, yes."

"But?"

"I worry about our future. Do you really see yourself plowing this road in the dead of winter when you're in your seventies and eighties?"

"By then we'll have hover cars that can skim over the snow."

"Be serious, Jonny Quest."

"We don't have to live here year round. We could travel more or get a second home in a warmer climate."

"And what about the horses?"

"We can stable them. Linda would look after them."

"You saw how the other horses abused them. Do you really think that's wise?"

"Then we get a horse trailer and take them with us. I've not really thought about it."

"Don't get irritable."

"I'm not irritable."

"You sound irritable."

Bill placed his hands gently on my shoulders and stared into my eyes. "What do you suggest we do, Nancy?"

I didn't want to say, but he kept looking at me. He wanted the truth. "I think we may have to consider moving…permanently."

Bill removed his hands and leaned back a little. I waited for the blowback. Instead he simply asked, "Are you unhappy here?"

"Bill, when we first moved here it was a great adventure. There was so much to learn, so many challenges to face, and the girls were still young. But that's all changed. I really love our home; I love the view, the evening sunsets, the starry nights." He kept looking at me, waiting for the rest of the story. "And most of all I love you. I don't want to spoil your dream. And I don't want to make you give it up because I fear you would resent me from then on."

There was long silence before he replied. "But we're not getting any younger, is that it?"

"That's part of it. Every time you go out to plow I worry something might happen to you, and yes, I worry about what I'd do then. I can't manage this place alone. And what happens when you're no longer physically able to plow, or drive thirty miles to shop, or a hundred miles to see a specialist? I don't want the years to creep up on us and force us into selling. I'd rather consider our options now and plan for our future—whether it's here or at some new homestead."

"Anything else?"

"As much as I love our privacy, sometimes I feel isolated from the world. For as long as we've lived here, we've never been fully accepted. We're pretty much on our own." There, I'd finally said it. It was my greatest disappointment of all. I was forever to be branded an outsider. Was this to be our future, living at Cimarron alone, comforted only by the surrounding wildlife, horses, and beauty of the mountains? Or would we pull up stakes, sell our home, and travel the country until we found another homestead and started a new life with new adventures? It was the unanswered question. It remains the unanswered question.

All was silent once more. Bill did not respond. He now sat quietly, pondering what I had said. I waited, worried I had angered him. After an eternity of a few minutes he spoke. "Nancy, I will consider it. As long as we are together, I have what I most need in this world."

I breathed a sigh of relief. I knew I would never make him give up what he loved. If we ever did leave, it would be because we both had found something better to share together. For wherever we are is our home, and home is where our story begins…

Epilogue

AS I PEN THESE final thoughts, a new comet has recently been discovered, C/2020 F3, more popularly called NEOWISE, after the space-based telescope that discovered it, the Near-Earth Objects Wide-field Infrared Survey Explorer. Unaware of its presence, we were startled to see it plainly visible in the night sky. More amazing is the fact that its long parabolic orbit means it won't be seen again from Earth for 6,800 years. It is events such as this on our rural mountain that have blessed us in ways that are not easily expressed or understood. There is always a price to be paid when you live a lifestyle outside the norm. Our experiences have forged us into individuals shaped by hardship, toil, tears, joy, jubilation, failure, and triumph, each measured in its own private way by the person affected. The years to come will continue to shape us, and though I do not yet know just how, I still look forward to the future and all it holds. Is it destiny or desire? I cannot say. I only know I feel bound to take that next first step with faith in my heart that we are up to the challenge.

I am blessed to awake every morning to the sight of vast miles of mountains, and I find it to be an uplifting experience. We must conform and live with the rhythm of the seasons, just as the natural world around us does. We too press on with a bustle of activity that ensures the treasured gift of life continues for another day. I find great comfort in the knowledge that, together, we all can live and grow under the big skies of Montana.

Brothers at heart.

Recipes

I HAVE A PASSION for baking. The long winters give me plenty of time to create new recipes in my kitchen. Each creation has a story behind it that is part of the family history I have related in my books. I hope you enjoy these new favorites, prepared with ingredients easily found in your pantry.

More fun and informative baking demonstrations are available on my internet channel *Nancy Quinn–High Mountain Homesteading.* Wildlife and nature, tea recommendations, gardening, and arts and crafts are also featured in my videos. Visit *quinnwildlifeart.com* for more information.

⭑ Fresh Blueberry Cookies ⭑

1 cup softened butter
1 cup granulated sugar
¾ cup brown sugar
2 eggs
2 tablespoons vanilla extract
2 cups all-purpose flour
1 cup almond flour
½ teaspoon baking soda
1 teaspoon salt
2 cups fresh blueberries

Preheat the oven to 350 degrees and line baking sheets with parchment paper.

In a large mixer cream the butter and sugars until light and fluffy. Add the eggs and vanilla, and continue mixing. In a separate bowl stir together the flours, baking soda, and salt. Add these ingredients to the large mixer before blending everything thoroughly at low speed. By hand, gently stir in the blueberries. The goal is to keep them whole, not crushed into the dough.

Scoop out a generous teaspoon of the dough onto the baking sheets and bake for 12 to 14 minutes.

Cool cookies on a wire rack.

⭑ Lemon Bars ⭑

Base
1 cup all-purpose flour
½ cup softened butter
6 tablespoons confectioners' sugar
1 teaspoon lemon extract
1 teaspoon lemon peel
2 tablespoons lemon juice
2 tablespoons flour

In a bowl combine all ingredients with a large spoon. Pat the mixture into an ungreased eight inch square pan and bake at 350 degrees for 20 minutes.

Filling
2 eggs
1 cup sugar
2 tablespoons flour
½ teaspoon baking powder
2 tablespoons lemon juice
2 teaspoons lemon peel
1/4 teaspoon lemon extract

Beat eggs in a bowl. Add sugar, flour, baking powder, lemon juice, lemon peel, and lemon extract. Beat until the mixture looks frothy. Pour over the crust and bake for 30 minutes.

Cool in the pan, then cut to desired size.

⭑ Painted Cookies ⭑

¾ cup butter
2 eggs
1 cup sugar
2 ½ cups all-purpose flour
1 teaspoon baking powder
1 teaspoon salt

Sift together flour, baking powder, and salt. Add remaining ingredients to bowl and beat with a mixer until smooth. Chill for at least one hour. The dough needs to be cold (it will also hold for several days in the refrigerator, if need be).

Roll out the dough onto a floured board and cut into shapes with cookie cutters. Place on an ungreased cookie sheet. Add egg yolk paint.

Egg Yolk Paint
1 egg yolk
¼ teaspoon water
Your choice of food colorings

Remove the egg white from the yolk. Divide the yolk into separate cups, one for each color you plan to use. Add a few drops of food coloring of your choice to each cup. Red, green, blue, and yellow colorings all bake up beautifully. I like to use several different colors on each cookie.

A set of soft paintbrushes used only for food will give you the best control, or you can apply colors with several small spoons. Try the paintbrushes; I think it makes for a more fun experience.

If the paint thickens too much, add a few drops of water.

Bake the cookies at 400 degrees for six minutes

Cool on a wire rack.

The cookies may be frozen.

Wilson: *Look—cookies! I love cookies!*
Star: *I love cookies more!*

www.hellgatepress.com

Made in the USA
Monee, IL
30 December 2020